T4-ALC-266

MARCEL ROETHLISBERGER–BIANCO

CAVALIER
PIETRO TEMPESTA
AND HIS TIME

UNIVERSITY OF DELAWARE PRESS

1970

FOR LAURA

© 1970 BY THE UNIVERSITY OF DELAWARE PRESS

ALL RIGHTS RESERVED

LIBRARY OF CONGRESS CATALOG CARD NUMBER: 78-101052

PRINTED IN THE NETHERLANDS BY JOH. ENSCHEDÉ EN ZONEN, HAARLEM

CAVALIER PIETRO TEMPESTA AND HIS TIME

OP
25·

CONTENTS

CAVALIER PIETRO TEMPESTA AND HIS TIME

INTRODUCTION

L'immortale, e non mai lodato abbastanza Cavalier Tempesta
(Maggi, Memorie sulla vita di Ag. Bertelli, Brescia 1794, p. 4)

SCOPE OF THE BOOK

This study deals with a hitherto almost unknown aspect of late 17th-century painting. Its core is a monograph of Cavalier Pietro Tempesta (Haarlem 1637–Milan 1701), illustrious painter of marines, landscapes, and animal genre. In addition, the artist is presented within his time; a large place is allotted to precursors, related contemporary masters, pupils, and followers in the fields of marine, landscape, and animal painting. Since most of the material is new, the book assumes a broader survey character for those areas.

Tempesta's importance can be summed up as follows: he is the leading landscape painter in northern Italy between 1670 and 1700. He is the link between Roman landscape of the mid-17th century and landscape of the next century in Venice – the link between Gaspard, Claude, Rosa on one hand, Marco Ricci, Tavella, and later artists on the other. He is the main force in marine painting in Italy.

The two central chapters of the text deal with Tempesta's position in his time and with his oeuvre; the first of them describes the sources for his art and the environment in which it developed, the second analyzes his oeuvre. This is preceded by chapters on his father, on the literary sources, and on his biography. His widespread influence is traced in a separate chapter. The catalog follows the sequence of the plates; it includes detailed information about the artists surrounding Tempesta.

I am only too conscious of the limitations of this study. Not everything by Tempesta is good or important; many of the good paintings are still badly disfigured by varnish; and some of the school works are of little merit. I also know that further research may render obsolete some of the information given here about artists in Tempesta's orbit. Critics will therefore find it easy to point out the limited interest of certain marginal aspects. But the phenomenon of 'Tempestismo' could not be demonstrated differently in its full range. And rather than offer a selection of Tempesta's masterpieces in splendid isolation, I have attempted to give an adequate image of the surroundings in which he was active. Above all, it is hoped that the shortcomings will be offset by the novelty of the entire subject, by the historic importance of Tempesta, and by the superb quality of his major paintings. Of the hundreds of illustrations, no more than three dozen have been reproduced before; paintings by Tempesta previously reproduced number about a dozen.

A special word concerns the American scene. Art history is here oriented on a set of few 'great' masters. Museum holdings, university curricula, textbooks, all have come to establish this set in the awareness of the history of art with a kind of finality that seems to exclude the possibility of changes and reevaluations. In this view, the 'local schools' of Europe become a negligible chapter of second-rate art. It is not sufficiently realized that the wealth of those local schools makes instead the true substrate of the pattern of art history. This volume will illuminate several of these local schools with numerous masters not as yet known.

The periodization by centuries and epochs of style, adopted in our textbooks and our minds, has made it virtually a 'fact' that baroque landscape came to a close in the latter part of the 17th century, after the death of Poussin, Gaspard, and Claude, and that a new start took place only with Watteau, Boucher, and Canaletto. The decades around 1700 are tacitly regarded as a sort of dormant, colorless transition period in which painting had neither significant masters nor a clear direction. It is true that the towering masters of the earlier seventeenth century were supplanted at its close by specialists who proved, on the whole, less inventive. The creations of the late masters had nonetheless a unique flavor, as different from the previous and subsequent generations as was the case in any other period. We can speak of neither a gap nor a decline in landscape painting at 1700. Demand and production were, on the contrary, ever increasing. We are also becoming conscious of more and more links between the two centuries. Tempesta is a key figure in this context. The book should then, from its angle, contribute to a new and more appropriate understanding of the late 17th century.

NAME

Before we enter further into the subject, it is necessary to be clear about the name of our artist, which has often given rise to confusions, most frequently with Pieter Molijn and with Antonio Tempesta. He was born in Holland as Pieter Mulier (the younger). In Italy, he is generally known as Cavalier Tempesta (more rarely as Tempesta di Genova) or as Petrus de Mulieribus, which is the proper latinization of the name (Pieter of the Muliers), a form proudly carried by the artist himself and only coincidentally, if fittingly, also meaning 'of the women.' In the 18th and 19th centuries he was mostly called, by confusion, Molijn the younger (such an artist in fact never existed) or Pieter de Molijn, in France usually Tempesta de Gênes. He must be distinguished from some artists whose names sound similar and several of whom moreover influenced him: his father, the marine painter Pieter Mulier the elder; the landscape painter Pieter Molijn; the famous Florentine engraver and painter Antonio Tempesta (1555–1630); the classical landscape and figure painter Pietro Testa (1611–1650); the Tuscan portrait painter Domenico Tempesti (c. 1655–1737); finally, Tempestino, who was Tempesta's pupil and brother-in-law.

During his lifetime and for a century afterwards, Tempesta was extremely famous. The reason is easy to understand: he was a splendid and prolific painter whose landscapes appeal immediately to the eye. Formed in Holland as a marine painter, switching in Antwerp to monumental Flemish animal painting, then emigrating for life to Italy, there from the outset successful with seastorms, landscapes, and animal pieces, active for forty years in Rome, Genoa, Venice, Milan, and Lombardy, he had much to offer on many sides. In addition, the saga of his life provided the biographers with welcome, unusually colorful traits. He was convicted for the murder of his wife, spent eight years in prison, later engaged in renewed adultery, enjoyed the protection of the highest nobility, kept a zoo in his garden in Milan, at various times accumulated great wealth and suffered utter misery. No wonder that throughout the 18th century the *cause célèbre* of the murder kept the memory of the artist as much alive as did his artistic oeuvre. Painters with murders and manslaughter on their conscience are, after all, a rare breed (their ranks include Caravaggio, Cornelis Schut, Jacques van Loo, Francesco Bassi, Marco Ricci, Antonio Calza – the latter three in the very orbit of Tempesta). It took an age as disinterested in biographical anecdotes as ours to forget altogether a story of life so rich in ups and downs. The only work of fiction dealing with our artist is the eccentric short story *Die schöne Insel* (Isola Bella) by Uffo Daniel Horn, published in Germany in the middle of the 19th century, when historic novels were at their zenith (no copy available in America).

It is no exaggeration to say that Tempesta is nowadays unknown outside of Italy. How this came about requires a word of explanation. The scarcity of an oeuvre would normally be the most common reason for ignoring an artist; this applies indeed to many of the minor names discussed on these pages. Of Tempesta, we have instead a most enviable number of excellent, large paintings; we even have some fifty letters by him, which is without parallel in Dutch art. One of the main causes for his almost total oblivion amounts to the same as would the loss of his works: by far the greatest part of his extensive oeuvre is still being kept in old Italian private collections, which are, for many reasons, shrouded in secrecy or, at least, do not seek publicity. Many of the finest Tempestas are therefore of difficult access, especially to non-Italians. Other paintings of his are scattered in museums all over Europe, more often stored in deposits than on exhibit. The Metropolitan Museum recently sold the only Tempesta then in an American public collection, without keeping so much as a photograph. Some works have in the past few years come on the Italian art market, where they command, not surprisingly, very high prices; on such occasions, about a dozen paintings have been published in local Italian papers. To give a measure of the artist's present reputation in other countries, it is sufficient to say that he was not included in the exhibition of Dutch Italianizing artists at Utrecht in 1965 and is quoted neither in Rosenberg and Slive's book on Dutch Art and Architecture nor in Stechow's book on Dutch Landscape Painting, both of 1966.

LITERATURE: ACHIEVEMENTS AND LACUNAE
This brings us to the art-historical research of our time, from which the topic derives its actuality. In the past decade, 17th-century landscape has received the widest public and scholarly attention. We

need only mention the recent monographs, books, and exhibitions centering on classical landscape from A. Carracci and Domenichino to Claude and Poussin; on Rosa, Pietro da Cortona, Elsheimer, Bril, Dutch landscape in general and Dutch Italianizing landscape, the Bamboccianti, van Laer, Il Sestri, Flemish landscape of the baroque age, and the much overrated Monsù Desiderio, to name only a few. For the early 18th century too, the list of books and exhibitions is not negligible; they deal with Vanvitelli, Magnasco, Marco Ricci, Zuccarelli, Carlevarijs, Busiri, Venetian landscape in general, not to mention the Venetian Vedutisti.

In spite of so many endeavors, there remain notable gaps in our knowledge. Much research still needs to be done on Gaspard, Grimaldi, Mola, on Dutch masters, on Roman 18th-century landscape. Above all, the entire field of later 17th-century landscape painting has been strangely neglected. Neglected areas are, furthermore, marine and animal painting. While the range and extent of Dutch marine painting is well known, even if little study has gone into it so far, the Italian counterpart is next to unknown. Yet Genoese, Roman, Tuscan, and Neapolitan marine painting of the 17th century exists in countless examples, often of gigantic dimensions. Sooner or later, it will be 'discovered' with the same amazement that accompanied the revelation of Italian still-life painting in the exhibition at Naples, 1965. As to animal painting, it was represented in every respectable dining room of the past; artists such as Rubens, Castiglione, Giordano contributed to it. The Flemish animalists were studied by Greindl, but no comprehensive attempt exists for Italy, where the genre was in fact no less common (only on Roos and Scorza are there studies). In most of the cited areas, the difficulty for the student lies in the overabundance of the material, not in its scarcity.

METHOD

With an artist like Tempesta, who worked rapidly and used collaborators, and whose production was at times uneven and was widely imitated, our standards in matters of authenticity, chronology, and completeness must needs be different from what they are with Claude or Poussin. While the major portion of Tempesta's oeuvre is of a high personal quality and poses no problem of attribution, we are also faced with a borderline area, in which the question of authorship remains insoluble. The chronology is largely hypothetical. Most of the extant oeuvre was produced between 1685 and 1701; within this period, it appears impossible to press for a precise sequence of works.

This book was designed in the first place to be an illustrated compendium of Tempesta and his entourage. It is conceived from the plates, to which the text serves as a comment. Plates and catalog have the same order and numbering. The arrangement is chronological, by large sections. The precursors are listed in the sequence of their importance for Tempesta, not by their birth date; the marines are grouped together, including predecessors and followers; the bulk of Tempesta's oeuvre is basically arranged by picture types and such natural criteria as subject, pairs, size; the contemporary and later artists likewise are presented in groups and by school affiliation. For the precursors and comparative examples, the choice has consistently stressed works not previously reproduced. As regards completeness, further works by Tempesta must surely survive in Italian and probably in foreign collections.

Since Tempesta learned his art from his father, following, at first, in his footsteps, it seems advisable to make up here for the total lack of literature on Mulier the elder. Complete enumeration of the oeuvre is not attempted, however; only twenty out of sixty to eighty paintings known today are reproduced (46–65).

Despite the widespread appeal that Dutch marine painting has always enjoyed, it has up to now been the subject of very little scholarly work. Almost every museum and private collection of old painting, especially in England, contains a selection of Dutch marines. We seem to know the masters very well, but on closer inspection there is hardly any literature on them, although there are at present indications of a coming change. The prevailing attitude has been that marines are to be looked at rather than studied. To this day, the only serious book on the subject is the brief study by F. C. Willis, published over fifty years ago. His paragraph on Mulier the elder (p. 60) and Fokker's entry in Thieme-Becker (1931) are almost the only titles forming the bibliography on our artist.

To begin with, the biographical data are these: Pieter Mulier (Molier) was born in Haarlem at an unknown date, presumably about 1610. He was the son of Pieter Joostensz. Mulier, a refugee coming from the southern Netherlands, obviously under the stress of the religious persecution that drove so many of his compatriots northward. (I am indebted to C. A. de Goederen van Hees for this archival information.) His Flemish ancestry is important for the art of Mulier the elder, for Tempesta's early sojourn in Antwerp, and for his adoption of the Flemish manner in painting. The family were Baptists (*Doopsgenooten*, in a reference of 1647 contained in the Bredius files at The Hague). Mulier the elder was married on 25 February 1635 in Haarlem to Maycken de Graet, also born at Haarlem. Two years later, their son Pieter (Tempesta) was born, and within the same years a daughter, Anna Maria. In 1638, the father was first recorded in the local St. Luke's guild. These dates suggest a birth date around 1610. After 1638, he was regularly mentioned at Haarlem. Frans de Hulst (1610–69) was a pupil of his. In 1647, Mulier seems to have stayed temporarily at nearby Amsterdam. A Pieter de Mulier (ours?) made his last will on 27 August 1669 at Leiden. The artist died in 1670 at Haarlem. The manuscript archival excerpts in the Bredius files contain these further details: in 1640, Mulier had a pupil, Frederick Cornelisz. (unknown); on 11 April 1652, Pieter Molier (hardly the son) was fined for having insulted someone; on 3 November 1654, he settled a bill for beer with pictures; in 1658, he was entitled to sell his pictures by advance of price.

The early biographers mention him briefly, without any details. Soon, he was being confused with the Haarlem landscape painter Pieter Molijn, possibly because of the same initials (which resulted in Tempesta being called Molijn the younger). Thus, Houbraken does not seem to distinguish clearly between Mulier the elder and Molijn (to whom he also refers), although the former did only seascapes, the latter only landscapes.

Mulier is a typical Dutch specialist of marines of high artistic distinction, if more limited in his range of image types than such great masters as his contemporary Bonaventura Peeters or the somewhat later Bakhuyzen and Cappelle. His preference for sea storms and heavy seas may have been a heritage of his Flemish ancestry. In Flanders, agitated seapieces were favored in the decades around 1600 (Eertvelt, Porcellis, the Peeters family). His pictures, almost all on panel, are signed with the monogram *RΛ*, which includes all the letters of his name. His art derives from Porcellis (born in Flanders in 1584, deceased in Holland in 1632). Among his contemporaries, he comes closest to Claes Wou, who practiced similar picture types and a similar style, and to Simon de Vlieger, both of whom were born half a generation before Mulier. Judging from his rather small oeuvre known so far, Mulier's favorite type was the stormy sea built on the motive of a single span (or two spans) of waves extending across the entire foreground, with strong contrasts of dark corners and a brightly lit depression of the wave in the center. This is a highly personal, effective, and bold device found, for example, in the Dresden picture and in no. 46. It is between this type of image–no doubt Mulier's strongest contribution to Dutch marine painting–and Tempesta's sea storms that one can sense a family resemblance, an affinity of temperament, however different their works are in technique and style. Another group of Mulier's pictures shows rough seas with smaller waves and a straight horizon line. Occasionally the light is rather even (51), but most often we find the familiar scheme of an illuminated area following abruptly upon a dark, diagonally cut foreground (55–57), invariably resulting in a poignant illusion of depth. In both the tempestuous and the rough seas, the entire character of the pictures is dramatic. The agitation of the elements is felt in a vital manner, which again relates Mulier to the sea storms of his son. The ships are kept small and distant; the foreground sometimes contains a boat. The anecdotal theme of men in shipwreck, so keenly exploited by the masters of the following generation, is kept to a minimum.

While landscape and figure painting lead to much discussion of thematic questions, pure sea pictures confront us more directly with matters of style. As in a large part of Dutch 17th-century painting, the novelty of invention from picture is no measure of quality. What do count, however, and make the essence of such works, are coloring and atmosphere–aspects, that is, which are difficult to put into words. Mulier's brushwork is substantial, the range of tones goes from dark brownish hues in the foreground to a soft, silvery grey for the distance and the cloudscapes. The light is not indifferent; he always rendered a loaded mood. Handling and coloring are of an unmistakably personal quality that conveys to the oeuvre a distinct sense of unity.

A few examples of two further picture types practiced by Mulier exist. The coast view with shipwreck or calm sea (61–65) belongs to the repertoire of every marine specialist, but is perhaps best known from van Goyen and Salomon van Ruysdael of the Haarlem School. Finally, fig. 59 is an example of the calm, shallow sea in the manner of van Goyen, from whom it also borrows the translucent brownish tints. Other similar works by Mulier may well exist under the name of van Goyen.

Mulier's individual pictures show, then, great refinement and a high artistic level, while the oeuvre as a whole does not equal that of the most renowned masters. Enough signed pictures of a coherent style survive (but not a single dated one) to give us a good idea of the artist's personality, though not of his evolution. No drawings are known. Regarding the son, whose debt to the father will be summed up later, one question remains: since both used the same monogram (cf. no. 148), some of the father's marines may in theory be youthful works by the son done before his departure from Holland. While the bulk, and the best, are, for intrinsic reasons, clearly the father's works, one may well raise the question of father or son in works such as the somewhat less refined no. 48 or the coast view no. 65, which is like a foretaste of Tempesta's Italian works.

THE SOURCES

This chapter contains translations *in extenso* of the major 18th-century biographies of Tempesta in chronological order, with brief comments. The principal source is Pascoli. While the material available today allows us often to be more complete and exact than the historiographers of the past, the early sources will always remain of fundamental importance. Their more genuine spirit and liveliness make up for their faults. Rather than relegate them to an appendix (which diminishes their significance), I chose to give them precedence over our own reconstruction of Tempesta's life, to which the next chapter is dedicated. And instead of the original Dutch or Italian texts, most of which may be consulted in good libraries but which are not intelligible to all students, an English version is offered. The sequence of these Lives constitutes at the same time a history of Tempesta's survival. This is completed at the end by a survey of the scarce modern literature.

P. Orlandi, *Abecedario Pittorico*, Bologna 1704, p. 119.
> Pietro de Mulieribus, called il Tempesta, painter of marines, sea storms, vedute, landscapes, and animals. He was born in the year 1637 in Haarlem, Holland. Converted by a Carmelite monk from Calvinism to the Holy Faith, he came to Italy, being already trained in painting. He was received in Rome by the Duke of Bracciano and stayed a long time in the service of that benign maecenas of the arts, who rewarded him with a knighthood. He then left for Venice, moved to Vicenza, Brescia, Milan, and Genoa, where he was jailed for five years, convicted of having had his wife killed. Finally freed thanks to the intervention of the Count of Melgar, governor of Milan, he moved again to that city, where he died in the year 1701. He lived in a grand manner, with carriage, liveries, a numerous family, and a menagerie of animals that he kept in order to paint them from nature. And indeed he was a great painter and landscape artist.

For all its brevity, in keeping with the other entries of Orlandi's dictionary, this first biography contains the basic factual information that served as a base for all later Italian writers.

Natale Melchiori, *Vite de' pittori veneti*, manuscript of 1728, copy of 1790 in Venice, Biblioteca Marciana, *cod. marc. it.* IV, 167 (5110), pp. 405–406. This entry copies Orlandi, but adds one passage, a bit of first-hand information from Melchiori.
> . . . He then left for Venice, where he made his talents known. From there he arrived at Castelfranco, his new home, where he formed an intimate friendship with Mr. Donato Fabris, a dilettante of painting, who at Cole di Musone near Castello di Asolo owned a delightful residence.

Tempesta enjoyed staying there for some time, inspired by his friend as much as by the site, which was conducive to depicting from nature the fine views of those hills. Fabris was compensated by Pietro with several of his works, which now belong to his son, Dr. Don Francesco Fabris, provost of the cathedral of Asolo. Hence he moved to Vicenza, Brescia, ...

These paintings cannot be traced.

A. Houbraken, *De Groote Schouburgh,* vol. III, Amsterdam 1721, p. 183.

> Same and same fits best, goes the Dutch proverb. This is also true of the competent animal painter P. Molyn, who had the surname Tempeest in the painter's union. He was a native of Haarlem, the son of Pieter Molyn the elder, and was born about 1640, since in the year 1697, when Isaac de Moucheron was in Rome, he was a man of some fifty years. Of his art, there is to my knowledge nothing in this country, as he went early to Italy and elsewhere. His brush could represent everything, but he excelled especially in painting boar hunts in the manner of Frans Snyders. The peak of his career, in luck and misfortune, was his years in Genoa. Misfortune, I say, since, presumed to have killed his own wife, he was jailed for life. (Others hold that it was his mistress whom he had killed by two or three scoundrels hired for this purpose, after having grown tired of her.) There, his Dutch companion Jan Visser, alias Slempop, a landscape painter and pupil of Mommers, often went to visit him. After sixteen years in jail, he was given freedom in the year 1684, when the French bombarded the city ('the pain of the one is the luck of the other'). He went to Piacenza in the state of Parma, where he died. Until his old age, he loved the arts, and when he lost his eyesight and could no longer see with any spectacles, he placed two of them on his nose when painting. He was, according to the testimony of those who knew him, a great lover of the arts and likewise of Venus.

Houbraken's short entry is the first Dutch statement on Tempesta. Its message recurs in practically all later Dutch biographers. It is merely a string of marginal and mostly wrong information and in no way attempts to evoke a personality. In this, it is no different from many other entries on artists about whom Houbraken knew little. He calls the artist Molyn the younger and knew of no works of his in Holland. Though his brush could 'represent everything,' Houbraken mentions neither the landscapes nor the seascapes, only the boar-hunts and animal pieces. These, produced during Tempesta's early sojourn in Antwerp, before he proceeded to Italy, where he turned mainly to landscape, were clearly the only echo of the artist in Holland. From the Italian years, Houbraken ignored everything. The information about the failing eyesight is confirmed by Tempesta's letters. As to Jan Visscher (c. 1636–after 1692), he was an engraver after Berchem and others and, later in life, an animal painter, but he is not known to have been in Italy, and Houbraken seems to confuse him with Theodor Visscher, called Slempop (Haarlem 1650–1707), painter of animal pieces in the manner of Berchem. It had not been known that he also stayed in Genoa and that he was the pupil of Mommers; no works of his can be identified.

Exclusively borrowed from Houbraken is the page dedicated to Tempesta in 1729 by J.C. Weyerman, *De Levens-Beschreyvingen der nederl. Konst-Schilders,* vol. III, The Hague, p. 23.

L. Pascoli, *Vite de' Pittori, Scultori, ed Architetti Moderni,* vol. 1, Rome 1730, p. 177.

Of Pieter Mulier. In the years around 1637 came to light at Haarlem, a town situated on the river Sparen, three miles from Amsterdam in Holland, known for its strength as much as for having been the place of origin of many famous masters, a child named by the parents, who were merchants, Pieter. As he came of age, they wanted him to join their business, in which they had instructed him since childhood by teaching him arithmetic, good handwriting, and the rules of mercantile correspondence. But as he learned to write and his teacher recommended to him the imitation of the models, he began right away to imitate the lettering and the frontispieces of the books, which he soon copied admirably in pen. From frontispieces he proceeded to copying some marines kept in the house of his parents, and, not satisfied by drawing them in pen, he got hold of pencils and thus drew them. Subsequently his urge to draw, and especially to represent after nature the various effects of the sea storms, grew to the point that he would often leave home at dawn and go to draw to the coast, which lay just under a mile from the city; and watching in the green pastures on his way the splendid cattle so plentiful in Holland, he also began drawing those. The parents were delighted with his application, believing that he spent his time in school, not being notified as to his absence by the negligent teacher. But as he some-times failed to return in time for dinner because of his passion, they began to suspect that he went astray or gambling with other boys. They followed his steps, and aware of what was hap-pening, they scolded him bitterly, although he did no evil. They complained to the teacher and henceforth had him accompanied to school. Distressed at no longer being able to go drawing to the shore and the fields, he began to deceive the teacher and the parents, and with his wits he often found some pretext for getting out of school. Hurrying out of the city gate, he drew for a short while from a distance what he was forbidden to draw from close-by. The teacher noticed this, and seeing that also in school he drew on every occasion, no matter how often he scolded him, advised the father to leave the son to his vocation. And the father, taking his sound advice, called him one day and said to him: 'Since you have this great urge to draw and to go sketching to the shore, have your will and go where you want to. But I want you to have a teacher also in this.' And he recommended him to a painter friend of his, who taught him to paint and to draw figure compositions. But being more inclined toward animals, landscapes, and the stormy sea, he did more by his own observation than by the lesson of his teacher. With time, he became that excellent and worthy master, who for his singular ability to represent truthfully from nature animals, landscapes, marines, and particularly the various accidents of the tempests, was no longer called Pieter Mulier but Pietro Tempesta. He remained in Holland until almost the age of thir-ty, always wandering from one place to the other in those beautiful, wealthy and populated provinces, and always painting and leaving his pictures everywhere. He then went to Antwerp in order to meet some masters with whom he already corresponded and to see the country of origin of Rubens, van Dyck, and other famous painters produced by that fruitful land. There he was lucky to make friendship with a Carmelite monk, who cautiously began to persuade him and finally brought him to renounce the dogma of Calvin, in which he had grown up, and to

9

espouse our faith. The monk suggested to him to come to Italy for the benefit of his profession and recommended him to various clerics at different places, especially to some in Rome. As soon as he arrived, these introduced him to the Duke of Bracciano, who immediately assumed his protection, and in his presence he was converted. His first paintings met with great applause in Rome. The duke was delighted to protect him and made him continually work for himself. With time and growing experience, by which he refined himself, the fame of Pietro increased beyond measure; and with the reputation grew the love and esteem of the duke, who provided him with other protections and other commissions. He produced many works for many clients. Noteworthy were the last that he had to do for the duke and for the Contestabile [i.e. Prince Colonna]. I shall not mention others, for they are almost innumerable and are in private houses, not easily accessible. I shall, however, say that he always had so many at work that he took to being helped by pupils in order to complete them in time. Above all others, he esteemed one who was then called the Tempestino, with whom he continually dealt and conversed, thus also gaining access to his sister, with whom he fell so much in love that he wanted to marry her. But as the marriages which are contracted only for love often arouse shadows and suspicions, he grew jealous of her soon after marrying her, and the jealousies gradually turned into bitterness and continuous trouble. Pietro trembled, talked, and did strange things, as do those who are obsessed by this kind of meditative madness. Agitated by somber thoughts, he decided to leave Rome and immediately solicited permission from the duke, who would hardly have conceded it to him, had he not seen him resolutely decided to leave, with the promise to return soon. But though not denying it, the duke never granted final permission. Instead, he sought with new commissions to alter his intentions. But while he served him, Pietro renewed his demands more fervently; and the duke found no further means to persuade him. One day, he called him and said: 'By my reluctance to grant you the leave you so often solicited, you can measure my displeasure. Yet I shall have to agree in order to satisfy you, much as my heart tells me that I shall not see you again, and that you will suffer infinite disasters elsewhere. If I did not love you, if they dragged you out of my house, if the artists conjured against you, if all of Rome did not mind so much what your good nature and your singular virtue rightly demand, if you were in need of money, if you had no friends, if you were without protections, I would say: by all means leave, look for other quarters and abandon these too crude ones. But you, who have nothing left to hope for from others, it seems to me that you are wrong in your compulsion to leave. Therefore, think of a better way, and bear in mind that precipitous resolutions almost always lead to regrets. As to me, I leave you in full liberty and grant you ample permission.' And taking a fine cross with a necklace, ordered for the occasion, he hung it around his neck and declared him a knight, making him also further gifts. Pietro remained speechless and thoughtful in the face of these new attentions and generous demonstrations by the duke. He was deeply tormented by two passions: one urged him to leave at all costs, as every moment of indecision seemed to him a thousand years, for too much against his will he stayed; the other admonished him to remain, in order not to lose the wise advice and the continuous kindness of the duke. Yet the first urge won. He thus took leave from him, telling his wife that he would soon send for her, and he went straight to Venice, where he remained for some days, then proceeded to Milan and from there to Genoa. His fame having preceded him there, he was immediately employed by several gentlemen and at the same time received commissions from others. He thus worked untiringly and he often delighted in conversations with friends. It happened that in talking often to a young woman he fell in love with her. Not knowing how to satisfy his desires, and not being on good terms with his wife because of the said jealousy, he decided to have his wife killed in order to marry the other one. He contracted with a villain, whom he sent to Rome in order to fetch her, with the command that he do her in on the way, wherever convenient. In Rome, the assassin immediately went to see her, presented her husband's letters, and told her to be ready to leave at the earliest; for he was in a hurry and could remain but little. The poor woman grew suspicious of that dreadful face. Conscious of how little her husband went along with her, she delayed the departure as long as she could. But having received also by mail his explicit order to leave without delay, she readied herself, though unwillingly, for the journey and left with the abominable killer, who brutally murdered her in Sarzana. The horrible news spread in Genoa, and Pietro, who imprudently solicited the new marriage, gave to all a motive of suspicion of what had happened. Even those who in public tried to defend him thought him guilty. So much was talked, so much was murmured about it, that Justice finally laid its hand on it and Pietro was imprisoned. At the trial, he was not only suspected but fully convicted, and after some time also condemned to death. Numerous friends arranged at that moment that the verdict was not executed with the habitual speed. And as the defense did not cease to insist strongly and to incite the court, the execution was delayed. But the verdict was not revoked. Nor would the excellence of his art have saved him from death on the strength of the law 'Ad bestias ff. de poenis,' had not after five years of imprisonment his pardon been obtained through the intervention of the Count of Melgar, governor of Milan, and of Count Borromeo. During all that time he painted continually. It was then that he filled the city with his pictures, partly giving them away, partly selling them. And it is held that those were his most beautiful. Yet I fail to understand how he had the heart to paint with the leash on the throat. But also the death-bound hope until the last moments to live, and nature, which wants them to live, illudes them, so that very few believe those moments to be the last. How many times, however, in that miserable state, or rather in that long agony, did he regret the sojourn in Rome and think of the admonishments given by the duke on his leave. Only too gladly would he have gone to see him, if the obligations to his liberators, to whom he owed nothing less than his life, had not called him to Milan. Emerged from prison, he thus stayed little in Genoa, but went to thank the Count of Melgar and Count Borromeo, by whom he was kindly received. He entered so much into the favor of the first that he did much work for him and through him received many other commissions, in particular from Count Pietro Scotti, so that he earned immense sums of money. But living in grand style, without putting aside so much as a penny, he spent it with the same facility as he earned it. He held a carriage, liveries, lived in a splendid house, where he made a fine seraglio which he filled with animals in order to paint them; and he rendered them so naturally and lively that he had only few equals. But while he thus lived in magnificence and splendor, his poor second wife, already abandoned by him, went almost begging. And without minding in the least, he happily enjoyed new friendships and amused himself. Finally his means began to dwindle, for being already old, he was not in sound health because of his disorderly life, and he could not apply himself with the earlier vigor. Thus he too saw himself reduced to misery at the end of his life. Continuing all the same to get himself into trouble and to spend the little which either was lent to him by friends or he drew from pawns, he contracted an acute fever at the age of 64 and passed away on 29 June 1701. His body was brought to the parochial church of S. Calimero, where he was buried under a white stone with the following [Latin] inscription:

Cavalier Pietro Mulier
Called Tempesta
who in painting marines and landscapes
added admirable suavity
to the elegance of colors,
great also in small things,
illustrating Italy with distinguished works.
The name passed to immortality,
the body to this tomb
in the year 1701.

He left a single daughter, aged 15, who was said to be a natural child. After his death, she took what little was left over by the creditors and departed with a mistress of the father and with a pupil who was in the house and whom she married on their arrival in Piacenza. Numerous young pupils frequented his school, but none, to my knowledge, emerged with an ability worthy to be remembered. Pietro was well-shaped in face and body and also in advanced age preserved his natural beauty, elegance, and verve. Fortuna loved him in his youth, but he did not recognize her, and by his imprudent and dissipating conduct did not know how to take advantage of her. She scorned him for some time in his maturity, then took to love him with renewed strength. But it did not last, for illuded by her love, instead of intimidated by her contempt, he left himself to be guided by the former rather than by the latter.

This is by far the longest *Vita* of Tempesta and gives a measure of the high esteem in which he was held at the time. The correct interpretation of the text presupposes a familiarity with Pascoli's *Lives* as a whole. This historian was particularly interested in landscape painting; the eight pages allotted to Tempesta compare with ten given to Claude, five to Grimaldi, six to Gaspard, twenty-five to Rosa (whose life offered the most anecdotes). Like all of Pascoli's biographies, it is eminently readable and written with much verve. It has neither the penetrating thought of a Bellori, nor the classical equilibrium of a Baldinucci, but is a more urbane, bubbling conversation, which it is impossible to render adequately in English. The text is far from balanced and yields much less accurate information than its length would lead one to expect. Pascoli's drawback is his delight in story-telling. In this case, the greater part of the description is taken up by four episodes–school, Duke of Bracciano, murder, and final decay. The story of the boy running away from school belongs to the classical 'legend of the artist.' The parents are called merchants, whereas the father was in reality a marine painter. Possibly the father engaged in some business besides painting, as did so many Dutch painters of the time (A. van der Neer, Hobbema, Steen, etc.). That the son was apprenticed to a painter friend of the father is unlikely, all the more so as the alleged teacher remains nameless. The emigration from Holland did not take place at age thirty, but more than ten years earlier. Little information about the sojourns in various Italian cities is offered. The debauchery may be somewhat overplayed, and so is the final decadence, which achieves a fine moralizing effect. Pascoli must have been familiar with some portions of Tempesta's work; but nothing at all is said about the paintings or the frescoes themselves, and no particular pictures are listed. Declining to 'mention others, for they are almost innumerable,' means in fact that the author knew them only from hearsay. Had he known personally any of the large groups of Tempestas, he would have quoted specific works and collections, as he did in other *Lives*. Yet for all the lacunae, Pascoli shows himself very interested in the artist and reasonably well informed about him.

R. Soprani, *Delle vite de' pittori, scultori, ed architetti genovesi,* vol. II, by C. G. Ratti, Genoa 1769, p. 332. Of Pietro de Mulieribus, called il Tempesta, Dutch painter. Also the famous painter Pietro de Mulieribus, a native of Haarlem in Holland, came to Genoa toward the end of the past century. But if only he had not come! Unluckily he had to stay for five years in prison. The reason for this only-too-justified stay in prison I have not the courage to expose. It is well reported by Pascoli, by the author of the Museo Fiorentino, and by that of the Abecedario Pittorico, where those who are curious to know may investigate it. What is extraordinary is how in those five years of anxiety and of fatal danger he could work so excellently, painting so many superb pictures for these citizens, where they are still conserved and kept in high esteem. Prior to his imprisonment, this painter withdrew to S. Giacomo di Carignano, where he painted for those Fathers a semicircular canvas which still survives in the guest house. This canvas represents a maritime tempest. And because such subjects were those which he practiced most commonly and with special mastery, he was named il Tempesta, which is why certain authors have occasionally confused him with the Florentine painter Antonio Tempesta. De Mulieribus finally left prison thanks to the mediation of the Count of Melgar, governor of Milan, who obtained his pardon from our Most Serene Senate, and took him along to Milan; where he lived from then on in good conduct and with every facility. And here his life ended, after many excellent works, in the year 1701, in his 64th year.

Essentially a shortened compilation from Pascoli, this *Vita* shows the esteem in which Tempesta continued to be held in Genoa, but adds nothing new, except for the mention of a painting in S. Giacomo di Carignano, Genoa, a church long since destroyed; this picture is first mentioned in Ratti's *Istruzione di quanto puo vedersi di più bello in Genova,* 1766, p. 54. One of the references concerns Gori's *Musaeum Florentinum,* Florence 1772, where the engraving of Tempesta's self-portrait is accompanied by a short *Vita.*

Aimo Maggi, *Memorie sulla vita di Agostino Bertelli Paesista Bresciano,* Brescia 1794, p. 4.

> Tempesta's ingenious and forceful manner of coloring had struck Agostino Bertelli. And indeed, who does not behold with amazement in the large paintings of Tempesta those burning tints of the horizons, that frank touch of the brush in the rocks and abysses, that force and variety in the various levels, in short that radiation descended, so to speak, with such force and truth upon his paintings? Although Bertelli for those reasons embraced blindly the manner of such a master, he soon grew aware of a certain dryness in Tempesta's distances, in his cascading masses of foliage and the crude masses of the heavy clouds which almost always mark the character of the otherwise immortal and never enough praised Cavalier Tempesta. I said never enough praised, for who will be able to equal those lively and breathing animals with which he used to adorn his landscapes? In Genoa, Tempesta painted the majestic sea storms which will always be admired by anybody not entirely ignorant in matters of painting.

Much of this text is copied verbatim from Carboni, 1776 (p. 47; see the Bibliography). Though not in a *Vita* proper of Tempesta, it is an interesting document of his reputation in Lombardy throughout the 18th century. The text does not consist of the usual repetition of biographic anecdotes, but is a statement of art criticism which forms a significant complement to Lanzi.

L. Lanzi, *Storia Pittorica,* Bassano 1795; ed. 1809, vol. II, p. 201.

> Similar to Tassi by talent and much worse for his delinquency was the Dutchman Pietro Mulier, or de Mulieribus, called il Tempesta because of his well-painted sea storms. His pictures frighten one to the utmost, as one watches a loaded and threatening sky bursting onto the ships with furious clouds and lightning, causing fires, while stirred from the depth the sea rises furiously against the ships, collides with them or submerges them in its whirls. In the galleries, Tempesta is represented more frequently than Tassi, for he almost always worked in oil. In this activity he was helped in Rome by a youth who thus got the name Tempestino, although he more often practiced Poussinesque landscapes. He also married this youth's sister, whom he had killed by a scoundrel. For this deed he spent five years in jail in Genoa, barely escaping death. The tempests which he painted in jail with a fantasy increased by the horrors of the place, by the well-deserved suffering, and by his guilty conscience, were extremely numerous and resulted in his finest works. He also excelled in painting animals, a great number of which he kept in the house for the convenience of his studies. Lastly, he is very notable in landscapes. In several galleries I found him to be a good follower of Claude on account of the compositions formed by a great variety of hills, lakes, and fine small buildings, although he remains behind the model in the effect of the coloring and in the refinement of the work. He makes it up, however, in the figures, to which he gives a mixed Flemish-Italian character, full and gay features, well varied. More than anywhere else I have seen examples of all the said abilities of his in Milan, where he spent

the last years of his life, and in the neighboring towns, *viz.*, Bergamo and especially Piacenza. His epitaph can be read in the Guida di Milano on page 129.

Lanzi, the creator of modern art criticism, gives for the first time an appreciation of Tempesta as an artist, based on a personal contact with his paintings. He mentions the sea storms, animal pieces, and landscapes and relates the latter to Claude. Always sound and well informed, he avoids anecdotes.

Tempesta is mentioned briefly in many other 18th-century sources under other artists. As an example, G. B. Zaist (*Notizie istor. de'pittori ... cremonesi,* vol. II, 1774, p. 113) cites in the *Life* of F. Bassi 'Cavalier Tempesta, called de Mulieribus, who did animals, figures, sea storms, and excelled in every kind of painting.'

The biographers of the 19th century, ever increasing in number, provide for our artist mere compilations of earlier writers. Even Ticozzi, a Milanese generally well informed about local art, heaps error upon error in his *Dizionario* (1832). Some other examples are Nagler's *Künstler-Lexicon,* 1840; Descamps, *Vie des peintres flamands et hollandais,* vol. II, Marseille 1842; Immerzeel, *De levens en werken der hollandsche en vlaamsche kunstschilders,* Amsterdam 1842 (he confuses Genoa with Gouda in Holland, etc.). No new facts emerge; Nagler lists five engravings after paintings by Tempesta. We have to turn to our own century for some further information.

Fokker, much interested in Dutch-Italian relationships, was the first to draw attention to the Colonna frescoes (1929). His entry in Thieme-Becker's *Künstlerlexikon* (1931) is factual and lists a number of pictures in museums (no mention of the Borromeo collection), summing up the artist's style as 'crude and superficial.' Of greater significance are Hoogewerff's archival findings reported in the next chapter (1942). Nicodemi published five pictures in 1958; Bonzi reproduced a few works in Genoese newspapers. For further marginal mentions of Tempesta in old and new local literature, in handbooks on landscape painting, or in connection with such artists as M. Ricci and Magnasco, see the Bibliography. Putting it simply, there is virtually no modern literature on the artist.

THE LIFE

On the evidence of the preceding *Lives,* of archive material, letters, and further pertinent sources, we can now sum up the known facts about Tempesta's life.

1637–c. 1655 Haarlem and travels in Holland

1655 or 1656 Antwerp

c. 1656 (or 1655)–1668 Rome

1668–1684 Genoa (1670 Rome?), 1676–1684 in prison

1685–1701 Milan, with sojourns in Piacenza, Parma, Modena, Venice (1687–1690), the Veneto, Brescia (c. 1692, 1697), and some other places.

Pieter Mulier the younger was born in Haarlem in 1637, the son of the Haarlem-born parents Pieter

Mulier the elder (whose father was Flemish), marine painter, and Maycken de Graet. He grew up in Haarlem. By 1656 at the latest, he must have been in Rome, for in 1663 he is recorded as having a son aged six by his wife, who was the sister of his Roman assistant. Settling in Rome at age nineteen, taking an assistant and a wife, must have demanded some time. Before going to Rome, he sojourned long enough in Antwerp to be profoundly influenced by Flemish animal painting. And still earlier, in Holland, he was 'always wandering from one place to the other ... and always painting and leaving his pictures everywhere' (Pascoli). This makes our artist very precocious. To fit all this activity into his youth, Pascoli had him remain in Holland 'almost until the age of thirty'–a claim that may sound convincing, but is wrong, for both the birthdate and the arrival in Rome can be confirmed with about a year's accuracy. The family were Baptists (Doopsgenooten), a sect whose members were not baptized at birth. Hence no birth record exists, and his epitaph does not state the age or the birth date. But his parents were married in February 1635, and during the sixties, the annual Roman census mentions his age several times, with implied birthdates ranging from 1637 to 1640, so that the traditional date of 1637, already given by Orlandi and Pascoli, cannot be questioned. As to the arrival in Rome, a drawing by Tempesta is signed *Roma 1659* (148). There is no reason to surmise that he might have arrived only in 1659 and that the son of his wife was not his son.

Our artist learned painting from his father, whose manner he adopted at the beginning. Both were members of the Haarlem St. Luke's Guild ('Pieter Molier' and 'Idem de Jonghe' are mentioned there without date; see Bredius, *Künstlerinventare,* vol. VI, The Hague 1918, 2219). That he learned from a friend of his father's, as Pascoli states, is rather doubtful. The son must have been gifted and restless at an early age. We can assume that between the age of 15 and his departure to Antwerp at about 18, Mulier traveled and painted a good deal in Holland.

From Antwerp, he journeyed to Rome in the company of a Carmelite monk, who succeeded in converting him to Catholicism at the beginning of the Roman years, and who provided him with the first recommendations. He was immediately patronized by the Duke of Bracciano, who knighted him upon his departure in the late sixties. By an odd contrast, almost no paintings of his Roman years are known, although we are better informed about the circumstances of his life during that period than for any other time. Our knowledge is based on the *stati d'anime,* the annual parochial lists of inhabitants published by Hoogewerff, 1942, pp. 48–51, 66, 76, 142–150:

1663 – Parish of S. Lorenzo in Lucina. Vicolo del Carciofano: Pietro Tempesta, painter. Lucia, wife. Carlo Antonio, son, 6. Maria, mother, widow. Domenico, son. In the same house: Pandolfo Resci, painter (i.e. Reschi; see no. 426).

1664 – La Selciata towards the Trinità: Pietro Tempesta, painter. Lucia. Elisabetta, sister. Carlo Antonio, 8.

1666 – Parish of S. Maria del Popolo. Corso, no. 26: Pietro Mulier, Dutch, 26. Lucia, wife, 30. Carlo, son, 9. Elisabetta, her sister, 22. In the same house: Giovanni, Fleming, painter, 25. Giacomo, Fleming, painter, 25. Another Fleming, 26, and a Roman pupil, 14.

1667 – Corso, towards the Babuino, no. 34: Pietro Tempesta, Dutch, painter, 30. Lucia Rossi, Roman, wife, 30. Carlo Antonio, son, 10. Maria Tempesta, of the late Pietro, Dutch, 32.

Elisabetta, his sister-in-law, 24. Maria, widow, mother-in-law, 60. In the same house: Cristo-foro Botteli, Fleming, 30. Ignatio Crono, Fleming, painter, 26. Giovanni Suinchi, Fleming, 25. Gregorio, pupil, Burgundian. 4 May: baptism of Flavio Francesco, born 27 April, son of Pietro Mulier alias Tempesta, Dutch painter. Witness: Duke of Bracciano, represented by Carlo de Mauris.

1668 – Corso, no. 43: Pietro Tempesta, Dutch, painter, 30. Lucia Rossi of Faenza, 34. Carlo Antonio, 11. Flavio Francesco, son, 1. Maria Molier, sister of Pietro, 28. Elisabetta Rossi, Roman, widow of Giovanni Cortina, 25. Maria Gordini, widow of Antonio Rossi, 60. In the same house: Giovanni, Fleming, painter, 25, and a young Italian couple with daughter.

1669 – Corso, no. 43: Pietro Tempesta, 30. Lucia, 34. Carlo Antonio, 12. Flavio, 2. Elisabetta, 24. Maria, sister of Pietro, 26. Maria Gordini, 60.

1670 – Corso, no. 42: Pietro Tempesta, 30. Lucia, 35. Carlo Antonio, 13. Flavio, 3. Maria Molier, 27. Elisabetta, 25. Maria Gordini, 60. 10 July: Carlo Antonio, 14, died.

1671 – Parish of S. Lorenzo in Lucina. Corso, from S. Giacomo to the Arco di Portogallo: Lucia, wife of Pietro Tempesta, painter. Flavio Francesco, 4. Maria Tempesta, absent, sister of Pietro.

1672, 1673, 1674 – the same three persons.

Summing up this information, the following facts emerge. Pietro lived in Rome for a dozen years, from at least 1656 to 1668. He is recorded there in 1663, 1664, 1666–1670; actually he was absent in 1668/69 (see *infra*) and perhaps left permanently in 1668, but his family stayed on. He lived in the artists' quarter, changing his address a few times. His wife was Lucia Rossi, a Roman, born in 1635, recorded in Rome until 1674 and murdered near Sarzana (Massa) in 1675. During the eight years of his absence, i.e. from 1668 onwards, Tempesta supported her by means of one hundred Genoese lire (document of 1683 and letter of his sister of 19 July 1682). While he was away, she bore three more children. He had met her through his assistant called Tempestino, whose sister she was; surprisingly, Tempestino himself is not mentioned in the house (or is he the Domenico of 1663?). Tempesta's first son was Carlo Antonio, 1656/57–1670. A second son(?), Domenico, is listed only in 1663. Another son, Flavio, was born in 1667. Also in the household were Elisabetta Rossi, sister-in-law of Pietro, Roman, born 1644, recorded 1664–1670 as widow of Giov. Cortina; (Anna) Maria Mulier, sister of Pietro, born 1635/40, recorded in the house 1667–1674, married in 1675 to Guido Francesco Beltrami of Turin; and Maria Rossi, mother-in-law of Pietro, widow, born Gordini, recorded in the house 1663, 1667–1670.

Our knowledge about the subsequent thirty years of Tempesta's life is very vague. The main lines are known, but precise information is to a great extent lacking. Most helpful are the indications contained in his letters and in those of his second wife. He must have left Rome in early or mid–1668 and settled in Genoa, abandoning his family in Rome. The reason was apparently jealousy regarding his wife, who was said to be a prostitute. According to Pascoli, this jealousy led to some kind of mental trouble or nervous breakdown. The young man certainly had a large family and a full house to care for. Existence had probably become unbearably complicated, leaving him with no other solution than to escape. As to his itinerary, we are somewhat uncertain; Pascoli mentions a visit of a few days in Venice, then Genoa. The Ligurian capital must have proved the most promising market for his art. His letter dated 7 September 1669 to Cardinal Giberto Borromeo in Rome informs us that he had at that time been in Genoa for eleven months and was planning to return to Roma via Milan and Parma, two cities that he had not previously visited. Whether or not he actually returned to Rome is not certain: probably he did, since he was still officially registered there in 1669 and 1670. He must have left Rome permanently in 1670 or 1671, as in the following four years only his wife, son, and sister were registered there. He was living in Genoa by 1675, and in all probability during the preceding years too. Before his imprisonment, he lived for some time in the monastery of S. Giacomo di Carignano, Genoa (here pp. 13, 137).

It was in Genoa too that he met and fell in love with Anna Eleonora Beltrami, from Turin, who had abandoned, or was abandoned by, a first husband; her brother, Guido Francesco Beltrami, married Tempesta's sister in 1675. In the same year, the artist sent for his wife in Rome; on her way to Genoa, she was murdered near Sarzana, in the dukedom of Massa. He immediately solicited a marriage with Anna Eleonora, who already lived with him. Rumors about his alleged instigation of the crime having spread, he was jailed in the tower on 13 January 1676. At the trial on 27 September 1679, he was found guilty and sentenced to twenty years, despite a strong defense by Count Borromeo's lawyer Giovanni Della Torre. In the same year, while in prison, he married Anna Eleonora. As a result of strong protection and years of high-level negotiations carried out above all by Count Borromeo and also by the Spanish governor of Milan, the Count of Melgar, Tempesta was pronounced innocent and freed on 15 October 1684, having served eight years in prison. That he was freed at the bombing of Genoa by the French, on 17–22 May 1684, as has often been said, is inaccurate. During his prison term, he kept painting frantically, apparently producing many of his finest works. His letters from prison, excerpts of which are quoted in a subsequent chapter, give a telling picture of the mental and physical hardship suffered by the artist during those years. In particular, he complained several times (e.g., on 20 December 1682) about his failing eyesight, which must have improved in later years, as some of the paintings dated in the very last years are also richest in minute details.

Tempesta soon left Genoa for Milan, where he was by Christmas of 1684, in order to thank his benefactors, Borromeo and Melgar. He spent the remaning 17 years of his life in the Lombard, Venetian, and Parmesan territories, often moving around. There is very little precise information as to places and dates. In Orlandi's and Melchiori's enumeration, Venice, Castelfranco, Vicenza, Brescia, and Milan precede the years in prison. But this order should not be taken literally. Tempesta may indeed have visited those cities between the Roman and Genoese phases. Houbraken has him moving from Genoa to Piacenza. From late 1684, he almost certainly remained for two years in Milan in the service of his benefactors. A Borromeo inventory records him at the Isola Bella in 1685. On 26 October 1686, in Milan, he solicited from Count Borromeo letters of recommendation for Modena and Parma and promised to visit Isola Bella after his return. Indeed, he worked in Modena for Marquess Montecuccoli (and sold two pictures to Prince Foresto d'Este), and he stayed for some time at the convent of S. Giovanni in Parma where he was befriended by the art-loving Abbot Angelo Maria Arcioni. By March 1687, he and his wife lived in Venice in the house of his protector Nicolò Contarini, who had invited him there. He then rented for a year a house at the Fondamenta Nuove, near the Gesuiti, 'where one has a beautiful view, for one sees in the distance the mountains of Germany and the sea on the other side' (his letter of 15 March 1687). He is registered from 1688 to 1690 with the Venetian Fraglia, the local guild of painters (see T. Pignatti, 'La Fraglia dei pittori di Venezia,' in *Boll. dei Musei Civici Veneziani,* vol. x, 1965, no. 3, p. 36). In May of 1688 however, his wife wrote that he was at that time constantly in Milan, where he was having an affair with a young woman. In December 1689, he was again living in Venice. In his usual manner, he had immediately made many contacts. 'Here in Venice there is no lack of superb pictures to be seen every day in private houses, where as a connoisseur I sometimes go to pass the time with the greatest delight' (*ibid.*).

We know from Dal Pozzo, who wrote as early as 1718, that Pietro Cignaroli (born in 1665), after a first apprenticeship, 'went to Cremona, Pavia, and elsewhere in the company of Tempesta,' whose pupil he became, settling later in Milan. A later source, Zannandreis (1834), reports slightly differently that Cignaroli and his servant shared Tempesta's house, first in Piacenza, then in Milan (see p. 59). This happened between 1685 and 1695.

For the last decade, we find Tempesta in Bergamo, Brescia, and above all Milan. About 1692, he stayed in Brescia, where Roncelli was his pupil (the date can be inferred from F. M. Tassi's biography of Roncelli). In 1695, Tavella returned from Genoa to Milan 'in order to study further under the direction of the famous Pietro de Mulieribus, Fleming, called Tempesta. He was well received by that great artist and copied many of his paintings' (Ratti's *Life* of Tavella). Having then spent some time in Bergamo, Tavella went to Brescia 'only in order to see Tempesta again, who lived there at that time' (this about 1697/98; Ratti, *ibid.*). A prolonged sojourn in Brescia is also confirmed by Carboni (1776; p. 46), according to whom 'paintings by Cavalier Tempesta were no rarity there, Brescia being well provided with them because of the several years passed by the great painter of landscapes in that city.' A painting by Tempesta is in fact dated *Brescia 1697* (326). In his last years, spent in misery, he very likely lived in Milan. In 1700, at about mid-year, Tavella returned to Milan, 'where he lived in the house of Tempesta' until 1701 (Ratti, *ibid.*).

All this gives us the impression that Tempesta traveled around rather restlessly, which probably had to do with his irregular way of life, perhaps even with his amorous affairs; the reason cannot have been a lack of commissions. In the end it makes no great difference to us whether at a given moment he was in Milan, Bergamo, Piacenza, etc., as these towns are but a short distance from one another and shared in the same culture. His family life must have been far from exemplary. From the letter of his second wife to Count Borromeo dated 1 May 1688, we learn that he had dissipated her fortune, defamed her in Milan and Venice in order not to have to restitute her dowry, behaved immorally, abandoned her heartlessly to poverty (Pascoli), and taken a young mistress. His sister, Anna Maria Mulier-Beltrami, followed Tempesta all his life. She was in Milan by 1682 and died there in 1689.

Tempesta died in Milan on 29 June 1701 and was buried in the small church of S. Calimero. His simple Latin epitaph was placed inside the church, on the right side near the choir, at a height of about three feet, where it remained until the restoration of the church in 1830 (Ticozzi, vol. III, 21). It then disappeared for some time but is now relocated on the outside of the church. The inscription is quoted by Pascoli and in C. Bianconi's *Nuova Guida di Milano,* 1787, p. 129. His crested shield bore a bend charged with three estoiles. On the occasion of his death, Pascoli mentions a mistress of his and a daughter, his natural child, aged 15, who was to marry one of his pupils.

Tempesta appears to have been a very versatile and extroverted character who had the ability to make friendships easily. His letters are spiced with greetings to numerous persons—artists and noblemen. These loquacious letters also show him in perfect command of the Italian habits and of the local forms of human relations. Except for the earliest letters, his Italian is as genuinely idiomatic, colorful, and rich as is his pictorial language. It would be a mistake to see him mainly as an adventurer. His paintings and his friendships with such men as the Duke of Bracciano and Count Borromeo speak to the contrary. But he did not manage to keep the wealth that he earned and often got himself into material and other difficulties.

PATRONS

Turning to his patrons, and first of all to those in Rome, we have a few names of famous noblemen who bear witness to the artist's success. His principal protector was the Duke of Bracciano—actually not one, but two in succession: don Ferdinando Orsini, who succeeded upon the death of his brother Paolo Giordano II in 1656 as the fourth duke and died in 1660; he was followed by his son Flavio, fifth and last Orsini Duke of Bracciano, born in 1611, married first in 1642 to Ippolita Ludovisi, widow of Prince Aldobrandini. Flavio died in 1698 without progeny. He abandoned the old family palace on Monte Giordano in Roma and made the Orsini-Sangemini palace in Piazza Pasquino (near Piazza Navona) his residence. He engaged in insane expenses to adorn his palace, where he held a brilliant court. No study of his art patronage has as yet been made. The Orsinis of Bracciano were one of the most famous families of Rome, but in those years already deeply indebted and on the decline. By the 1680's, their financial collapse had begun. It ended at the close of the century with the sale of the entire property and titles to various buyers. In 1688, the palace on Monte Giordano passed to the Gabrielli della Regola (after 1888 property of the Taverna, since 1958 of the Gallarati Scotti); the castle of Bracciano and its titles passed in 1696 to the princes Odescalchi, who still hold it. The Gabrielli immediately proceeded in a lavish redecoration of their palace, including in one salon large landscape frescoes in the manner of Onofri. None of the works that Tempesta did for the Duke of Bracciano can be identified at present, nor is anything known about their fate, but it would appear that they were dispersed with the Orsini patrimony at the end of the 17th century. Though Tempesta did not live in the Orsini palace, but in the artists' quarter of the city, his employment must have been of the type of *servitù particolare* then quite common, by which a young artist became a member of the household of the rich patron, with all the advantages (assured income) and disadvantages (limited freedom) that this involved. His only other known patrons in Rome were Prince Colonna, for whom he did a set of frescoes in the late sixties, and Cardinals Giberto

Borromeo (letters of 1669) and Aloisius Homodei, both illustrious Milanese patricians. In 1661, Homodei also commissioned four large works by Gaspard, Mola, and Rosa (14). Most likely, Tempesta also worked for the Doria-Pamphilj.

For Genoa and Venice, we are almost without notice regarding patrons. In Castelfranco, Tempesta worked for his friend Donato Fabris, who is not otherwise known, and in Modena for Prince Foresto d'Este and Marquess Gio. Batt. Montecuccoli. In Venice he was received by Nicolò Contarini and Nicolò Micheli, and he often frequented noble houses.

In the Milanese period, three of the most important noblemen patronized him: don Giovanni, Count of Melgar, who was the Spanish governor of Milan from November 1678 to April 1686 and then ambassador in Rome until 1687; he was instrumental in liberating Tempesta from jail, possibly at the instigation of Count Borromeo. Nothing else is known about his patronage of the arts or the fate of his collection. Count Pietro Scotti, a leading figure in Milan, commissioned many pictures from the artist, about which nothing is known today (they are not in the collection of Duke Gallarati Scotti).

The major patron of the later years was indubitably Count Vitaliano IV Borromeo (1620–1690), whose intimate friend the artist was. The relationship with the family dated back to the years in Rome, where Tempesta was familiar with Vitaliano's elder brother, Cardinal Giberto (1615–1673, created 1652), for whom he painted a few small works. In 1669, the Cardinal recommended Tempesta to the Count (see the Letters), but the artist did not meet the Count before being jailed. Their exchange of letters only started in 1679, immediately before the election of the Count's uncle, A. Spinola, to the office of doge of Genoa (which he occupied until 1681). Understandably, Tempesta did not fail to exploit 'so favorable a conjuncture' (letter of 6 August 1679) in order to gain a much needed protection. Thereafter, he also came to know the Count's nephew and heir, Carlo II (1657–1734). Vitaliano was half a generation older than Tempesta, died unmarried, was Imperial Commissioner in Italy, Spanish Privy Counselor, and general of artillery. He assumed the defense of the artist at the trial and by means of long negotiations was most instrumental in achieving Tempesta's final liberation from prison. Afterwards, he did not chain the artist to his household, providing him, on the contrary, with other clients and giving him freedom to leave Milan for Venice and other cities. We know neither the precise facts behind the Count's protection, nor the dates and exact terms under which the pictures entered the collection. There is no doubt that, owing to this Count, about 80 paintings by Tempesta entered the family collection, where they are still kept *en bloc*. Besides a genuine affection for Tempesta's work, the Count had at that time a demand for paintings in considerable quantity, for it was precisely in those years that he built the palace at the Isola Bella. 'In the 1670's, '80's, and '90's, the Count went into such expenses there as to preoccupy even a sovereign, collecting objects for which he was envied by the most refined and magnificent gentlemen' (C. Bianconi, *Nuova guida di Milano,* 1787, p.268). No artist is represented nearly as extensively in the collection as Tempesta, and to my knowledge hardly any other old collection preserves today an equally large share of one artist. (The situation was not, however, unique in the past; in the mid-18th century, De'Franchi in Genoa owned 300 Tavellas; the Colonna and Doria galleries still have some dozen Gaspards each, the former also some dozen Vanvitellis). Tempesta proved faithful to his promise of life-long servitude toward the Count. Borromeo family tradition has it that the artist bequeathed all his pictures to the Borromeo (he died in utter poverty). No research has been done on the history of the large Borromeo collections, the core of which consists of 17th-century Lombard art. Vitaliano played the major role in its formation. Tempesta's pictures were surely supplied over a number of years, but no documents concerning them exist. Though the letters from prison occasionally mention a picture done for the Count, the bulk dates from his Lombard years. It may be added that all these pictures have hardly been mentioned until now; they are only cited *en passant* by C. Amoretti, *Viaggio da Milano ai tre laghi,* 1801, p.27; Wurzbach, 1910, p.210 ('several pictures'); Giolli, in *Rassegna d'Arte,* 1914, p.278; and Bonzi (on Tavella).

Because of the numerous evocations of the murder of Tempesta's wife in the past, it may be desirable to sum up what is known about it from the correspondence and from the detailed defense act by the lawyer Giovanni Della Torre (a lengthy printed document, which must date from 1679 and is preserved at the Isola Bella). In his letters, Tempesta never admits or speaks of his guilt. Lucia was lured to Sarzana with letters said to have been written by Tempesta. At the fatal moment, she was in the company of Guido Francesco Beltrami and of his wife Anna Maria, Tempesta's sister; the killer was Angelo Luigi da Valle Rustica, a soldier from Corsica, accompanied by Massimiliano Capurro, an adolescent. The Beltrami couple and Capurro were arrested on the spot. Condemned *in contumacia* were the killer and, as having been instrumental in sending the letters, Anna Eleonora Beltrami, Tempesta's second wife-to-be, who lived in his house in Genoa and was the sister of Guido Francesco; she fled, whereupon Tempesta was jailed. The defense pleaded innocent on the grounds of incompetence of the Genoese court, of insufficient evidence, and various unlawful procedures: the murder did not take place on Genoese territory, but at the border of the dukedom of Massa; the authenticity of Tempesta's signature on the letters was questioned; there was no complaint in Genoa, as an accusation from Lucia's brother in Rome (Tempestino) arrived too late. Lucia's last words were to the effect that she recognized Tempesta as the instigator of the murder.

Despite these objections, the court condemned Tempesta to twenty years in jail (see document of 1683; Pascoli's mention of a death sentence is not accurate). The idea to get rid of Lucia was very possibly his, but can we be sure? Lucia was hardly of the choicest breed, as she was called a prostitute and bore three children during the years of Tempesta's absence from Rome. On the other hand we may assume that his sister, her husband, and the sister of the latter, who was the new mistress and subsequent wife of Tempesta, all had an interest and a share in the affair. As far was we can estimate it today, there is the possibility that the murder was arranged by these relatives without the artist's knowledge or instigation.

The letters from prison contain such passages: 'I cannot leave my room and I am afraid that they shall lock me up in some tomb where I shall have news from nobody or shall have to die from hunger and misery, and this innocently … But with the time my innocence shall be known … Thus I come to the feet of yr. Exc. with tears of blood, that yr. Exc., by the five pains of God, help me now to make known my innocence and show that you do not protect a scoundrel, but a poor artist and honored man' (4 August, 1681).

TEMPESTA'S POSITION IN HIS TIME

The aim of the following pages is to see the artist in relation to his time. I shall attempt this by describing the artistic climate in which he was active, the types of images that he practiced, the influence of previous and contemporary masters upon him, the significance of his own contribution, and the impact that it exercised in turn on his surroundings. The discussion follows naturally the various centers in which he worked–Haarlem, Antwerp, Rome, Genoa, Milan and northern Italy. Each of these places represented a distinct cultural *ambiente* in response to which the art of Tempesta was shaped. The subsequent chapters will offer a detailed analysis of his oeuvre and a survey of his influence.

Tempesta belonged to the century that brought about the richest variety and the greatest propagation of landscape painting in all the leading schools. Through his Dutch origins, his further formation in Flanders, and his permanence in Italy over more than four decades, he participated as an international figure in this development. A brief *tour d'horizon* of the range and the achievements of 17th-century landscape will help to put things into proper focus.

Holland, the country of origin of our artist, contributed, above all, the realistic rendering of the local scenery by masters ranging from Esaias van de Velde and Buytewech to Jacob van Ruisdael, Hobbema, Molijn, Wijnants–to name just a few. No less important was the idealizing counterpart to this trend, the Italianate landscape with its evocative ruins and sunsets. Poelenburgh, Jan Both, Berchem, the Moucheron are some of the most succesful representatives of this direction. By contrast with his descriptive landscape etchings, Rembrandt created in his painted landscapes a unique type of visionary views. Special picture types were developed: the riverscape and the shore view by van Goyen, Salomon van Ruysdael, Aelbert Cuyp; the nocturne, with Lucas van Leiden and Elsheimer among its ancestry, embodied to an almost exclusive degree by Aert van der Neer; the winter landscape, based on Brueghel, later spread by Avercamp, Jacob van Ruisdael, van de Cappelle; the mountain landscape of A. van Everdingen and H. Saftleven; the farm house of the Ostade; animals in a landscape, represented by Potter in the Dutch vein, by Berchem, Dujardin, and so many others in the southern vein; the townscape and the topographic prospect, the battle scene, and others. The vast domain of marine painting, of importance also in the context of Tempesta, is, in quality as well as in quantity, the prerogative of the Dutch school. Here again, various types developed: beach views, lake scenes, the calm and the rough sea *per se,* sea storms and shipwrecks, shipping, portraits of ships, historic scenes, harbor scenes in Dutch or Italian (Lingelbach, J. B. Weenix) style, naval battles real and imaginary.

Flemish landscape had its greatest examples in the large panoramic views, farm views, and nocturnes of Rubens and his continuators (van Uden, Teniers). Beyond this circle, many specialists also practiced other types. The mountain landscape flourished in the early part of the century (Momper, Bril). D'Artois, followed by Huysmans and so many others, painted the wooded Flemish scenery. The Italianizing landscape came to bloom in the latter part of the century, assuming more classical and heroic forms than the Dutch.

Not equally important, the French landscape (exclusive of works by French emigrants in Rome) led from the classical landscapes by La Hire and Francisque Millet to an increasingly delicate classicism, influenced by Rome (the Patel, the Pérelle). Tempesta's art shows no specific contact with France.

The widest range of landscapes belongs to the Roman scene, enlivened by the presence of northern artists. When Tempesta arrived there shortly before 1660, the pioneering spirit of the innovators at the beginning of the century–Elsheimer, Annibale Carracci, Domenichino, Tassi, Claude, Breenbergh, and others–had given way to a broad stream of landscapes in firmly established styles. By 1660, Claude had arrived at his most heroic manner, while classical landscape gained ever more ground in Poussin's last years. Gaspard carried on his classical style without much change until 1675. Rosa, Mola, and Cortona all were to work for another decade, too. The classical trends increasingly dominated the field of landscape until the end of the century. By the time of Tempesta's death in 1701, numerous specialists were active in various centers. Rome remained the stronghold of the classical tradition under Orizzonte and was the theater for Vanvitelli's Vedute. Magnasco and Marco Ricci set the stage for the Venetian landscape of the 18th century, Tavella worked in Liguria, while Mehus, Reschi, and Onofri ended their career in Florence.

At the close of the 17th century, landscape continued to flourish in each country. For sheer volume, the output probably surpassed all previous epochs. A vital expression of its time, landscape around 1700 had, with all its ramifications of styles and types, an undeniable identity. A refined classicism set the general tone, but realistic aspects went side by side with it. No decline and no gap interrupts the continuous flow of landscapes that we can follow from the 17th to the 18th century. The binding forces of tradition become increasingly apparent to us. Thus, the heritage of Gaspard leads from Onofri and Orizzonte to Locatelli; the tradition of Rosa to Panfi, Reschi, Peruzzini, Magnasco, and Ricci. Codazzi and Cerquozzi lead to Panini and Ricci, Vanvitelli's Vedute to those of Carlevarijs, Marieschi, and Canaletto; Teniers and Francisque Millet lead to Watteau. Teniers was widely repeated in Flemish and French tapestries of the 18th century; Bloemaert's landscapes were imitated by the young Boucher; Dutch landscape continued vigorously all through the rococo age; Tempesta leads to Marco Ricci, Tavella, J. Vernet, Londonio.

YOUTH IN HOLLAND

Mulier grew up in Haarlem. Well before leaving for Flanders at age 17 or 18, he was already actively painting and traveling across the Dutch provinces. Only a few drawings, but no paintings, are at present known from those years. He was trained and most decisively influenced by his father, a marine specialist who, without being one of the foremost names, shared with his fellow artists the immensely cultivated métier and the sensitivity for hues and atmosphere that mark the Dutch school of sea painting altogether. The most personal pictures of the father are rough seas with waves sweeping in one or two wide bends across the entire foreground. Somewhat more than in other marine painters, we thus find in them an emphasis on the agitation of the elements that the son was at first to imitate, then to develop, to the exclusion of all other types of marines, into dramatic storms with shipwrecks. Beyond this link, there is, on the other hand, a profound difference between the father's characteristically Dutch technique of painting on panel with translucent layers of color in monochrome values, and the son's Italian technique of painting on canvas with opaque, but bright, colors. From the point of view of the elder's refined execution, the younger's early shipwrecks with their harsh highlights on waves and clouds appear crude.

The artistic *ambiente* of Haarlem provided other influences active upon the young man. Landscape was then at its peak, many of the greatest representatives having settled in town. Among them were Salomon van Ruysdael, Pieter Molijn, Jan Wijnants, Jan Vermeer of Haarlem, the animal painter Philips Wouverman, and several of the Italianizing landscape painters, above all Claes Berchem, his pupils Mommers, Wm. Romeyn, Thomas Wijck. Mulier must have been familiar with all of them. Moreover, Amsterdam with its flourishing school of marine and landscape painting was only a couple of hours away. Two artists need to be singled out specially – Berchem with his large animal scenes in an Italianate surrounding, which must have made a lasting impression on the young Mulier; and Pieter Molijn, whose influence is revealed in his earliest drawings; the link between the two artists is indirectly confirmed by the frequent confusion of which they have been the object (no doubt also because of the identity of their initials), to the point where Mulier was long regarded the son of Molijn. Until the end of his life, we can observe in Tempesta an echo of the Dutch farm houses so often represented by Molijn. On the whole, we may assume that the early paintings by our artist consisted of marines in the manner of Mulier the elder and of landscapes in the manner of Molijn. They were probably neither of outstanding quality nor distinctly personal; some may survive anonymously.

ANTWERP

The first foreign journey brought Mulier at the age of about 18 to Antwerp. This move was certainly in part due to family ties of the artist, whose paternal grandfather had emigrated from Flanders. Besides, there had always been close ties between the Dutch and Flemish schools, and many artists transferred from one to the other, for a few years or permanently (F. Hals, Brouwer, Lievens, etc.). Quite a number of young Dutch landscape artists extended their journeys into Flanders (van Goyen, Esaias and Jan van de Velde, Everdingen, Ro. Roghman, A. Waterloo, etc.). But if these were not deeply affected by Flemish art, the Antwerp sojourn, however brief it may have been, left the deepest impact on Mulier's art. Indeed, his painting shows in many respects Flemish, not Dutch, traits: the broad handling in a thick paste, the preference for grainy canvases of large size, a taste for sea storms and for certain rustic motives in his landscapes, an earthbound gravity, saturated images instead of the airy, spacious landscapes and marines favored by the Dutch – all this amounts to a basic affinity of temperament with Flemish art in general. Some reproductions ranging from d'Arthois to Huysmans may here exemplify this basic link (4f., 432f.).

A subject treated by Mulier in Antwerp was, in particular, the large animal battle as developed by Rubens, by the great specialists Snyders, Fyt, Paul de Vos, all of whom were then still alive, and by numerous imitators surrounding the masters. Houbraken mentions Mulier's 'boar hunts in the manner of Frans Snyders'; actually, the substantial handling of Fyt may have been even more to Mulier's taste. Only two large canvases with ducks can at present be identified as by him among the countless anonymous works of this kind. The type grew out of the monumental Brussels hunting and animal tapestries of the mid-16th century from the succession of Orley (such as the Hunts of Maximilian and the sets at Cracow and the Isola Bella). The Dutch equivalent of the great hunting still life, represented above all by Melchior d'Hondecoeter and the two Weenix, reached its full bloom only toward the end of the century. Tempesta had a special gift for the realistic representation of animals in life size. This predilection was to continue all through his life, either in straight animal pieces, or in the form of large groups of animals placed in the foreground of landscapes.

ROME

At the age of 19 at the most, Mulier journeyed to Rome, where he was to remain for a dozen years. Nothing was more common for a northern artist at the time. Indeed, the tradition had already prevailed for two centuries. The chapter of Italianism in Dutch art is reasonably well known, at least in its general outlines, and there is no need to trace it here in detail. A hint at the major steps in the field of landscape will suffice. The Romanists and antiquarians of the 16th century (Scorel, Heemskerck) already had a long heritage of Italianism behind them. A new wave set in with the brothers Bril and their wide surrounding (J. de Momper, Wm. van Nieulandt the younger, G. Terborch the elder, etc.), followed by the numerous Bambocciantti (van Laer, Miel), by the more modern approach to nature of Poelenburgh and Breenbergh, then by the continuators of Claude from the thirties and forties (Jan Both, Swanevelt, Asselijn) until later in the century (Jan Hackaert, Wm. de Heusch, I. Moucheron). There were specialists of Mediterranean seaports (H. Verschuring, Lingelbach), topographers and antiquarians (L. Cruyl, later B. van Overbeek), and other subcategories. Next to Claudianism, the main trend in Italianate landscape of the mid-century was the idyllic pastoral in the manner of Berchem (Mommers, J. B. Weenix, Dujardin). In the years of Mulier's Roman sojourn and in the next two decades, this direction was in turn giving way to classicist landscape with antique figures as we find it represented by the brothers van der Kabel, A. Meyering, Jacob de Heusch, the brothers Glauber, and others.

Such was the climate of Dutch Italianism when Mulier arrived in Rome. It is indicative that in the recent literature on the group of Dutch landscapers in Rome, his name hardly ever appears. He does not, in fact, qualify as an Italianist in the usual sense. He was an émigré who became completely assimilated into the country of his choice, comparable in this to Stradanus, Calvaert, or Sustermans before him, Vanvitelli and Orizzonte afterwards. How deliberate a turn this was is apparent from the beginning: right away he converted to Catholicism, took an Italian wife, and succeeded in entering the service of a Roman duke; he remained for life in Italy, painted only for local patrons and lost almost all ties with Holland. In his art, the conscious Italianization soon became an accomplished fact, whereas most of his countrymen who went for some years to Rome were not profoundly affected by the Italian masters of landscape.

Together with Tempesta, there were some other Dutch landscape painters in Rome – mainly minor names such as Adriaen Honing (Honich, alias Lossenbruy), Wm. Schellinks, B. Appelman, Jan Grevenbroek (in Rome 1667/69). The most personal was the Fleming Giovanni de Momper, documented in town from 1663 to 1668; his paintings, done in a fluid, characteristic brushwork, share no common ground with Tempesta, but provide in their own way a bridge from the northern heritage and the influence of Rosa to Roman 18th-century landscapes (see last Salerno, in *Palatino* 1968, p. 22). From 1659 to 1666, Adriaen van der Kabel was in Rome; subsequently, he was to carry his refined classicism to Lyon and is known to us from numerous paintings and engravings of his French phase (see the good, forgotten monograph by R. Cazenove, Paris 1888). Other foreigners then in Rome included the Frenchman J.-B. Forest and the German Pandolfo Reschi (426), who in 1666 lived in Tempesta's house.

The real competition that Tempesta had to face was that of the outstanding Roman masters. His surname at the Dutch painters' guild, Tempeest, shows that he made his way at first by concentrating on the specialty of sea storms, in which he benefited from his native tradition, from a lack of rivals, and from the wide appeal exercised on the collectors by this type of image. The epithet Tempesta, occurring for the first time on a drawing of 1659 (148), leaves no doubt about the kind of pictures he painted. Although there are, from a later phase, several stormy landscapes by him in the manner of Gaspard, the word Tempest, as any Latin dictionary will bear out, was invariably taken to refer to storm at sea, not to landscape; the opposite, viz. Calm or Tranquillity, had the same maritime connotation. In the history of marine painting and engraving, the two often formed significant pendants (based on Matth. 8:23–27). Our artist avoided the calm seas, the only example of the two opposites in his oeuvre being the Colonna frescoes, where one wall represents storm, the other tranquillity.

The Eternal City provided no market for the atmospheric subtleties of small beach views or still waters in the Dutch manner. Rome is not a maritime city, and marine painting had not flourished there before. The art historian will, of course, point out certain prototypes: the 16th century had created, especially in Rome, a number of gigantic frescoes of naval battles of the past (school of Raphael, Giulio Romano, Salviati, Vasari, etc.); the Armada and other historic feats gave rise to a wave of illustrative painting. But marines for the sake of their painterly values were introduced in Rome only by Bril, who did harbor scenes and sea storms (e.g. in the guise of the story of Jonah; see no. 66). His school took up the novelty: Nieulandt; Filippo Napoletano (on whom see exh. Florence 1969, p. 23); Hendrik C. Vroom, the first marine specialist in Rome; and above all Bril's pupil Tassi, whose most characteristic shipping pictures show huge prows of ships outlined as dark silhouettes against the distance. The marines of Tassi were continued by Claude; the coast views and the few sea storms of his first years soon gave way to the imaginary harbor scenes that made his reputation and that again derive from Tassi. Dutch marine painters who visited Rome included Abraham Willaerts, Reinier Nooms, the Beerestraeten, and Lieve Verschuier. On the level of engraving, sea storms appear with Callot, Stefano della Bella, and several specialists in their circle (Parigi, Silvestre, Ercole Bazzicaluva, Pietro Todeschi), and with Joh. Baur, Barrière, Hollar, etc. But all this is of marginal importance with regard to Tempesta. One source of real consequence for him must be mentioned here, though it will be discussed in more detail under the landscapes – Salvator Rosa. No pure marines are known by him, yet his large harbor scenes and coast views and the generous freedom of his brushwork affected Tempesta in a lasting way.

Sea storms and shipwrecks are only a minor aspect of Dutch marine painting. Not infrequent in the early phase, towards the close of the 16th century, they subsequently disappear in favor of the calm sea; this is not contradicted by the fact that every marine painter also produced a few tempests, some (e.g., Bakhuysen) more than others. Sea storms continued to be the preferred type in Flemish marine painting, e.g., with Eertvelt, the Peeters family, Caspar van Eyck. The Flemings also excelled in fictive naval battles, a genre not represented by Tempesta, who likewise kept away from terrestrial battle scenes. Unlike most of the Dutch marine specialists, several Flemish marine painters spent many years in Italy: Cornelis de Wael lived more than forty years in Genoa, which had traditionally strong artistic and commercial ties with Flanders; Eertvelt and G. van Eyck were his pupils there. De Wael played a leading role in paving the ground for marine painting in the Ligurian capital. A painter of great merit and exceptional versatility (67), a figure with European connections, De Wael was the leader of the Flemish colony in Genoa, then lived in Rome from 1656 until his death in 1667, during the same years, that is, as Tempesta, who must surely have met him. (De Wael's death inventory included a sea storm by Tempesta.) One of the few Dutch marine painters who had several times been in Rome and produced sea storms was Jan Blanckerhoff (1626–1669; see no. 68). But the closest prototype for Tempesta's sea storms was provided by two northerners: the Fleming Mathieu van Plattenberg (1608–1660; see no. 74), who was in Italy at about age 20, apparently not for very long, then resided in Paris until his death; and the Dutchman (or Fleming?) Monsù Montagna, active above all in northern Italy and deceased in Padua in 1644 (see no. 85). Tempesta can have met neither of them personally. The names and works of Plattenberg (Plate-Montagne) and Montagna were often confused in the past; Montagna's works were in turn frequently confused with Tempesta's, but cannot be identified today. Tempesta must have seen samples of them in Rome and northern Italy, and Montagna may indeed have been his most direct precursor. Plattenberg's sea storms survive in a number of examples; their splashy and rhetorical style represents an immediate anticipation of Tempesta. In this whole area, the borderlines between the artists remain uncertain, all the more so as the individual paintings are not distinguished by great artistic refinement.

The foregoing remarks remain somewhat up in the air because of the lack of certified Roman works by Tempesta. We know that he specialized in tempests. 'More than in any other way, he excels in painting landscapes with marines and lakes, and he works for a very advantageous price' – in these terms, Cardinal Borromeo referred to him in a letter of 1669. When it comes to actual works, we only have on one hand a masterpiece from the late '60's – the fresco decoration of a salon in Palazzo Colonna with tempests and calm seas, on the other hand a few drawings and some ungainly, blackish *burrasche* on canvas. This is what remains from a period of 12 years. Where are all the works done for the Duke of Bracciano, which were surely among his best? They were probably included among the Duke's properties sold to the Odescalchi in 1696, but there is no further trace of them.

Going by his drawings and his post-Roman oeuvre, it can be taken for granted that Tempesta also produced landscapes and animal pieces in Rome. The most telling indication is the fact that all his later landscapes gravitate between the poles of Gaspard and Rosa, the two masters who have since become synonymous with a classical vs. a romantic approach to landscape. While this contrast indeed exists, it should not be forgotten that there are also many points of contact between Gaspard and Rosa. The two occasionally worked on the same commission (see no. 14); Gaspard produced wind-swept stormy landscapes (derived from Poussin), the late Rosa imitated the landscape and figure style of Poussin. In retrospect, the dominating stream of landscape in the latter part of the century derived from the art of Gaspard, whose classicism contained *in nuce* the main trends of the decades around 1700 as seen in the large, decorative works of the Roman school (Onofri, Orizzonte, Locatelli) and in the refined style of the French and Dutch schools (Patel, Pérelle, van der Kabel, Eglon van der Neer, etc.). Despite some recent studies on Gaspard, we still have to defend his achievements against Claude, Poussin, Domenichino and Rosa. The 19th century was a better judge of Gaspard's importance. On the last pages of the *Cicerone,* discussing briefly Poussin and then at length Gaspard, Burckhardt put it this way: 'In him, nature speaks the sublime language which still resounds from the mountain ranges, oak forests, and ruins of the surroundings of Rome. ...The pictures of Swanevelt, of Joh. Both, of Tempesta-Mulier, until the improvisations of Orizzonte ... all merely reflect single rays of the light that had collected so forcefully in Gaspero and Claude.' Both Gaspard and Tempesta were fast-producing masters whose single works can at times be slight and superficial, whose oeuvre does not stand out as neatly against the imitators as that of Poussin or Claude, and whose art remained rather static during their last 20 years, thus rendering the study of their chronology difficult and of lesser importance.

An exterior contact between Tempesta and Gaspard is provided by Tempesta's Colonna frescoes placed in a suite of rooms decorated by Gaspard and pupils of his. The Dutchman's work is a genuine contribution to Roman decorative painting, for it is the first example of sea storms and coast views on this scale. Motives for some of the images derive from landscape and sea storm frescoes by Bril (66) and from the early harbor views by Claude (7), with whose highly personal art there is otherwise no immediate contact in Tempesta. From Gaspard's model of a dozen years earlier, Tempesta took over the basic decorative pattern and the concept of a continuous view extending over an entire wall. Also in his post-Roman landscapes, Gaspard's example continued to determine the basic structure of the pictures: static composition, orthogonal layout, massing in clearly contrasted forms, a saturated greenish coloring. At times, we find more specific evocations of Gaspard, as in the stormy landscapes (276) or in a few particularly classical compositions (219). But while Gaspard limited himself to landscape (and a few isolated architectural views), Tempesta's repertoire included in addition, coast, lake, and river views, figure and animal scenes, and miniatures – a versatility which likens him in turn to Rosa, whose range of subjects was even wider.

A further, indirect glimpse into Tempesta's Roman production can be gained from four large landscapes at Burghley traditionally known as Tempestinos (364). Except for a rougher brushwork and a more obvious Gaspardism, they are extremely close to Tempesta's late landscapes. But they can only reflect Tempesta's otherwise lost landscapes from the Roman years, thereby proving that already in Rome the master must have produced excellent landscapes in a manner to which he was basically to adhere for his whole lifetime. This assumption rests on the old and reliable attribution of the Burghley pictures to Tempestino. Yet the master did not remain stagnant, as his later landscapes gain considerably in refinement and comprehend a wide range of possibilities.

The influence of Rosa, which again we can grasp only in the post-Roman oeuvre, is, so to speak, superimposed on the fundamentally classical conception of Tempesta's landscapes. It appears in a general liveliness and gracefulness of the image, in an emphasis on pleasant forms, in the painterly freedom of the brushwork, and in the vivid coloring of the foliage, clouds, and skies. Rosa also provided the model for the type of coast and estuary views (20 f.) that proved enormously successful not only for Tempesta, but for an entire century to come, from Montanini, Reschi, J. de Heusch to Manglard, J. Vernet, J. Goupy, and so many others (134 f., 426 f.).

We can only surmise what other contacts our artist may have had in Rome. They included no doubt Pietro da Cortona (28) and Mola (26), with whom he had a basic affinity of temperament; Poussin from the 'Venetian' phase to the late landscapes; Testa (18); and Filippo Lauri (42). As we know from old inventories, Roman collections contained countless Venetian pictures. It is above all the Bassanesque type of landscapes with large animal scenes that must have appealed to Tempesta.

Rome had only minor animalists of its own. The genre had been imported by traveling northerners: Snyders (1608) and Fyt (before 1641) had visited there for short times, Castiglione was in town for several years around 1640. The Dutch contributed J. B. Weenix, in Rome from 1643 to 1646, and the low-class genre pictures of van Laer with his followers. Luca Giordano, who occasionally did large animal scenes, visited Rome around 1650, Joh. Heinr. Roos sojourned there in the mid-fifties. A native specialist of animals and still lives was Michele Pace (i.e. Michelangelo Pace da Campidoglio, 1610–1670); among his few certified pictures are four large, dynamic works with Cerquozzi-like hounds in a heroic landscape reminiscent of Gaspard and Mola (Ariccia, Pal. Chigi); they suggest that Tempesta may well have received the inspiration for comparable pictures such as no. 319 from Pace (on whom see Faldi in *Arte antica e moderna*, 1966, p. 144, repr.). Upon Tempesta's departure, two northern animal specialists came to town: the Fleming David de Coninck (1636–1699), a pupil of P. Boel, active in Rome from 1670 to 1687; and Karl-Andreas Ruthart, the German specialist of exotic animal battles, who spent his last 30 years until his death in 1703 in a monastery at Aquila. All this remained, admittedly, a minor aspect of Roman painting. Tempesta must have been struck by the manner of Castiglione, but had no part with the Bamboccianti and the other Dutch animal painters. The real wave of animal painting was only to set in with the 30-year-long activity of Rosa da Tivoli (the son of Joh. Heinr. Roos) at the end of the century.

Tempesta spent nearly sixteen years in Genoa, from late 1668 to late 1684, the first period perhaps interrupted by a short Roman sojourn, the last eight years in prison. The Genoese school of painting, then still at its peak, constituted an artistic climate very different from Rome. It was not in the same way at the crossroads of international influences, except for the traditional links with the Flemish school, which had forcefully been renewed by Rubens, van Dyck, and numerous followers. The three genres which Tempesta had to offer – marine, landscape, animal painting – were unevenly represented. Marine painting was in effect introduced and made fashionable by Cornelis De Wael. With his superior ability for sea storms, Tempesta clearly filled a gap and found in the rich maritime capital a more receptive audience than in Rome. Not by chance are all the paintings under his name in old local collections tempests. The surprising fact is rather that Genoa had not already produced a school of marine painters long before him.

In the field of landscape painting, no Italian city of the time could rival Rome. Though Genoese Renaissance masters such as L. Brea had invented admirable Flemish-style landscape backgrounds for their altarpieces, the specialty as such was introduced by foreigners: around 1610 by Tassi, who decorated some of the villas and garden casinos on the Ponente side of town, now all lost; in the 1610's by Cornelis De Wael and Jan Wildens, who stayed in town apparently for several years, and by whom Palazzo Rosso still conserves an excellent set of landscapes; and during a sojourn of Tassi's pupil, the German Goffredi Wals, who excelled in tiny landscape paintings, none of which can be identified today. Tassi and Goffredi contributed to the formation of Il Sestri (Antonio Travi, 1608–1665), the only Genoese landscape artist before Magnasco (see on him Delogu, 1931, p. 43, and Bonzi's unsatisfactory pamphlet, Genoa 1964). But his art, delightful as it is, moves on a restricted local scale, and he is in fact a painter of ruins in landscape rather than of pure landscapes. Nor did Castiglione practice landscape in the Roman sense. For the rest, landscape only occurs at times in an accessory role with Gregorio de 'Ferrari and with Bacciccio, who in spite of his Genoese upbringing belongs altogether to the Roman school. In this domain too, Tempesta was thus without a competitor. Only in the last decade of the century began the revival of Genoese landscape with Magnasco and Tavella.

The animal genre, on the contrary, was flourishing. The foundation was laid by Scorza (dec. 1631) and Jan Roos (Giovanni Rosa), first a pupil of Snyders, then active in Genoa from 1616 until his death in 1638. Scorza (34), himself indebted to Flemish animalists, popularized the Orpheus and Paradise images that Tempesta was to continue in a more modern way. Another Flemish master of the animal still life who had sojourned for some time in Genoa around the middle of the century was Pieter Boel (1622–1674; the Louvre preserves over 200 drawings of his). Between Scorza and his gifted follower Antonio Maria Vassallo (see Delogu, 1931, p. 52, and exh. Genoa 1969, p. 87), whose activity immediately preceded that of Tempesta, stands the dominating figure of Castiglione (39). A universal artist, a great painter and an inventor of new types of images, he broke the traditional limits of the landscape and the animal piece. Although he left the Ligurian capital permanently around 1640, his art, which echoed well into the 18th century, was the major impulse received by

Tempesta in Genoa. The previous contact with Rosa made Tempesta all the more receptive to the painterly qualities and the liberal handling of the Genoese. And he took over the type of pastoral scenes with generic Old Testament themes. The elegiac, yet festive mood so typical of Castiglione can still be felt in several of Tempesta's best works from the post-Genoese phase. Vassallo and Castiglione having died in the sixties, Tempesta found an open field for his specialty.

Marines, pastorals, and landscapes were thus in great demand at the time of Tempesta's sojourn in town. Some of his most personal paintings fit stylistically into this phase (201 f.). But faced with a complete lack of dated pictures from Genoa, we remain rather uncertain about the full scope of his Genoese production. Almost the only pictures known to have come *ab antiquo* from old local collections are a dozen tempests of such inferior quality that they either are not his or, more probably, are the result of his worst days in prison.

Several dozen letters illustrate the artist's painful existence during the prison years. We learn that he kept painting in the measure of the possible; his production must at times have halted altogether and was probably of very uneven quality. On one hand he had to satisfy the influential persons on whom his liberation depended; the pictures done for this purpose were surely of fine quality. We are not surprised to read several times that he had been working for months on one canvas; only one such work is mentioned by title–an Ark of Noah. On the other hand he was obliged to paint for sheer survival and in order to pay his debts, a situation that would account for hasty execution. Pascoli confirms that Tempesta partly gave away, partly sold his pictures, and goes on to say that the works done in prison 'are held to be the most beautiful that he did.' This is certainly an overstatement, for the dated pictures from the last years of his life are inferior to none. The artist, at any rate, was capable for years to produce tempests and landscapes in confinement, cut off from any contact with nature.

MILAN–VENICE–NORTHERN ITALY

The extant oeuvre of Tempesta is mainly that of his last 16 years. So far we have to point out our uncertainty regarding the production of his Netherlandish, Roman, and Genoese phase. We are hardly better off with dates for the Lombard period; but the Borromeo group, and with it most of the other similar works, cannot precede the Lombard phase. The peak of the artist's activity can further be narrowed to the decade between 1685 and 1695. Pascoli reports that Tempesta was immediately in favor with Count Borromeo, whose protection resulted in numerous other commissions and immense gains for the artist. He soon lived in great style, in 'magnificence and splendor,' with a superb house, carriage, servants, and a seraglio. Following his biographer, this had already happened before he abandoned his second wife, which became an accomplished fact between March 1687 and May 1688 (letters of 15 March and 1 May). In these years, the artist was frequently on the move in northern Italy: in 1687 for a short time in Modena and Parma, from 1687 to 1690 in Venice, with frequent stays in Milan, in the early nineties in Brescia; and also in Castelfranco, Vicenza, Bergamo, Piacenza. Success was not to last. 'Finally his means began to fail him' (Pascoli), his health and eyesight declined, painting slowed down, utter misery preceded the end. In looking over the artist's late years, we are thus faced with a master who displayed an astonishing activity within a relatively small lapse of time. Yet–if we want to be the critics of his way of life–his natural talents could have led to an even larger and better oeuvre. Our opinion must in the end concur with Pascoli's assessment: 'Fortuna loved him, but he did not recognize her, and by his imprudent and dissipating conduct did not know how to take advantage of her.'

From Genoa, where life was obviously impossible for him, Tempesta would have returned to Rome, had he not been obliged to serve his benefactors in Milan. While we do not know the extent of his work for Counts Melgar and Pietro Scotti, he must have been working for the Borromeo over a long time. The Count's efforts on behalf of the artist were being well rewarded.

Milanese painting of the last 15 years of the century was at a low ebb, particularly after the death of Frc. del Cairo and Nuvolone. Tempesta was to meet no challenging inspiration, all the more so as his specialties had no tradition here. In a province without access to the sea, marine painting would not be a flourishing genre. Admittedly, all of Tempesta's best marines–presently about nine pieces (110 ff.)–date from this phase. But they represent only the smallest part of his post-Genoese output, while he must have concentrated on marines far more in Rome and Genoa. Nor had landscape played any part in Milanese Seicento painting. Milan had had some contacts with earlier Flemish landscape, of which a number of examples are still preserved in old private collections. What worked instead for Tempesta was the fact that the taste for landscape was 'in the air' at the time. Hardly any other senior landscape painters are then recorded in Milan, certainly none of Tempesta's stature. During the eighties, we find there the Dutchman Jan Grevenbroeck (il Solfarolo; 129), who specialized in sulfuric sunset effects. His manner was continued in the nineties by his pupil Tavella (born in 1668) and by Roncelli (born in 1669; 400), who, also in the nineties, became Tempesta's pupil. The young Genoese Magnasco (born in 1667) spent most of the century's last two decades in Milan, but his contact with Tempesta was marginal at the most. For Marco Ricci, who probably sojourned in Milan during the nineties, the intercourse with Magnasco as well as with Tempesta was to leave a permanent mark. Into the years around 1700 falls the Milanese activity of Frc. Peruzzini, teacher of Marco Ricci (see last exh. Florence 1969, p. 70). Only passing through was Vanvitelli, who in 1688/90 did several pictures and drawings of the Isola Bella and other points of Lago Maggiore. Soon after 1700, landscape specialists in Milan grew more numerous; 'many were at that time the painters in Milan, who had the figures of their marines and landscapes painted by Magnasco. … It would be long to enumerate them' (Ratti, *Life* of Magnasco). In the animal genre, which later became a flourishing Lombard specialty, Tempesta was once again the first exponent.

The other north Italian cities in which Tempesta worked for short periods all had local schools of a distinct, if somewhat provincial character. We need not be concerned here with their individual peculiarities, as Tempesta's specialties were hardly represented anywhere. But one overall trend must be pointed out. It is the well-known inclination of the Lombard schools toward realism in various aspects (still life, genre, battle). Only by the first half of the 18th century did Lombard realism attain its full blossoming in animal painting, genre figures, and portraiture. Yet the naturalism of Tempesta's landscapes and animal scenes had already fallen on receptive ground and became in turn a step in the development of the coming realism.

33

Venice is the only city to give lieu to some further remarks, because of its tradition and of the length of Tempesta's sojourn (two to three years). We have his own word regarding the reason for his prolonged stay: 'My arrival in this city has been appreciated by many dilettanti and gentlemen, because there are enough figure painters, but none of landscapes and marines and small animals, or those who are here, are no good, for which reason there is no want of work, thank God' (his letter of 15 March 1687). Despite the monopoly enjoyed by Tempesta in Venice, Venetian painting on the whole was, at the close of the century, by far the liveliest of northern Italy; the most comprehensive surveys of this subject are by Pallucchini (1960), Martini (1964), and Donzelli-Pilo (1967).

The maritime orientation of Venice provided fertile waters for marine paintings, though not the Dutch kind of easel paintings with atmospheric subtleties. The local version was the monumental historic naval battle, deriving from Tintoretto's huge Lepanto battle in the Sala dello Scrutino of the Doge's Palace; the same *salone* harbors other, equally gigantic examples, going from Andrea Vicentino (ded. 1617) to the Victory of the Dardanelles of 1656 by Pietro Liberi, who died in the year of Tempesta's arrival. Our artist engaged neither in battle pieces nor in historic subjects, but he must have been as keenly interested in the Venetian grand style as the local market was, in turn, in his pictures. Two minor sea storm specialists preceded him in Venice: the already named Monsù Montagna, whose name occurs frequently in old north Italian collections (see no. 85); and Giacomo Maffei, whose praise is sung by Boschini (1660), where we also find the only reproduction of one of his works.

In landscape, the heritage of the masters of the Venetian Cinquecento–Titian, Campagnola, Dossi, Veronese, Tintoretto, Paolo Fiammingo, Pozzoserrato, Sustris, etc.–remained alive throughout the 17th century. As one among many examples, a series of 53 fine engravings by Valentin Lefebre after Titian and Veronese went through numerous editions in Venice from 1680 to 1749. The most decisive impact on Tempesta came from the Bassano. Their influence spread widely for more than a century, over Rosa, Courtois, Giordano, to Seb. Ricci and Boucher. Tempesta made the spirit of the Bassano his own. Jacopo da Ponte as well as his sons–of whom Gerolamo and Leandro lived until the 1620s–excelled in a type of image that proved important for Tempesta: the large, broadly painted landscape with animal groups in the foreground, a religious subject in the distance, the whole often rendered as a nocturne with the light breaking dramatically through glorioles of clouds. Landscape and animal genre are here united. Though Tempesta must have been exposed to works of the Bassano before his sojourn in Venice, their example, combined with that of Castiglione, became as determining for his late years as Gaspard had been for his Roman landscapes. Tempesta's subject matter is mostly simpler and does not involve any cycles such as months or elements. His Entry into the Ark and his Sacrifice of Noah (241), a Bassanesque pair owned at the time by the Venetian Count Algarotti, were almost certainly done during the Venetian years.

There are some other, minor aspects of landscape in 17th-century Venice, which may here be mentioned. (See also Donzelli, 1967, p.41). The genre flourished mainly in the early years, from Elsheimer's visit to Fetti. Boschini's poem of 1660 praises three northerners then active in Venice: the Frenchmen Monsù Cussin, whom I believe to be Noël Cochin (412), Monsù Giron, and the German

Conrad Filger, whose specialty was the effects of the sun. None of Giron's and Filger's works is known at present; their name does not occur in old inventories, and Boschini's reproductions make them look like outdated imitators of Bril. Landscape painters settled in Venice at the time of Tempesta were Giovanni Eisman (424), a native from Salzburg, and his adopted son Carlo Brisighella, called Eisman. Among the few Dutch landscapers who came to Venice, Livio Mehus (Oudenaarde 1630–Florence 1691) worked there at a young age, then propagated his outspoken Venetian style in Florence, where many of his attractive works survive (see exh. Florence 1961, p. 61). Joh. Glauber was in town in the seventies, Dujardin died there in 1678. Landscape had, furthermore, an important place in the classicizing, sometimes Poussinesque, figure compositions of Giulio Carpioni (1611–1674), who was active mainly in Vicenza. In this context it is significant that Tempesta was associated in Venice with another figure painter of prerococo elegance, Antonio Bellucci, to some of whose figure paintings he contributed the landscape setting (see 349c). The class of landscapes that in the following century was to overshadow all others, the Veduta, never occurs in Tempesta, although at about the time of his Venetian phase his compatriot Vanvitelli painted the first great examples of Venetian Vedute, a type in which the pedestrian Josef Heinz (dec. 1678) had preceded him. In the last decade of the century finally, we witness the beginning of the great revival of Venetian landscape with Bartolomeo Pedon (born in 1665), Luca Carlevarijs, and Marco Ricci (born in 1676).

Regarding the animal genre after the Bassano, it will be recalled that Fyt, Karl-Andreas Ruthart (1652/59), Luca Giordano, and the Dutch poultry specialist Giacomo Victor (1663) visited Venice. Boschini (1660) also cited, and reproduced a composition of, Domenico Maroli (1612–1676), an animal specialist from Messina who had worked in Venice. In the end, all this goes to prove that Tempesta was, as he claimed, unrivaled in his specialties at the time.

THE OEUVRE

This chapter offers a discussion of Tempesta's oeuvre, its stylistic characteristics, and its development. While the bulk of the oeuvre is formed by the paintings, the early Dutch and Roman phases are known to us almost exclusively from the drawings and the frescoes respectively, which are therefore given precedence here.

DRAWINGS
Unlike his paintings, Tempesta's drawings are hardly known to us and are revealing only for his early years. About 15 sheets bear his signature or old inscriptions of his name; some two dozen more can be ascribed to him on grounds of style or traditional attribution. All the signed sheets, and a selection of the others, are reproduced here (140–169). It seems that they all belong to his Dutch and Roman years, except for the animal studies. We are thus faced with the odd situation that from his Dutch beginnings only a few drawings, but no paintings, exist, while virtually no drawings are

preserved from the years of his maturity as a painter. This is surely owing to the hazards of preservation, for we know also from Pascoli that the artist drew eagerly in his late years. But we can infer that, in true conversion to Italian artistic life, he did not regard drawing as an end in itself and as a source of income, as was customary in Holland (attested, e.g., by the numerous pictorial drawings of Molijn, van Goyen, Berchem, and others).

Tempesta's drawings do not show a tight stylistic unity. Small groups of them reveal various artistic origins, which confirm in a more explicit way what we likewise observe in his early paintings. In view of the scarcity of dated works by Tempesta, five dates from the fifties and one from the next decade assume particular importance; unfortunately, the reading of the last digit is unclear in several cases, but the basic trends leave no doubt. As is to be expected, his beginnings are entirely rooted in the Haarlem school. The Dutch riverscapes and village views from the mid-fifties, done in soft chalk and light wash, imitate the style of Pieter Molijn, who was the leading local landscape artist and an assiduous draftsman (136–139). It may not be by chance that Molijn, who had the same initials as Mulier, very often dated his drawings in the mid-fifties, rarely at other periods. There are borderline cases in which it is difficult, if not impossible, to separate the two hands. Tempesta's drawings also resemble ipso facto certain sheets of van Goyen and Hermann Saftleven. Since our artist left Holland at the age of about 18, we have a clear terminus for his Dutch scenes. As works of a very young man, almost an adolescent, they are very respectable (140–143). If the riverscapes could be termed Molijn redone in a prettier fashion, the village roads and houses are a type of image familiar to us from Isaac van Ostade. What we cannot assess is the influence of Tempesta's father, by whom no drawings are as yet known. Very likely he too worked in the van Goyen–Molijn manner. Tempesta's drawing of a coast view (150) is close to his father's painting no. 60; but the Mulier signature of the drawing cannot be that of the father, as the handwriting is the same as the Tempesta signature on no. 148. Pascoli speaks of Tempesta's journeys across Holland. His Dutch scenes bear, in fact, all the marks of nature drawings. Yet in two instances of two almost identical and apparently genuine drawings, one of the two sheets must be the repetition done at home after the other. As to Tempesta's paintings from the Dutch years, which are still unknown to us, it is only logical to assume that they too belonged to the artistic ambience of Mulier the elder, Molijn, van Goyen, and Ostade.

From the beginning, the attractive settings and the evident technical ease of these drawings betray a contact with such Italianizers as Berchem. In the early Roman years, from 1656/57 onwards, Tempesta was not yet the Italian classicist of his later phase, but a romantically inclined Dutch Italianizer. Two views of 1657 and 1659 (145, 148) are telling examples of this transition: the scenery is now imaginary (or at least seems to be so), a few Italianate buildings have been introduced, but style and layout still follow the undulating pattern of Molijn in the first case, already show a firmer framework inspired by classical landscape in the second case. The picturesque no. 147, too, is an Italianizing work in the taste of Berchem and Dujardin.

The next step is marked by the influence of classical landscape. Only at this stage do we begin to grasp Tempesta also as a painter. Not by chance the technique changes now from the soft chalk and wash to pen and wash. The two nature views, nos. 151 f., one dated 1662, have the tight setting of drawings by Claude from about 1640 without their poetic sensitivity. It was not the elevated and personal art of Claude, but the more imitable language of Gaspard that the young Tempesta took to heart. Two studies of rocks and torrents (156 f.), probably dating from the later sixties, belong to a type of image that leads from Flemish prototypes (Bril) to Claude–who around 1640 created the boldest examples–and from there to Gaspard, Swanevelt, and Vanvitelli. The colorfully contrasted wooded scene, no. 158, also echoes Flemish landscapes in its curvilinear framing, casting at the same time its shadow far ahead to Marco Ricci; among Tempesta's paintings, no. 287 represents a somewhat more advanced compositional parallel. A further species of his drawings are the animal studies which, according to Pascoli, he must have practiced extensively but of which only a few fine examples in chalk are known at present, dating almost certainly from the late years.

Among the certified drawings, some are outstanding in quality. The unsigned sheets with old attributions to Tempesta show certain disparities of style that raise here and there doubts as to his authorship. Basically we have to allow for quite a wide range of possibilities in the artist's young years. Not a single sheet corresponds to a painting. Was he, then, not in the habit of preparing his paintings with drawings? While he surely did not work out each picture by a series of penetrating studies, as Claude did, it is also clear that he did not abandon drawing in his later years. His name occurs occasionally in old drawing sales; the greatest single batch figured in the S. van Huls sale at The Hague, 14 May 1736, which lists 54 sheets of 'Tempeest', in particular the following subjects: several battles, the children of Niobe, the Red Sea, a boar hunt in pen and one in wash, a lion hunt, a hunt, a landscape, St. Francis, a monk in agony, a saint with herdsmen, the conversion of St. Paul, the life of a saint in 8 sheets, another in 10 sheets, the life of Christ in 14 sheets; all are lost. (The same sale comprised 206 drawings by Molijn.) The series suggest that Tempesta may also have prepared book illustrations.

FRESCOES

Our present knowledge of Tempesta immediately begins with his masterpiece–the decoration of a salon in the Colonna palace in Rome (173–181)–which remains a unique work within his oeuvre. All at once it is his earliest certified painting, his largest and most stately achievement, his only extant work done in fresco, and the only major monument known from his sojourn of a dozen years in Rome. Earlier dates only appear on a few drawings. Besides, a mere handful of rather minor, darkened sea storm paintings in the Colonna and Doria collections can safely be attributed to his Roman phase on the strength of their provenance. The frescoes do not stand isolated in the history of Roman wall decoration, but have their place within the extensive Gaspardesque landscape cycles of the time.

To begin with, a word about the literature. Although the frescoes bear no signature and no documents are as yet available from the Colonna archives, there can be no doubt about Tempesta's authorship; it is confirmed by the style, by family tradition, and by old references in the guides. The biographers do not mention the frescoes. But in speaking of the Roman sojourn, Pascoli (1730) reports that 'noteworthy were the last works which he had to do for the duke and for the Contestabile' (i.e., Prince Colonna). The frescoes are first cited in the Additions to Titi's *Descrizione della Pitture … in Roma,* 1763, p. 482, which say of Palazzo Colonna: 'The ground floor apartments are enriched with wall paintings by Poussin (i.e., Gaspard), Tempesta, Stanchi, and others; and one room is in the manner of a hermitage painted by Pietro Paolo Scor' (Schor; in the index, Tempesta is wrongly listed as Antonio). Summary mentions appear in later guidebooks. More explicit is the Colonna catalog of 1783, which describes the palace room by room; in this instance: 'The marines and sea storms in all the wall frames are by Tempesta of Genoa. The decorations of the walls are by mediocre authors. The figures in the two ovals of the vault and the trophies of all the lunettes of the said vault are by Pomerancio. The rest is by mediocre authors.' The next reference to be more than a mere repetition of previous quotations is by Fokker, who in 1929 drew attention to the frescoes (see Bibliography). Being in the private apartments, they are not mentioned in the modern Colonna catalogs. A photograph of the room appeared in *Connaissance des Arts,* March 1957, p. 68, and in *Great Family Collections,* ed. D. Cooper, London 1965, p. 25, both in color. Finally, an article of mine on the frescoes was published in *Burlington Magazine* 1967, p. 12.

The salon is on the ground floor, vaulted, 9.5 by 5.5 m., lavishly decorated from top to bottom with an architectural framework adorned by caryatids, putti, and floral still lives. The only older part is the vault, adorned with armors and Etruscan decors; it was painted, like the ceilings of three adjacent rooms, by the late mannerist Cristofano Roncalli, called Pomarancio (1552–1626). The collaboration of specialists of quadratura, figures, landscape, flowers, and decorative work resulted in a perfect unity and in one of the richest room decorations in all of the Roman baroque. The walls were obviously planned and executed in one go. The captivating effect is heightened by the freshness of preservation and the strong coloring. Tempesta's contributions are the marines–six lunettes measuring 3.15 by 2.20 m., plus a strip along two doors. Clockwise, one long wall shows three fields of stormy seascapes with shipwrecks in a continuous space (175, 177 f.; two thirds of the left hand field are occupied by a door). On the narrow wall to the right follows first a window, then a serene coast view (179), whose space carries over to the second long wall with its three fields of a continuous, imaginary coast view (180 f., 174). On the remaining narrow wall is a harbor view (176), flanked on either side by a window from which the real as well as the fictive illumination for the whole decoration comes. The perspective of the painted architectural framework is focused on the center of the room; the horizon is at eye level. The decoration contains two contrasting parts–one wall with the tempests, in bluish-grey tones, the other wall and the lateral frescoes with calm coast views; the predominant tones are green, yellowish-green, and some brown; the water is green, the clouds are violet. Except for some damage in the lower part of no. 176 and for some cracks, the condition is good.

With perfect taste, Tempesta succeeded in blending the landscapes with the rest of the decoration. His light and airy views strike exactly the right key and are conceived in the proper spirit of fresco work. More than half of each field is occupied by sky and water–a spaciousness that contrasts markedly with the pictorial saturation of his canvas paintings. What impresses the viewer

38

most, even today, is the illusion of a vast, life-like expanse of space beyond the arcades of the festive loggia. A daring and unique effect is the coloring of no. 179 in luminous hues of a sun-bathed atmosphere with the sea in yellow and white, the sky in pink and light blue. The most forceful composition is undoubtedly the tempest, which justifies the artist's high repute for such scenes. Masses of rocks, water, and clouds are dramatically built up in oblong, triangular areas of contrasting tones and directions. The coast views, on the other hand, also reveal the limit of Tempesta's compositional means: foreground and sea are separated in them without any binding elements such as large figures or buildings.

Regarding the date, Pascoli's statement suggests that the work was done at the end of Tempesta's Roman sojourn, i.e., either shortly before his departure for Genoa in mid-1668 at the latest, or, less likely, between his return about early 1670 and his final departure, apparently in 1670 or 1671. There is a profound difference of quality and conception between the frescoes and the drawings from the first Roman years (dates ranging from 1657 to 1662).

The artistic sources for the individual images go back to the fresco works of Bril and Tassi in the early part of the century. This heritage has been lightened under the impact of Claude's art of 1640, of Gaspard, and to a lesser degree of Rosa. The only prototype for the sea storms is Bril's example in the Scala Santa (see no. 66). Flemish elements are particularly noticeable in another image (180), characterized by romantic scenery composed of rocks, broken trees, a bridge, and a torrent. At the same time, the basic decorative quality of this fresco brings to mind some of Veronese's lofty landscape frescoes at Maser, although there can have been no direct link. Tempesta's other two coast views are directly inspired by similar subjects of the early Claude (7). With his Dutch background, the young Tempesta must naturally have felt a closer affinity to the world of the young Claude than to the elevated classicism of Claude's works done at the time of these frescoes. What differs in the Colonna cycle from the preceding generation is the ease and grace in the design of the coast views with their luminous coloring and open space. Their elegance points into the future, toward Manglard and Panini.

The major significance of the frescoes lies in the spatial illusion of the whole room. It is, therefore, appropriate to consider the origin of such comprehensive landscape decorations. Nothing in his Dutch heritage prepared the artist for this task. The Colonna salon is very likely the earliest example of continuous marines, although much research is still needed before we can claim to have an adequate knowledge of Roman decorative painting of the seicento. Rooms with continuous landscapes (as opposed to seascapes) have a long history from Etruscan and ancient Roman examples (the finest being the 'Wintergarten' of the Villa of Livia at Prima Porta, now in the Museo Nazionale, Rome) to late medieval and renaissance hunting décors (Aosta; Leonardo's *Sala delle Asse* in the Castello Sforzesco). In the 16th century, painted landscapes encompassing entire rooms are rare. Decorative schemes consisting of large, though not continuous, landscape areas which create a room-wide illusion of spatial expansion are found in some famous villas: first in the Farnesina, with Peruzzi's perspectives, furthermore in some rooms at Caprarola, Bagnaia, Maser (Veronese), and others. A smallish room in Villa Imperiale at Pesaro, the *Sala delle Cariatidi,* decorated in fresco c. 1530 by

39

Dosso Dossi, affords the most complete landscape illusion of its time: painted caryatids in the foreground, growing out of trees, strengthen the spatial unity of the view.[1] More important for the genesis of the room opening up into landscape are numerous sets of Flemish and some French and Italian 16th-century tapestries with hunting scenes, noble park views, or *verdures,* destined to cover the four walls of a room. What must have been, a generation before Tempesta, a major example of a room with continuous landscape frescoes all around is a decoration by Claude Lorrain in a rustic house of the Muti in Rome. From his teacher Tassi survive two grandiose ensembles of continuous landscapes and coast views opening up behind painted double arches in the Lancellotti palaces ai Coronari and in Piazza Navona, Rome.[2] It would be fascinating to follow in detail the idea of the comprehensive landscape decoration from its origins in the country villa to its penetration into the city palace. Among the Roman palaces, that of the Colonna has in its design, its decoration, and its vast, sloping gardens particularly strong affinities with the suburban villa.

Tempesta's Colonna salon is part of a suite of six rooms, all lavishly adorned with landscape frescoes by different hands in a Gaspardesque taste. This is certainly the most important ensemble of landscape decorations of the time, and only in this context is it possible to understand the achievement of the young Dutchman. Since the whole series is unpublished and hardly any scholars have so far been granted access to it, a summary description may be justified. The suite begins with two small rooms showing landscapes in the manner of Tempesta, the first a little weaker (the second was the bedroom of Maria Mancini); the vault is by Pomarancio. The third room is identical in size to the Tempesta salon. Our unsatisfactory reproduction (170) will at least suggest its general scheme: the lower part has a festive, painted loggia with four columns per bay and a continuous panoramic landscape consisting of low hills, water, and some trees in yellowish-green tints. The outstanding quality of this landscape supports the traditional attribution to Gaspard; the vault is in the Etruscan style by Pomarancio. After the adjacent Tempesta room follows the fifth room, twice as large, with four wall-size frescoes of park views, fluffy trees, and a fountain, in yellowish-brown tones and a unique impressionist handling (a detail is reproduced in *Connaissance des Arts,* March 1957, p.71). According to the Colonna catalog of 1783, this room is again by Gaspard; to my mind, it cannot be by the same hand as the third room, but is either repainted or by an extremely gifted pupil of Gaspard. The battle scenes in the lunettes are by Allegrini (d.1663), the decoration of the vault is by Cavalier d'Arpino. The sixth salon is by far the largest and is made up by partly curved walls in a rectangular scheme; four large frescoes of continuous landscapes in a classicizing taste are by Crescenzio Onofri (also according to the description of 1783), the figures on walls and ceiling by Carlo Cesi (d.1686) and Giac. Gimignani (d.1681).

Tempesta's room, which is second to none of the others in quality, is thus incorporated into a whole scheme in which Gaspard was the guiding force. As to the date, Baldinucci reports that after the San Martino frescoes, which have now been proved to date from 1648/1651 (*Burl. Mag.* 1964, pp.58, 115), Gaspard was commissioned by Prince Colonna 'to paint also in his palace several rooms

1. See last F. Gibbon, *Dosso and Battista Dossi,* Princeton 1968, p.79. The ceiling represents a pergola.
2. See Mussa, in *Capitolium* 8–9, 1969, pp.41 ff., figs.23 f., 28.

in fresco, with further friezes and sopraporte.' We also know that in 1654, long and extensive transformations of the palace were undertaken. Gaspard's work can thus be dated in the mid-fifties and ipso facto precedes Tempesta's activity.[1] A further work by Gaspard in this taste was the fresco decoration of the entire Sala del Principe in the Doria palace at Valmontone, done in 1658 for Prince Pamphilj and again based on the device of dominating painted paired columns opening up into a view with trees and distant mountains (see L. Montalto, in *Commentari*, 1955, p. 279, repr.). What Tempesta took over from Gaspard was not the classical character of the landscape, but the convincing illusion of a continuous space. Room five may well be contemporary with Tempesta, and the Onofri room very likely belongs to the later decades of the century, as do apparently Onofri's Theodoli frescoes at San Vito Roman.

Other examples of wall decorations with landscapes from the time are a room with four landscapes by Grimaldi in Villa Doria-Pamphilj done between 1644 and 1652; the decoration, c. 1650, of the Sala di Galatea in the Farnesina, one of the largest landscape cycles done by a still unidentified artist from the surrounding of Gaspard (171 f.); an interesting salon in Corso Umberto, Rome, by another Gaspardesque master (182), possibly preceding Tempesta's frescoes; and two rooms by Gio. Paolo Schor (d. 1674), which, to my knowledge, no longer exist: one in the same Colonna palace, done as a hermitage, and one in the Altieri palace, Rome, done in imitation of a grotto (both are quoted by Titi). Finally, the Colonna cycle was to exercise its impact for over a century. It will be sufficient to refer here to two such works that are indebted to it: the elegant spatial effect of Panini's frescoes in a mezzanine salon of the Quirinal, done in the 1720s,[2] and the marines by Manglard covering the walls of a large hall at Palazzo Chigi (185) in a style that alludes directly to Tempesta's frescoes.

The Colonna cycle was ordered under Cardinal Girolamo (d. 1666) and Prince Lorenzo Onofrio (1637–1689). This is not the place to reiterate Lorenzo's well-known predilection for landscapes, which made him the principal patron of both Claude (from 1663 until the artist's death) and Gaspard. For the young Tempesta, the commission must have meant a great gain in prestige. Most probably he also did a number of canvas paintings for the prince; five marines by him are listed in the Colonna catalog of 1783 (see here p. 136). In the same years as Tempesta, Rosa and Schor were also, among others, employed in the Colonna palace (Schor in 1665/1668 for the decoration of the gallery).

Tempesta must surely have had some previous experience in fresco work before being entrusted with this important task. He is recorded to have done some apparently minor work at Palazzo Chigi, Ariccia, in 1665, and some minor fresco work at Palazzo Borghese, Rome.[3] More surprising is the fact that after this success he never reverted to the technique. Was it for lack of suitable commis-

1. Rooms three and five are credited to Gaspard in passing references by Waterhouse (*Baroque Painting in Rome*, 1937), Sutton (in *GBA* 1962, p. 286, as early 1640's), and Arcangeli (exhib. Bologna 1962, p. 270), but have never been discussed.
2. See Briganti, *Il Palazzo del Quirinale*, Rome 1962, pl. xxiii.
3. Palazzo Chigi: V. Golzio, *Documenti artistici sul seicento nell'archivio Chigi*, Rome 1939, pp. 239, 246: among the artists having worked at the palace were Pietro Tempesta, Bastiano Ciardi (unknown), and Jan de Momper (March 1665). In March 1665, 'Pietro Tempesta Pittore' received 6 scudi for work at Ariccia. The kind of work is not specified; it seems that there was a marine on canvas by him. While the landscapes by Jan de Momper are still in the palace, no works by Tempesta can at present be identified there. Palazzo Borghese: Titi mentions

sions? Fresco was as much *de rigueur* in Genoese palaces as in Rome. But it is true that Lombardy did not provide nearly as many opportunities for fresco decorations. His subsequent limitation to the canvas must have been primarily a matter of choice. It is to the canvases that we must now turn to trace his further artistic development.

PAINTINGS

Before entering into the subject, it must be emphasized how much the appreciation of Tempesta's paintings is impaired by the present unsatisfactory condition of many works. Not that they are damaged, but most are covered by thick layers of old varnishes and dirt and have not been touched for generations. Instead of their original fresh look and brilliant coloring, they have a dull, yellowish or brownish appearance with insufficient contrasts and lack of clarity. Some of the early works have to some extent deteriorated; worst in this respect are the Genoese sea storms. Natural darkening, too, has often contributed its share. Understandably, this state of affairs does not help the reproductions. To what extent the average picture differs from its original look appears by comparison with works recently cleaned, such as nos. 265, 276f. It cannot be stressed enough how different and much more impressive Tempesta's oeuvre would look, were all the pictures similarly cleaned.

Any monographic study will in the first place be concerned with the questions of authenticity and chronology. To begin with the attributions, the oeuvre of Tempesta is large and characteristic enough to put us generally on safe ground. Problems arise in the following areas: the Dutch, Roman, and Genoese years, because of an almost total lack of certified works; the prison years, because of erratic quality; the Roman and late years, because of gifted imitators. During the prison phase, standards of quality derived from the late period cannot be applied; the best as well as the worst may be expected. If the Genoese sea storms nos. 94 ff. are indeed his, there is little hope of determining a sharp boundary against minor painters. As to the imitators, Tempestino (119) remains an enigma. In the Lombard years, the problem of imitators arises at a level of high quality. Tavella was capable of perfect imitations of the master's work; the same is reported of Pietro Cignaroli (p. 60). Yet, as pointed out, the bulk of Tempesta's extant oeuvre poses no major problems of attribution, nor do individual paintings show evidence of work by assistants. Fewer than two dozen pictures are signed, a dozen with dates; these inscriptions are inconspicuously tiny (306); some more may thus appear in future cleanings.

The question of dating is a more difficult one. Four drawings bear early dates; the Colonna frescoes can be dated in the late sixties; a dozen pictures–among the best–bear dates from the artist's last five years (1696: 320 and pendant, 322 and pendant 116; 1697: 326 and a now unknown work listed on p. 136; 1700: 291, 305, 315, 317 and pendant; 1701: 118, 267, 304, and a lost work listed on p. 135)–that is all. No evolution is recognizable within the dated group. It may be asked whether these dates record the time of execution or were applied at the moment of sale to earlier works kept

there 'many landscapes painted on the walls by Gaspard, Grimaldi, Tempesta, Filippo Laura, etc.' In this context, 'Tempesta' must mean Mulier, not Antonio listed in Titi's index. But nothing conclusive could be found out on the spot, and the extant landscape frescoes of the 1670's (especially two rooms on the mezzanine) are of modest merit. See also Hibbard, *The Architecture of the Palazzo Borghese*, Rome 1962, pp. 78, 80.

I (No. 280)

II (No. 265)

III (No. 116)

IV (No. 114)

V (No. 286)

VI (No. 270)

VII (No.273)

VIII (No.302)

in the studio. On one hand we are told that the artist was, at his end, a physically and financially broken man, on the other hand the dated pictures are excellent products, mostly of great refinement, showing no sign of a hurried execution or decline. They conform entirely to the general style of Tempesta's late years. All things considered, we may assume that the dates indicate indeed the year of the execution, with the conclusion that Tempesta preserved his creative forces and his métier to the very end.

The provenances lend some strength to this meager scaffold of dates. Three tempests *ab antiquo* in the Doria collection (88 ff.) and a coast view inscribed in Rome (87) are all that we have from Rome; while this is next to nothing, the pictures at least point out the direction of his Roman production. From old Genoese collections, we know a dozen tempests (94 ff.), which on account of their mediocre execution must be credited to the prison years. The first eight years in Genoa are almost unaccounted for; but a few strongly Genoese paintings (201 f.) give us an idea of his style at that time. The works in modern Genoese collections, where Tempesta is nowadays more sought after than elsewhere, offer no guarantee of a local origin. As to the Lombard phase, it can be regarded as certain that virtually the entire Borromeo group was done between 1685 and 1701 in dutiful recognition by the artist for his liberation from prison. Tempesta's letters from prison occasionally mention a painting done for Borromeo, yet there cannot have been many. Such examples may be nos. 108 f., which resemble the Genoese tempests. For the rest, the Borromeo group is stylistically uniform and in keeping with the works dated from the last five years. Since most of Tempesta's oeuvre corresponds stylistically to the Borromeo group, it follows that the bulk of his production dates from the Lombard phase. This is supported by old provenances from Milan (e.g., nos. 289, 310), Piacenza (242), Bergamo (301), Parma (279, 286), Brescia (281 f.), and Venice. Several pictures can be traced back to Venice in the 18th and 19th centuries and thus have a good chance to date from 1687–1690 (236, 239, 241, 255 f., 265, 292). Venetian traits are no more in evidence in them than in many others. That Tempesta's style should have changed notably in Venice was, in fact, hardly to be expected. And it will not surprise that the local provenances do not enable us to establish an internal chronology for the Lombard years. Listings in old inventories (p. 137) provide some additional hints. Thus, maritime tempests were predominant in Rome; landscapes, nocturnes, and animals in Venice; landscapes in Brescia. On the whole, Tempesta's oeuvre does not show an irreversible progression from year to year. For this reason, the quest for precise dates loses some of its significance.

Our discussion of the extant paintings follows, as a rule, the sequence of the illustrations. None of Tempesta's Dutch pictures being identifiable, our knowledge of his painting sets in with the large pair of wild-fowl scenes (188 f.) representing ducks and a heron attacked by a dog and a falcon respectively–fully competent, decorative works in the manner of Fyt, datable in Antwerp c. 1655. For an 18-year old, they are remarkable. Although there is no trace yet of any Italianism, Tempesta's personality can already be felt in the taste for large-scale, well-garnished and appealing imagery and in the gift for realistic rendering of life-size animals. The execution is still in fine strokes; the Flemish landscape background, above all, shows great delicacy in the design, the handling, and the atmosphere. More than the liquid handling of Snyders, it is the manner of certain works by Fyt (1) that is here imitated. Many similar works by Tempesta, including boar hunts, must have existed and may now be hidden under other names.

From the twelve Roman years, we have only a handful of works, none of them a landscape, and only one of interest. The outstanding quality of the frescoes, the fame of the artist, the Duke of Bracciano's protection–these provide the true measure for Tempesta's Roman production, of which the surviving works must be a mere shadow. The quality of the early Roman works may have been uneven. We also have to bear in mind the problem of Tempesta's lost Roman landscapes as reflected in four pictures by Tempestino at Burghley (364 ff.). Their execution is rather cursory, but their strongly Gaspardesque compositions already resemble certain works from Tempesta's Lombard years.

Among the extant Roman works, the small Coast View in Sens (87) shows facile effects in the use of a fantastic rock and in the nocturnal staging. Both elements are still derived from Dutch prototypes rather than from Salvator Rosa. The three *burrasche* (88 ff.) are equally brassy in their effects. The large Tempest no. 90, which is over 12 feet wide and can be dated in the late sixties, is the most representative work of its type, and probably of good quality had it not darkened so much. It comes closest to the storm scenes of the Colonna frescoes. The Italianization of the artist is here already an accomplished fact.

The Roman tempests, reflected also in two works by Tempestino (119 f.), are continued in Tempesta's Genoese sea storms (94 ff.). The brushwork varies here and there, but is generally rough. Some pictures are outright mediocre, which may be due to the stress of life in prison. To what extent Tempesta was here influenced by van Plattenberg and Montagna remains a question. The coloring does not aim at a smooth, monochromatic atmosphere, but acts with a rich range of individual hues. All this is no longer Dutch, but Flemish and Italian. The compositions are rather competent, either symmetrical or dominated by a diagonal with coastal mountains on one side. As an example, no. 94 contains in the center a carefully framed, swirling oval of wide waves and clouds, on the dark side a highlighted vessel, on the bright side a dark-silhouetted ship; this relationship is reversed in the two distant ships; the masts of the large ships are in contrasting diagonals, counterbalanced by the diagonals of the rain and the bright clouds. A few small marines from the Borromeo collection show the same flickering handling (108 f.), reminiscent of small works by Rosa, and may likewise date from the prison years. Five tempests with religious subject matter in Modena–a large one, and a series of four small ones (103 ff.)–seem similar in handling, but are more advanced in the setting and probably date from the early Lombard years. The lively alternation of colored surface areas combined with the evocative horror of the shipwreck scenes, always stressed in old descriptions, explain the immediate success of the Genoese tempests with the public. It was this kind of awe-inspiring scene, vested in the vastness of the ocean, which by the mid-18th century became the manifestation of the Sublime.

Among the smallish landscapes beginning with no. 190, some are still completely under the spell of Gaspard (190, 195) and probably date from Rome. As a rule, an outspoken proximity to Gaspard points to an early date. Some others reflect Castiglione (193 f.). One of the better pieces of this group is a Genoese animal scene in a landscape with classical motives (194). The set of landscapes at the Stuard Gallery in Parma (196 ff.) is hard to judge on account of its precarious condition, but may precede the Lombard years. All these works show a rather rough brushwork which is a mark of Tempesta's pre-Lombard production.

Two paintings of larger size, strikingly Genoese in character, stand out for their painterly quality: an animal piece in a landscape, with Noah sacrificing, and a Rape of Europa (201 f.). Their compositions and their vigorous execution represent a distinct advance over his Roman works, while still differing from the classicism of the Lombard phase.

The following group (203–215) contains works of classical tendencies. Some may still date from Genoa. The Storm Scene with flooding and lightning in the Hermitage (203) is a carefully composed, classical landscape in the manner of Gaspard. The same source can be felt in the two subsequent paintings. The technique varies from broad and fluid (208) to exquisitely fine (212). A pair, at Burghley (213 f.), consists of a Bassanesque nocturne and of a morning scene with strong classical echoes. Two elongated overdoors (210) belong to the artist's most classical compositions, with a strict emphasis on orthogonals and with motives borrowed from Carracci, Domenichino, and Gaspard. These inseparable sources as well as the influence of Poussin are equally evident in the Riposo no. 219. The Judgment of Midas (209) is one of Tempesta's few classical stories, but does not yet show the serene and firm composition of his late mythological pictures (289 ff.). The pastoral landscape in Vienna (215) has Tempesta's favorite device of a strongly articulated composition with contrasting stratification of the terrain over several levels. The Budapest pair (211 f.) belongs to Tempesta's most delicate creations. Gaspardesque and Claudian reminiscences are already fused into a personal style. Compared with Claude, Tempesta's inventions are less novel, more bound to formulas, and not imbued with the study of nature. But they have a painterly density of their own and point in their more idyllic settings to the future.

Ten upright landscapes at the Isola Bella (216 ff.), measuring in height from one to two and a half feet, form a consistent group of severe, heroic compositions flanked on one side by a tall tree. In keeping with their small size, the compositions are relatively simple. This type of landscape derives from Gaspard and Mola (26). In no. 220, the evocative setting and romantic coloring convey a Venetian flavor. In some, the principal motive is a winding, dead tree trunk, first rendered popular in small works by Rosa. One pair, of narrow format (226 f.), stands in the direct tradition of Gaspard (15, 17), but the pink coloring of the sky gives it a lightness anticipating Hubert Robert and Fragonard. Another landscape (223) displays in the foreground the characteristic farmhouse with tall, thatched roof, which occurs so frequently in Tempesta (213, 323). This farmhouse is unclassical, never occurs in Claude, Poussin, or Gaspard, but is a familiar motive in the school of Bloemaert and of the Bassano (31).

Three of these upright pictures are staged as nocturnes, one of the most common and striking effects in Tempesta, repeated in several dozen landscapes. In the century of Caravaggio, nocturnes were in fashion north and south of the Alps, though the masters of classical landscape shunned them: Claude, the artist of the sun, paints the moon only in a single painting; it appears with neither Carracci, Poussin, Gaspard, nor Orizzonte, and only in isolated cases with Rosa. Nocturnes had their first bloom with the tenebrists of the 16th century – the Bassano, Savoldo, Cambiaso, whose works must have been familiar to Tempesta. Moonlight landscapes appear then with Elsheimer, Aert van der Neer, the early Molijn, Aelbert Cuyp, among the Italianizers with van Laer, Berchem, Asselijn, also in Rubens and so many other artists. Later nocturnes appear in Magnasco, in coast views of Manglard and principally Joseph Vernet, in coast views of the Neapolitan Carlo Bonavia (mid-eighteenth century) and many more, but surprisingly never by Marco Ricci. In his time, Tempesta was the uncontested leader of lunarism, providing the link between the Venetian renaissance and the 18th-century Italian and French nocturnal park or coast views.

The three small tondi on copper with New Testament subjects (229 ff.) represent one of Tempesta's unusual facets. They are works of miniature-like refinement in handling and atmosphere. Their lyrical intensity stands in the line of Elsheimer, the Velvet Brueghel, Bril, and F. Lauri. There is an unmistakably northern feeling about them.

The next few works include some of Tempesta's suavest pictures (232 f.). In the lovely Flight into Egypt (238), the story is rendered with poetic embellishments that had been popularized by the Bolognese (L. Carracci, Mastelletta) and became dear to the whole century: the Holy Family is wading through a brook and is greeted by shepherds; or the Virgin, accompanied and surrounded by angels, is crossing a bridge (237).

The pictorially equivalent stories of Noah and of Orpheus (240 ff.) represent a fascinating type of image which embodies a rich traditional heritage. Animals assume an encyclopedic prominence in them. Far more complex than Tempesta's Animal Scene from the Genoese years (201), they can be dated in the Lombard phase on account of style and provenance. For numerous details as well as for the entire compositions, the artist drew not only on Genoese but on Flemish and Venetian traditions (33 ff.). His various versions of these subjects share many individual ingredients, but each work shows them amalgamated differently.

With the next works (243–248), we return to small landscapes of miniature-like execution and densely packed compositions. They include no. 244, with an orthogonal structure, and no. 247, tied together by a wide curve at the base. The intimacy of these surface-filling, wooded sceneries evokes the memory of Bril, certain early Claudes, the Frankenthal masters, even Altdorfer. At the same time, they have a unique, personal tone. Unlike Claude, Tempesta's mastery does not stem from the penetrating observation of nature. But on occasion, his rich human texture permeates and reanimates extant pictorial schemes. This, together with the excellent craftsmanship, accounts for the quality of the works under discussion. One may only deplore that Tempesta did not always maintain this artistic level.

A somewhat different type of image appears in no. 243: though of equally small dimensions, the setting develops over several levels and has the inner complexity of many large works. The scenery is, in the literal sense of the word, composed: the basic arrangement is symmetrical, with a central cluster of trees, framing trees along either side, and two enclosed vistas. Counteracting are the diagonals and the contrasts formed by the two halves: on the left, vertical, large motives (pastoral scene, hut, castello) under a dark sky, seen from close by; on the right, narrow, horizontal motives in distant view under a bright sky. The same elements, from the ducks in the brook (a Flemish note) to the trees, buildings, and figures, occur in variations throughout Tempesta's oeuvre (248). The landscape is not very 'natural,' there is no rendering of a specific atmosphere, but the whole not only makes a good image, it also captures ideally the landscape of northern Lombardy from the Brianza to the Veneto, even if this idealism is, for various reasons, less compelling than Claude's vision of the Campagna.

Surface-filling, wooded scenes with tiny figures and an unusually detailed handling, but now in the large format, also characterize the next group of works (249–254). The thick forest passages are imbued with the spirit of Flemish landscapes (compare nos. 4f., 432). Diagonally placed, dominating trees with battered trunks (251, 258), although existing in Italian art (18), appear especially in Flemish painting. In no. 253, a fine forest scenery forms a foreground curtain on the left half; the right half leads step by step into the distance; mid-way, flanked by slender birch trees, appears a towering building, as we find it in the Venetian Renaissance, later in Marco Ricci, but not again in Tempesta. The building stands out as a dark silhouette in *contre-jour*; the distant town is illuminated by the sun. This rich pattern of alternating highlights and shady zones is a conscious stylistic device of Tempesta. It accounts for the liveliness of the entire surface and, in his best examples, for the vibrating poetic tissue of the image. In the Wooded Scene no. 254, we find an unusual predominance of bulging foliage and shrubbery. The herdsmen driving their animals in the foreground – a century-old motive in pastoral and classical landscape – go here back to Claude and Gaspard. In no. 249, we meet a rich, symmetrically organized composition with echoes from Bril and Rubens. The same setting recurs in a smaller version (250), an unusual case of a genuine repetition. Normally, Tempesta's repetitiveness results from the frequent recurrence of individual motives in new combinations such as the foot-bridge found here and in nos. 213, 244, or the pair of flying ducks which appear, almost like a signature, near the bottom of the majority of his paintings (a detail faithfully imitated by Tavella).

True to his surname, Tempesta also did a number of landscapes with approaching storms. Unlike Rosa, who represented the impending tempest by atmospheric means and wind-swept trees, the more classically oriented Tempesta worked mainly with clouds and groups of frightened figures hurrying away (251), groups that may look similar in several works. Also lightning occurs at times (203, 252, 255, 340). In accordance with the stirred atmosphere, the composition of no. 252 is dramatic, the trees and the lightning enclosing a rhombic center area. The detail as well as the whole mode of this work constitute an astonishing anticipation of Marco Ricci. The smaller Stuttgart Tempest (255), linked with the large no. 276, is one of the artist's most refined and accomplished works, filled with form up to the top. Its undulating structure and sensitive handling points to the future, to Zuccarelli. An interesting parallel to this picture is provided by an early Tempest of Orizzonte (441) likewise derived from Gaspard, yet more classical and Roman than Tempesta.

While Claude refrained from painting lightning, it was Poussin who, after Giorgione, set the decisive example in his Landscape with the Struck Tree, a composition known to us from Chatillon's engraving and reflected in Tempesta's serene no. 249; also Poussin's tempestuous Pyramus and Thisbe at Frankfort belongs in this context. Tempesta's immediate inspiration for stormy scenes stems once more from Gaspard, whose several tempests ranked as his most famous pictures. Tempests and lightning later recur, still in a Gaspardesque vein, with Orizzonte and Marco Ricci (Mostra, 1964, no. 73), but their greatest vogue began with the cult of the Sublime in the mid-18th century and lasted throughout the Romantic movement.

The companion piece to the Stuttgart Storm Scene is a fine, bluish winter landscape (256), the only work of its kind by Tempesta. It, too, forms the link between two centuries; this time, it does not originate from Italian art, where winter scenes had been scarce, but from Dutch scenes as created by Cappelle and others. It gave rise, in turn, to a limited vogue for winter scenes in Tavella (382), in Marco Ricci above all, and in some other Venetian artists of the 18th century (Pedon, A. Diziani, Bison); even early Boucher winter landscapes with their Dutch flavor come to mind.

The influence of Castiglione's plentiful pastorals with generic Old Testament subjects (39) is felt in a number of Tempesta's most stately pictures (259–267). Among the richest examples is the large pair nos. 263 f., of contrasting layout, where the cortège of figures is emerging from depth to the foreground with a strong effect of perspective. In others, the composition is more tied to the surface. The masterpiece of the group is the Journey of Rebekah (265) – one of Tempesta's finest works altogether. Not unlike no. 264 in its right half, it assumes a new elegance and airiness due to the subtle articulation of space and the perspective of light. A very comparable work of the same large size, but carried out in a slightly harder manner, is no. 267, dated from the artist's last year. In other instances, the landscape captures an echo of the spirit of Giorgione (262), or an animal group is displayed with an elegiac breadth (266). Often, a group of mounted figures is crossing the image, directed by shepherds who are seen at rest in the foreground. In the last two examples, we find, so to speak, a pastoral version of the Flight into Egypt. The passing-by of figures, contemplated by some immobile spectators, adds a further evocative note of transience in permanence, an effect already exploited by the Bassano and by Castiglione. These works form an Italian counterpart to Berchem's animal scenes in a landscape. They are also among the most comprehensive demonstrations of Tempesta's art. Saturated in every part with vegetation, trees, rocks, water, mountains, palpably sculptured clouds, figures, herds, and buildings, with alternating surface and depth, light and shade, colors and hues, they embody his innate taste for abundance and realism. What does not show in our reproductions is the element upon which the appearance of the picture rests primarily – the substantial coloring and the surface texture. In many of the best pictures, the color creates a very special mood, as, e.g., in no. 259, where a somber, blue sky and strong brownish-red foreground tones account for a particularly solemn and grave character of the scene.

The subsequent group (268–280) brings us to the river, lake, estuary, and coastal views, several of which are paired with stormy landscapes or with pastoral scenes. Both combinations exist in the two pairs of oval-shaped works. The first pair is graver and more restrained, the second has a sparkling prerococo character. Both coast views are unusually calm in the scenery, with still water and shipping in the foreground, but are dramatic in the cloudscape. The second (280), made up of deep blue tones, is unique for showing, in the best Dutch manner, only the narrowest strip of a distant shore line; yet it exemplifies Tempesta's urge for loud, surface-filling images in the spectacular shaping of the clouds. Despite its theatrical effect, the basic tenor of the picture is strictly classical and symmetrical, the center emphasized as in convex mirror images. The whole character could not be more different from contemporary works by, say, Wm. van de Velde the younger, with their atmospheric subtlety but great compositional tension. Other river and coast views by Tempesta stand more conventionally in the tradition of Rosa (compare no. 21), except that they are usually nocturnes. Often, there is a large mass of rocks on the opposite shore, as in the repetitive nos. 271 f. Closely connected with each other, but larger and more elaborate, are the two nocturnes showing a ship being tarred (273 f.), with their startling effects of resplendent cloudscapes and fires reflected in the water; the theme had already been exploited by Dutch marine painters. The scenery of no. 278 and of a few other works seems to recall, with some fantasy, Lago Maggiore or the north Italian lakes in general, but we never find a topographic view.

The climax of coastal views is the large no. 277, a brilliantly colored sunset. It owes a debt to Rosa in the setting, to Claude in the ideal concept, to Bril in the trees; it is in its own right a beautiful, motionless, classical picture; and it anticipates 18th-century Italian landscape in setting, in technique, and in the decorative vein. From the viewpoint of Claude (7), this would seem a regression, inasmuch as the study of nature is replaced by formulas, and atmosphere is schematized (unlikely rocks, blue mountains, etc.). But the same is true of Marco Ricci, Zuccarelli, or Locatelli, and Tempesta's picture speaks too evidently for itself to be rated as regressive. If Claude's study of nature was a step beyond Bril and Carracci, Tempesta represents in turn an advance in the direction of rococo landscape. Herein lies his importance.

A theme connected with the coast views are the marines, of which a dozen specimens (110 ff.) date from the late years. Typically, all of them are dramatic tempests (*burrasche*), with tall coastal rocks reminiscent of the Ligurian shore on one side, repoussoir rocks in the foreground, and narrative details of shipwrecks. This type again differs profoundly from contemporary late-17th-century Dutch sea storms as exemplified by Wm. van de Velde the younger, who mostly dispensed with all accessories of coast, rocks, and shipwrecks, in order to concentrate exclusively – often with increased effect – on the tension of waves, light, and a sole ship in distress. But for all their apparatus, Tempesta's storms make superb oratory. There are small ones and large ones, somber ones with sweeping rainstorms and bright ones. With one exception, the composition is dominated by a diagonal. Oddly shaped, erect rocks in the foreground (111) still betray the heritage from Dutch masters, with whom such rocks are a common device. Two of the works are dated from the last years (116 – 1696; 118 – 1701); most others fall stylistically in line with them. The four largest are also the masterpieces. They are no. 113, the only orthogonal composition, which draws its unfailing effect from the resplendent prerococo color range of green and white for the sea, light violet and orange for the sky (the same tonalities, that is, that we also find in the most luminous of Tempesta's landscapes). The epitome of his dramatic shipwrecks are the symmetrically balanced no. 114 and the large, majestic no. 115. At the close of the century, these works recall to memory a singular creation from the beginning of the century done in Italy by a northerner under the impact of Tintoretto–Rubens' nocturnal Storm with Hero and Leander. Concluding this group of major works is no. 116, the artist's only imaginary battle piece, which echoes Venetian naval engagements. It is a busy, filled composition with a visionary sky of Tintorettesque derivation.

In connection with the coast views, I pointed out the artist's decorative approach, as opposed to Claude's study of nature. In the wide range of Tempesta's capabilities, we also find moments of a more direct contact with nature. I have already mentioned a few examples (246). Not by chance, it is in the small size where these fresh tones are seen. The most eloquent case in which we sense an immediacy of the feeling for nature, rather than an artful staging, is no. 270. Its naturalism still conforms, of course, to the framework of classical landscape, with such components as the two diagonal foreground coulisses and the road leading into the distance, the cluster of trees, the repoussoir shrub on the opposite side, the central rhombus of the vista. But this is unobtrusive. What conditions the viewer's impression is the organically fluid transition from one part to another, the sensitivity of the handling, the unified lightness of color. These peculiarities become apparent by comparison with the equally small no. 205, which shows a very similar, yet more conventional, composition.

Such naturalist traces are not unique at the time of Tempesta. They sprout here and there, first in the private domain of drawings in water color and gouache–van Dyck, Foucquières, Waterloo, Wildens, for example–then in the rare landscapes of François Desportes, leading to further 18th-century and later developments. But the importance of Tempesta does not rest on the forward-looking naturalist side. This is merely one of the possibilities among his extensive register. His forte is well-anchored in the tradition of his time: it is the richly filled composition, as embodied by the Stormy Landscape no. 276, the crowning piece of its kind.

Tempesta's most representative 'grand manner' shows up in the next 30 or so works, many of which are important and fairly large (281–311). They constitute the artist's mainstream–pastoral landscapes of classical conception, with vertical framing elements and a forceful horizontal structure accentuated by means of parallel levels of rivers, waterfalls, and river banks. Their merit does not lie in the capturing of a fugitive impression of nature, but in the mastery of composite assemblage.

A majestic grandeur worthy of Claude's heroic works emerges from the two mythological landscapes at Brescia (281f.). They are symmetrically contrasting compositions with large foreground trees on one side and a framed opening into the distance on the opposite side. The whole is rendered in moonlight here, under a hot sunset there. Carracci, Poussin, Claude, Veronese, the Bassano, Mola, all are incorporated in the ancestry of this pair. Directly dependent upon Carracci is also the Landscape no. 283 with its double-arched bridge and boat in the foreground. In the Landscape of the Liechtenstein pair (284), the symmetrical placement of two pairs of trees is so elementary and convincing that one is astonished at the complete absence of a close prototype, even among the Bolognese masters; the accompanying Nocturnal River View is a picture type of Rosa turned classical, with a burning citadel at the upper right.

Two important works at Parma form a pair of uncommon, unschematic compositions. The saturated Forest View (287) with a winding road derives ultimately from the school of Frankenthal, Bril, and d'Arthois, with an echo of Berchem in the mouth of the spring. A rich heritage links the picture with the past, but equally significant is its impact on masters of the early 18th century such as Tavella (383 f.). Likewise, the brushwork, consisting of short strokes and dots that remain thoroughly visible as such, is already that of many 18th-century landscapes (Zuccarelli, Panini). The pendant to this painting (286) is, by contrast, a more extended composition with a wide valley harmoniously framed on either side. An altogether outstanding and novel composition, it again is a direct forerunner of Marco Ricci (410), who knew to grasp the best of Tempesta.

In the subsequent examples, the setting and the figures aim consciously at a classical, bucolic, or elegiac mode reminiscent of the late Claude and Poussin (288 ff.). Most Claudian in this regard is the Landscape with Nymphs and Satyrs (290), serene and unusually calm in composition, superbly refined in execution. Equally meticulous in handling, but more traditional in its crowded layout, is the Landscape with Fauns and Nymphs dated from 1700 (291).

Next, we come to a group of works in which the landscape builds up over a cascade and high banks to an elevated plateau with buildings, the whole backed by a range of mountains (293 ff.). These are heroic pastoral landscapes in the truest sense. The apex among this group is the large no. 300. On a smaller scale, the same compositional density appears in no. 305, which is dated from 1700. An inevitable repetitiveness in the formulas of layout and of stage effects in no way diminishes the appeal of these most typical, stately works of our artist. The guiding classical concept results in a static firmness of the image, which is in keeping with the main trend of the epoch. To masters of the following age, such solidity must have appeared rigid. In some examples, awkwardly contorted tree trunks of a northern flavor rise large in the nearest foreground, as in no. 301, which anticipates the German 'heroic landscape' of the decades around 1800.

Closely akin to these works is a characteristic group of pastorals with rivers and lake views, almost all rendered as nocturnes (303–311). Some are large, some small; one is dated 1701 (304). Despite certain schematic traits, the effect of moonlight and of fires is exploited in a startling manner. Once again, such works lead into the future, through Ricci and Tavella to many Kleinmeister and Hinterglas specialists throughout the 18th century and the Romantic period.

At times, the stillness of the landscape and of the unconcerned figures in its midst are contrasted with a distant fire devastating the buildings (298, 300), an effect inviting the beholder to meditation. Burning citadels occur often (222, 285, 299), or the columns of smoke emerge from a chalk or brick kiln (309). The result is the same: a dramatic outburst of usually indomitable and destructive forces amidst peaceful, pastoral nature, a kind of Death in Arcady formula. It offered the additional pictorial advantage of introducing lively colors and rich masses of clouds. Startling effects of fires had existed since the Renaissance in Netherlandish art, especially with themes such as the destruction of Sodom (Lucas van Leyden, Patinir), then appeared with Pieter Brueghel the elder and the younger ('Brueghel degli inferni'), in the 17th century with Egbert van der Poel and other specialists, in Italy with Onofri (fire screens). But the only significant model for Tempesta's mostly nocturnal fires was the smoking St. Angel's Castle in Poussin's Orpheus and Eurydice (which is a daylight scene, the fire being thematically linked to the mythological event). Fires in the manner of Tempesta also reputedly became the specialty of Solfarolo and Tavella and spread widely in the 18th and early 19th centuries.

The Landscape with the dominating arched bridge (302) is a masterpiece *sui generis*. The setting has a fancifully unreal air announcing the 18th century. But the valley into which the bridge is placed breathes an unconventional freshness and delicacy, indicative of the artist's feelings for nature. The coloring in green tones for the hills, brown for the bridge and the framing rocks on the right, and yellow-violet for the clouds, contributes to the gay, decorative effect of the picture. The same tones are later taken up in many passages of Zuccarelli's and Hubert Robert's landscapes with bridges.

The late animal scenes (312ff.) bring us back to a specialty in which Tempesta had already excelled in his young years. A comparison with his pre-Italian animal pieces done in the Flemish manner (188) gives eloquent proof of his progress. The main difference lies in the sweeping painterly unity of the late works. Mild, poetic scenes with sheep have replaced violent combat episodes between dogs, boars, and birds. Typically, the two dramatic scenes, which still are represented, do not show an actual fight, but a contemplative mood: the wounded sheep (312) and the dying wolf (319) arouse the viewer's compassion. This very note points far into the future, above all to Londonio (438). Due to its large size and symmetrical layout, the painting with the dying wolf has the monumentality of Tempesta's classical landscapes. Purely idyllic are two pastorals with groups of sheep and some other animals, in which the distance is almost eliminated: no. 314 is a large, life-size work, the animals being displayed parallel to the picture plane; no. 315 is a smaller work, dated from 1700, in which the motifs are grouped in a more intimate, prerococo fashion. The animals demonstrate Tempesta's admirable skill in the realistic rendering of texture. The heritage of the Bassano and Castiglione and of the engravings after Bloemaert (recognizable, e.g., in the large, leafy plants at the bottom) is blended into a mellower, personal style announcing the next century. Particularly Bassanesque is the treatment of the Pastoral no. 313. The artist's two largest paintings, forming a pair, also produce the most striking effect (317f.); life-size cattle and sheep, but, exceptionally, no figures, are opposed to distant mythological scenes; the abundant color scale is cooler in one work, hot in the companion piece; the broad brushwork conforms to the oversize. No doubt commissioned for the decoration of a specific salon, the pair is undeniably successful.

If we try to define further the contribution of Tempesta's animal pieces in his century, we must compare them with the leading representatives of the genre – Paulus Potter, Berchem with his numerous followers, and Rosa da Tivoli (Roos) in Rome, all of whom produced at times large and even overscale pictures. Tempesta's largest pair, just cited, is so deeply rooted in Venetianism that it has little or nothing in common with Dutch works. There is a closer affinity with Rosa da Tivoli (436), who was younger but active at the same time, although Tempesta probably did not know Roos's production. Exclusively an animalist, and extremely fertile at that, Roos has always ranked as the main spokesman of the genre (to the point where he has become a collective name, behind which some works of Tempesta may still hide). When it comes to comparing individual pictures, Tempesta holds his own. His classical concept and thoroughness of execution convey to his works a quality unmatched by Roos, whose art consists of more schematic formulas rendered in a lighter, decorative spirit. Moreover, Roos used landscape merely as a stage foil, without attempting to incorporate his animal groups into a space environment; this admittedly had its positive side too, which was the anticipation of the spirit of early 18th-century pastorals.

There is no sharp borderline between Tempesta's animal pieces and some of his landscapes containing large pastoral motives. Animal groups very similar to the Pastoral with Sheep (315) will also be found inserted into wider landscapes. In a few very large pictures, dominating animal foregrounds are accounted for by a religious subject. An odd and startling example, compositionally as well as for the coloring in strong brownish tones with some blues, is the Annunciation to the Shepherds (316) or, more exactly, the Annunciation–minuscule, in the distance–watched by shepherds in the foreground. Animals and figures assume a compelling presence because of the life size, the view from close by, the tight filling of the image in a symmetrical layout, and the surface emphasis on composition and color. The painting stands at the end of a tradition traceable to Aertsen, Bassano, and Castiglione. It must have appealed to Milanese taste, which, a century earlier, had already welcomed the large, realistic genre pieces of Vincenzo Campi.

The Annunciation theme, ideally suited for an artist excelling in pastorals, nocturnes, and spectacular illumination, recurs in the large no. 323, the key work among the Borromeo Tempestas. The basic layout is the same, but the figures are now embedded into a landscape with the divine light emerging from the center. In the contrasting arrangement of the pendant (324), the foreground also shows a group of shepherds witnessing a distant religious event–this time the Crucifixion–and, in the distant city on the left, the earthquake. Another, larger version of this theme is no. 325; the setting is comparable, but the space is expanded, the foreground somewhat removed, and the figures do not react to the events of the background. Closely linked with the preceding works is the masterful Pastoral no. 322, dated from 1696 (the pendant to the Sea Storm no. 116): in one of Tempesta's most saturated compositions, a group of figures and animals in the foreground is contemplating the Holy Family passing by in the middle distance on the way to Egypt. In many late paintings of the artist, the figures show, incidentally, the same facial types: the old, bearded herdsman and the young, oval-faced shepherdess, whose lineaments resemble those of Tempesta's second wife (compare, e.g., nos. 314 and 186).

In the pictures just discussed, the splitting of the subject into two zones, one of action and a contrasting one of contemplation or passivity, produces a kind of 'play within the play.' This stage effect, exploited earlier by the Bassano and Castiglione, proved dear to the entire century. Its roots are complex. One of its most obvious meanings in the age of shepherd poetry must be sought in the escape from reality that the simplicity of rural life provided–a note to which Tempesta's patrons were no doubt sensitive.

The subject of the distant Annunciation witnessed by pastoral figures in the foreground occurs once more in 1696, now in near-square format (321). The pendant to this picture is an unusually dramatic figure scene from the Old Testament, Lot and his family escaping the destruction of

Sodom and Gomorrah (320). Strongly indebted to Cortonism and to Luca Giordano, this is one of Tempesta's most accomplished figure scenes. Very close to such works is also the Pastoral no. 326, despite the fact that no specific subject appears in the distance; the inscribed date, 1697, confirms the late dating of several related pictures.

Six works at Burghley House form a group by themselves. All are religious subjects apparently dating from the late years. The large Nativity (327) compares with the Geneva Flight of 1697 (322). The others are small, more intimate and ornate in style, bringing to mind Lauri and Trevisani. The Finding of Moses (329), in particular, shows in its flowery design and elongated figures the trend for precious refinement found at the turn of the century simultaneously in Venice, Rome, Holland, and France.

The remaining works grouped here under Tempesta's name (333–349) are for the most part pastorals in his Lombard manner. As explained under the individual entries, some belong to the border area in which we may recognize the participation of studio assistants.

This discussion of the individual paintings has yet to be supplemented by a number of more general observations. The first concern commissions and production in pairs. Given the subjects of Tempesta's paintings, it can be assumed that only a few of his works were done on specific commission. In all probability, the normal course of action was that Tempesta painted at his own initiative, then sold to his clients. In 1687 for instance, he reported bringing to Modena two paintings and finding a buyer for them in Prince Foresto d'Este. Works with special themes or of unusual size were no doubt ordered ad hoc (210, 317).

Under whatever conditions of patronage, a great many of his pictures were produced in pairs, to be hung symmetrically on a wall, or opposite each other, depending on the case. The same is true of numerous other Italian and French paintings of the time (in Holland, the practice was perhaps less common). Claude and Poussin are the predecessors who contributed most to the refinement of the century-old concept of pairs. Rosa and Gaspard also frequently produced pairs, though the principles governing their pairing of images are simpler. In the case of Gaspard, many works, now single, must have been done in pairs. We know about Tempesta's pairs only from those, fortunately quite numerous, that have remained united until today in the same collections. In cases of isolated pictures, we can only speculate about possible combinations. Pairs extend over Tempesta's whole lifetime, from his two earliest animal pieces to the last works. The guiding idea required that two companion pieces be the same size, basically similar in type, inner proportions, and subject matter, but within this similarity complementary in composition, atmosphere, and theme. While each picture can also be viewed as a self-contained entity, one will have a greater weight on the left, the other on the right (263 f., 317 f.); or one will have symmetrical accents on either side, the other a main accent in the center (323 f.). A pastoral may be matched by a sea storm, a green tempest by a calm winter scene (255), classical buildings in morning light by rural buildings in evening or nocturnal light (213), a cool landscape by a warm coast view (276), and so forth. The story of the abduction of Apollo's herds responds to the abduction of Europa (281), Noah's entry into the Ark to the exit from the Ark. We clearly recognize a system, although it is never a rigid one. To ignore the creation in pairs would be to miss an integral aspect of Tempesta's pictures. As applied by him, the concept derives, in essence, from Claude. It is carried on with little basic change by Tempesta's followers: Marco Ricci, Tavella (many pairs now separated), Roncelli, Orizzonte, Joseph Vernet, and others. Larger sets of pictures, such as four overdoors, occur only rarely in Tempesta (104).

As in the case of Claude and Poussin, there is not a single landscape by Tempesta without figures (Gaspard has a few exceptions). Where the figures are more than mere filling, they have an elegance affined with Albani and Lauri and anticipate Trevisani. Compare, e.g., Tempesta's nos. 267, 329, with Lauri (42 f.). In keeping with the basic character of his art, Tempesta's figures do not aspire to a classical idealization in the manner of Poussin. Instead, they are rural types, but rendered with serene, idyllic grace.

The buildings that are introduced in the distance of almost every picture also share classical and rural elements. The presence of architectural motives is common to classical landscape, but is not to the same extent a rule in Rosa or in Dutch realist landscape. On the other hand, Tempesta refrains from using ruins, or antique, or extant buildings. His small repertoire of buildings consists either of fortified farmhouses and castles with circular or square towers (204, 243, 281), or of huts with thatched roofs (323). There is an abundance of large and small bridges. Isolated examples show pyramids (Flight into Egypt), a Giorgionesque building (253), and a tent. Entire citadels placed on a hill (292) resemble those found in Poussin and Gaspard.

The range of literary and religious subjects illustrated by the figures is rather narrow, at least by comparison with Poussin and Claude. Tempesta's concern is with landscape. From a thematic point of view, the oeuvres of Gaspard or of Grimaldi are, however, considerably more limited. Old Testament subjects occurring in Tempesta are the story of Noah, the Finding of Moses (329), Moses and Aaron (lost), Sodom (320), Jonah, and various more or less explicit voyage scenes. From the New Testament are the Annunciation to the Shepherds, the Nativity, the Flight into Egypt, Christ and the Tempter (231), the Agony in the Garden, the Crucifixion, St. John, St. Anthony Preaching to the Birds (lost). The few mythologies comprise usual scenes such as Europa, Mercury and Battus, Midas, Diana, Endymion, the Rape of Proserpina (the latter three lost; see p. 137). But the theme does not condition the entire form of the composition.

Tempesta's landscapes, to put it in the simplest formula, stand in the tradition of Gaspard's classical landscape and are moreover influenced in certain realistic elements and in the painterly handling by Rosa, Castiglione, and the Bassano. The compositions are richly orchestrated, densely packed, and saturated with form (gaining, thereby, a certain affinity with Grimaldi). By comparison with the masters of nature study, his nature is staged, coloring and atmosphere are stereotyped. But taken at their best, Tempesta's landscapes, coast views, marines, and animal pieces have an unmistakably personal character and a decorative quality that explain his renown.[1]

1. Whether Tempesta also produced battle pieces, as Dal Pozzo (1718, here p. 60) and Campori (1855, here p. 138) report, is questionable. No battle pieces exist, although the combination of the landscape and battle specialties is a frequent one (Rosa, Reschi, Eisman, Calza). We know that Tempesta was acquainted with the Brescian battle painter Frc. Monti. North Italian battle painting subsequently came to flourish thanks to Courtois's pupil Ant. Calza and his major followers–Stom, Spolverini, Simonini, Zais, and others. Cf. also E. Martini, *Marco Ricci 'Battaglista'*, Venice 1963.

INFLUENCE

This survey of the impact made by the art of Tempesta on his own time and on the 18th century includes a variety of aspects, ranging from the precise influence upon specific pupils to a broad panorama of his artistic legacy. While concentrating on works that stand in his orbit, the discussion occasionally touches on somewhat different, contemporary trends. As in the preceding chapters, the text follows the places of Tempesta's activity in Italy. It is meant to supplement the illustrations, whose arrangement it parallels.

ROME

For most of his life, Tempesta must have been surrounded by pupils. Already during his Roman years, he was, according to Pascoli, so busy 'that he took to being helped by pupils,' of which only one, no doubt the most important, is known to us: his brother-in-law Tempestino (a relationship which brings to mind Poussin and his younger Roman brother-in-law Gaspard Poussin). No firm personality emerges from the handful of works attributed to this intimate and gifted collaborator of Tempesta (119f., 364–375). Some of them follow so completely in the path of the Gaspardesque landscape style which Tempesta must then have practiced, as to be almost indistinguishable from the master; some, probably later works, can in turn hardly be separated from Onofri.

It is nearly impossible to define Tempesta's influence on Roman painting. Not only is most of his production from his 12 Roman years lost and our knowledge of Roman landscape painting toward the end of the century still inadequate in countless details, but his contribution is inseparable from the influence of Gaspard and of Rosa. These two artists were still active at the time of his departure from Rome and were to determine the mainstreams of Roman landscape painting in the last decades of the century, to be challenged only by the growing importance of the Veduta from Vanvitelli to Panini. Tempesta's paintings stand, then, at the crossing of the most influential trends of the last third of the century. Not surprisingly, there exist numerous affinities between his works and those of later masters in Rome, but they are due less to a direct influence than to common sources in Gaspard, Poussin, Claude, Mola, and Rosa. In the animal genre likewise, Tempesta's share is absorbed by the growing tide of animalism under Rosa da Tivoli. However, Tempesta preceded him by twenty years and may well have helped to prepare the ground for the enthusiastic reception met by Roos (436).

One ramification of classical landscape was the increasingly composite and refined view with antique architecture, as it spread from Rome to France and the Netherlands with such artists as Francisque Millet, de Neve, Polydor, Cossiau, van der Kabel, Eglon van der Neer, Lemaire, the Patel (428f., 434f.).

The heritage of Gaspard was first continued in a 'hard line' by his only pupil Onofri (417), then, in a key more lyric than epic, by Orizzonte. Onofri spent the last two decades of his life in Florence. At the turn of the century, the Grand Ducal court attracted, besides him, such landscape artists as Mehus, Reschi, and the young Peruzzini, Marco Ricci, and Magnasco. Formed under similar conditions, some of these masters active in Florence offer in their works many parallels with Tempesta which are not the result of direct contacts. As an example, we find the same level of development in the paintings by the hitherto unknown Tuscan landscape specialist Romulo Panfi (418 ff.). Be it said by the way that another chapter of Florentine art is today even more ignored – the marine painting. Once flourishing and kept in honor also because of the ties of the court with the Order of Malta, it survives in very numerous examples which deserve to be brought to light again.

Orizzonte (Jan Frans van Bloemen) came to Rome just before Onofri's departure, twenty years after Tempesta's departure. He dominated Roman landscape for much of his long activity, preparing the ground for Locatelli, Anesi, Monaldi, and other masters. His art, illustrated here in figs. 440–445, was at first more exclusively Gaspardesque than was Tempesta's. As with Gaspard, his sole specialty was the green landscape. There is no rapport in style or subject with Rosa. Some of Orizzonte's early storm landscapes (441) show a close resemblance to Tempesta by virtue of their common dependence from Gaspard. From there, Orizzonte's art gradually evolved toward a more decorative elegance in the classical line of Claude and the late Gaspard. This trend was a phenomenon of the time. We have observed its beginnings in Tempesta, whose range of possibilities was broader and could aliment the painterly direction of Marco Ricci and Zuccarelli as well as the strictly Roman classicism of Orizzonte.

At the other pole, that of the succession of Rosa, several masters such as Montanini,[1] Reschi (426), and Jac. de Heusch (427) present affinities with Tempesta. From here, it is, moreover, revealing to glance at the basically similar development of the contemporary Flemish landscape, which was dominated by d'Arthois and his school represented by artists such as Cornelis Huysmans and A. F. Baudewyns, both born within ten years after Tempesta (432 f.).

One of the favorite themes of the school of Rosa was the coast view. First propagated by Tassi and Claude, it reached its highest fulfillment in two French specialists in 18th-century Rome, Bril, Adrien Manglard and Cl.-J. Vernet (134f., 185). Though separated from Tempesta by two generations, with apparently no Roman marine painting of any consequence being produced in the interval, the works of Manglard grew out of Tempesta's coast views, sea storms, shipwrecks, and moonlight effects. On viewing Vernet's marines, one is often struck by their similarity with Tempesta (whereas the few landscapes by Vernet follow a different path). Vernet's marines are, of course, more transparent and airy in setting and coloring, but their structure shares much with our artist, who thus had his greatest 'Nachblüte,' somewhat paradoxically, almost a century after his departure.

GENOA

Despite the length of his permanence, it is difficult to assess the trace that Tempesta's production of 16 years may have left in Genoa. The two pupils of whom we hear are of minor importance.

1. Pietro Montanini (Perugia 1626–1689), an immediate follower of Rosa, working in a slightly more lyrical vein. There are 34 small landscapes of his in the Cathedral Museum of Perugia. Two Coast Views are in the Pallavicini Collection, Rome. See on him Voss, 1924, p. 299, and Schaffran, in *Pantheon* 1960, p. 263.

Ratti mentions, in the *Life* of Tavella, that Niccolò Micone, called lo Zoppo (Genoa 1645/50–1730), studied under Tempesta. This apprenticeship can only have taken place in Genoa between 1670 and 1676. Micone subsequently imitated Tavella and is reputed to have done lovely landscapes with an artful perspective, but no works by him can be identified at present. Likewise in Genoa, the young Utrecht painter Jan van Bunnick (1654–1727) remained for some time with Tempesta, according to Houbraken, 1721 ('from Milan, he journeyed to Genoa, where he heard of the good painter P. Molyn, alias Tempeest, with whom he remained for some time and did various pieces. From there he travelled to Leghorn…'). Van Bunnick had been trained by Herman Saftleven, then spent several years in Italy, in particular eight years in the service of the Duke of Mantua (c. 1680; cf. Campori, 1855, p. 99), whereupon he returned to Germany and Holland. In Rome, his Bent-name was Keteltrom. His few extant landscapes–small, rather old-fashioned, panoramic mountain scenes with mannered trees–reveal no common ground with Tempesta.

The specialties of Tempesta did not belong to the core of genres treated by the local school. The most Genoese pictures which he must have done there, the pastorals with extensive figure and animal groups, have their place in the vast, long-lived following of Castiglione. Conversely, his animal pieces fit into the well-established Ligurian tradition of animal painting, which continued on a modest level throughout the 18th century (437). In landscape painting, the Genoese Tavella was Tempesta's greatest continuator, but their contact took place in their Lombard phase. Tempesta's principal contribution to Ligurian painting was no doubt the marine, which he helped to anchor firmly in Genoa. No research has yet been done in later 17th- and 18th-century marine painting of Genoa. The quantity of anonymous material, for the most part still kept in private collections, points to a significant influence of Tempesta, extending from small, dramatic sea storms to giant, monumental, convincingly realistic marines. Such examples are, for instance, a pair of large marines from c. 1700, consisting of a calm and a rough sea, each with Maltese galleys fighting Turkish frigates, in the entrance salon of Pal. Reale in Genoa.

LOMBARDY AND VENICE

Up to this point, the influence exercised by our Tempesta may have been more important in the domain of marine painting. By contrast, the Lombard phase presents us with an extensive radiation of his art. Several factors concur in this result: Tempesta had numerous pupils and several important followers there; he sojourned in many north Italian towns, leaving his mark everywhere; he was the unrivalled master of his specialties; and Lombardy proved particularly receptive to the realist side of his art; not least, his late phase is well documented and paintings by him and his school survive in great number.

The existence of exact copies by other hands after his originals is thus no surprise (360–363). Even works of much lesser masters are commonly found to have been copied. The extant copies are after late works and date from the period. Many of his own landscapes are variations on similar themes, but he must have produced identical repetitions only on rare and specific occasions. While his quality may at times fluctuate, a coarser second version of a refined original points unquestion-

IX (No.322)

X (No.455)

XI (No. 300)

XII (No. 277)

XIII (No. 323)

XIV (No. 276)

ably to an imitator. We are not faced with a complex atelier problem in the sense of, say, Rubens. If the pupils collaborated on his pictures, there is no visible trace of it.

In the decades at the turn of the century, we can observe a whole wave of 'Tempestismo' in northern Italy, manifest in a great number of anonymous landscapes of varying merit, a selection of which is reproduced in nos. 125 ff. (marines) and 350–359 (landscapes). Some may be copies of lost originals, others are less close to our artist. All stand to prove how widely his art was taken up and successfully imitated.

Speaking of the Lombard years, Pascoli reports that 'numerous young pupils frequented his school, but none, to my knowledge, emerged with an ability worthy to be remembered.' Our own judgment about their merit is somewhat different. The most important of the six pupils known at present from Tempesta's late years, Carlo Antonio Tavella (1668–1738), was a memorable artist in his own right, although he is still unknown outside Italy (121–123, 376–399). After a first training, Tavella joined, in the eighties, the Milanese atelier of Grevenbroeck (Solfarolo), who was renowned for his landscapes with fires. In the startling effects of light, a mutual exchange of inspiration may have taken place between Grevenbroeck and Tempesta. Between 1695 and 1701, Tavella was twice the pupil of Tempesta. He came to master the pictorial language of his teacher to the point where certain landscapes and sea storms of the two can hardly be distinguished from one another. With his enormous, always very cultivated and often marvelous production, Tavella contributed, more than any other artist, in transmitting to Genoa and to the 18th century the legacy of his teacher.

Less influential, yet a colorful, if uneven, personality was Giuseppe Roncelli (c. 1669–1729), Tempesta's pupil in Brescia around 1692. Like Solfarolo, he was to become famous above all for his inflamed sunsets, sunrises, and nocturnes (400–407). This alone indicates the large place that artifice and effects hold in his production. The romantically flavored landscapes known so far reflect even more the influence of Marco Ricci. Some of the heavily wooded, rocky scenes show compositional schemes rooted as far back as Flemish 16th-century landscape.

Before turning to Marco Ricci and the subsequent fate of Tempesta's heritage, we must give notice of his remaining pupils. An apparently gifted imitator was Pietro Cignaroli (Verona 1665–Milan 1720), a member of the widespread Cignaroli family of landscape painters, the most famous of whom was to be his great-nephew from the Turin branch, Vittorio Amadeo. No works by Pietro Cignaroli can at present be identified, but P. Dal Pozzo (1718, p. 193) supplies the following information about him: he was at first the pupil of his brother in Verona, 'then went to Cremona, Pavia, and elsewhere in the company of Pietro de Mulieribus, called Cavalier Tempesta, whose faithful pupil he was, learning his manner and succeeding with great ability in painting landscapes and animals. Finally he settled in Milan ...' Ratti cites him in the *Life* of Tavella as an 'illustrious pupil of Tempesta.' Zannandreis reports about him in the *Vite* of the Veronese painters (written in 1831/34, published in 1891, p. 326): 'Cignaroli eagerly endeavored to benefit from Tempesta's instruction, to the point where he reached such a degree of excellence that he was paid by his master, who gave him in Piacenza and in Milan, where Cignaroli followed him, one filippo per day, as well as food for him and his servant, as long as he lived in his house, which was for no little time.' Speaking of

Cignaroli's activity in Genoa by 1695, Zannandreis continues: 'His works were so much in the manner of Cavalier Tempesta that they deceived even the best connoisseurs. He himself fostered the ambiguity, since he owned two of Tempesta's paintings, hung in a room next to works done by himself, and he enjoyed watching the dilettanti prefer upon comparison his own to those of the master, as it happened at that time, among many, to the Swiss envoy, Mr. Tramendorf, and to the general of the Germans, Count Harrach. No wonder then, that France, Spain, and Germany aimed at having his paintings, which came to adorn the most famous galleries of the nobility.' In the *Life* of Lorenzo Comendù (Verona 1675–Milan 1720), Dal Pozzo (p. 193) and Zannandreis (p. 328) write that Comendù's battle pieces occasionally had the landscape painted in by Pietro Cignaroli, 'who prevailed in this kind of painting.'

Orlandi mentions another Cignaroli in connection with Tempesta–Scipione (nephew of Pietro and father of Vittorio Amadeo), 'called il Veronese, excellent landscape artist, pupil of Cavalier Tempesta,' who then went to Rome in order to study the works of Gaspard and of Rosa and later was active in Milan and Turin. Scipione's exact dates are not known; works are documented from 1726 to 1740. The birth date is believed to be after 1683, at any rate early enough for him to have been Tempesta's garzone. Possibly Orlandi confuses him with Pietro, whom he does not mention; but the early date of Orlandi's testimony, 1719, does not allow us to dismiss it. Scipione's art is known to us from a number of examples that show a distinct personality. The extant works no longer reflect the immediate radiation of Tempesta.[1]

Another, young pupil of Tempesta's last years was Tommaso Porta (Brescia 1686–Verona 1766), a landscape specialist of distinction, whose fine canvases and frescoes, still unpublished, survive in considerable number, especially in the region of Verona. The oldest source about him is Dal Pozzo (1718, *Aggiunta,* p. 20), according to whom 'he was a pupil of Tempesta, the famous painter of battles and landscapes; following his manner, he succeeded so well that he can equal the master. He worked in Brescia and in Padua. But finally he settled in Verona. He did a painting for Marchese Raimondo Gherardini, as a pendant to one by Tempesta, to which it measures up.' This is repeated by Zannandreis (pp. 364, 409). Tempesta died in Porta's 15th year, but in those days boys were apprenticed well before that age (so was Tavella). Porta's oeuvre developed in the general sphere of Marco Ricci, a proof of how the early training under Tempesta decisively determined his direction.[2]

Concluding this enumeration, an unnamed garzone lived in Tempesta's house at the master's death and subsequently married his daughter (Pascoli).

In the discussion of Tempesta's paintings, we have again and again been led to point out their importance for Marco Ricci (1676–1730; figs. 409–411). It was the genius of Marco Ricci, the towering Italian landscape painter of his time, which ensured the widespread propagation of Tempesta's heritage during the 18th century. The two artists probably met during the nineties in Milan. Without being his pupil, Ricci was deeply affected by Tempesta, who was forty years his senior. As

1. See Delogu, 1931, and L. Mallé, *Museo Civico di Torino, I Dipinti,* 1963, p. 254.–The first edition of Orlandi, of 1704, does not yet contain Cignaroli.–Cf. also Mallé, *Stupinigi,* Turin 1969, pl. 153–165.
2. On Porta and his son Andrea, who was a landscape painter in his footsteps, see Butturini, in *Arte Veneta* 1966, p. 287 (brief) and Udine, *Mostra di pittura veneta del settecento in Friuli,* 1966, no. 66.

happens so often in the history of art, the most significant continuator was thus not a servile apprentice, but a neighboring artist who grasped and brought to a new fulfillment the essence of Tempesta's art. Ricci was too great a master to be explained in terms of a few sources only, as can be done with Roncelli or even Tavella. Numerous trends and inspirations flew together in Ricci and were absorbed by his personality. Contacts with Sebastiano Ricci, Magnasco, Rosa, Titian, the Bolognese, Carlevarijs, and others are reflected in the rich and constantly changing amalgam of his art. Consequently, there are entire areas of his production that stand outside the orbit of Tempesta – the ruins, the gouaches, the battle pieces, the picturesque style, the etchings, topographic views. Already earlier writers have on occasion linked the young Bellunese master with Tempesta; the Ricci exhibition of 1964, for instance, opened with two paintings by Tempesta. But as the oeuvre of the latter was so far only known from a few examples, it was impossible to reach an adequate understanding of his influence on Ricci, which was thought to be of some importance only for his early phase. The plates of this book will give a somewhat different view: Tempesta's real influence is felt as a profound and lasting effect at various stages of Ricci's life, rather than as a specific action confined to Ricci's early phase. Ricci's beginnings, still elusive to us for lack of facts and dates, stand mainly under the sign of Magnasco, Pedon, and Peruzzini, an *ambiente* which shared much with Tempestism at large and in which it is almost impossible to isolate each individual's share. Ricci's early picture types not infrequently resemble Tempesta, but their entire artistic aim, from the romantic concept to the handling, differs; what in retrospect appears as a continuation, was for Ricci, then and there, a break with his predecessors. The closest early links with Tempesta exist in the tempestuous marines, which Ricci was later to abandon. Instances of a deep, inner affinity with Tempesta begin to appear a decade after the death of the latter, as a result of Ricci's gradual evolution towards calmer, bucolic, or more classical landscapes. It is by no means unique to find an artist receptive to the lesson of a great precursor only at an advanced stage; Carracci's and Domenichino's influence on the mature Claude, but not on the production of his youth, is a case in point. The mature Ricci must consciously have sought and found inspiration in some of Tempesta's best works. A comparison between a large, famous painting by Ricci and one by Tempesta, preceding it by almost a generation (284, 411), speaks for itself and stands for many similar instances. A future oeuvre catalog of Ricci might give even further evidence of this relationship.

The single most determining factor for the early Ricci was his contact in Lombardy with Magnasco who was nine years his senior (1667–1749). But although Magnasco and Tempesta worked contemporaneously for a decade or more in Milan, no significant contact between the two developed. The young, then still unknown Magnasco was a romantically inclined painter of Bamboccesque figure sketches in a landscape, rooted in the tradition of Morazzone, Cerano, and Cairo. In his vast oeuvre, there are inevitably a few compositional parallels with Tempesta. But it was left to Marco Ricci to assimilate both directions.

The same circle included, besides the still insufficiently known Peruzzini and Antonio Marini (on whom see Donzelli, 1967, p. 271), both active at the turn of the century in Milan, also Bartolomeo Pedon (Venice 1665–1733), an extraordinary bohemian, if ever there was one. The fewer than twenty known paintings by him—large, Bassanesque landscapes and stormy nocturnal coast views grouped around a documented set of six works done just after 1694 for Ca'Borini at Este—resemble in their fluffy, painterly appearance the contemporary works of Marco Ricci; the exchange may have been a mutual one. But the types and the compositions of Pedon's works reveal specific contacts with Tempesta, who had just spent a couple of years in Venice.[1]

Ricci and Pedon place us on Venetian ground. The widely felt impact of Marco Ricci on Venetian landscapes carries with it, as an integral component, the heritage of Tempesta, which also emerges at various points in its own right. A brief aperçu of this spread, by no means meant to be exhaustive, leads first to Luca Carlevarijs (1663–1729), whose occasional early, imaginary landscapes evoke in their firm structure the classical concept of certain works by Tempesta; reminiscent of his are in particular two early, Biblical scenes with landscape background in S. Pantaleone, Venice.[2] Although we still are in the dark about the beginnings of Carlevarijs and his early Roman sojourn in the eighties, the contact with Tempesta was already pointed out by Moschini in 1806 (p. 86): 'He then turned to painting, and for the most part his subjects were landscapes and seaports, although he did at times some battle pieces. In the coloring he tried to imitate Pietro de Mulieribus, called Tempesta.'

The blossoming of the idyllic, pastoral landscape under the never sufficiently praised Zuccarelli (1702–1788) and under Zais (1709–1784) shows, naturally, no immediate dependence from Tempesta. It is rather the difference between Tempesta's tightly filled classical landscapes and Zuccarelli's airy, open form and looser painterly handling that comes to mind; compare, for instance, the large, surface-covering forms of Tempesta's animal pieces (315) with the natural delicacy of no. 451. But there are moments in Tempesta when the gap of two generations melts away; a point in case is the sensitively done, smallish landscape no. 270, or the pastoral no. 232, which may be likened to Zais. Among the few examples of Venetian landscape given here, also Antonio Diziani (447), who already belongs to the late part of the eighteenth century, evokes, through Marco Ricci, a definite echo of Tempesta. The same could be demonstrated of the Cimaroli (especially Giovan Battista), Costa, Pecchio, and quite a number of other, minor landscapers of Venice. Finally, the sea storm and the stormy coast view, with which our artist set a precedent in Venice, were continued, beyond the rare examples of Pedon and the young Ricci, by Simonini, Frc. Guardi, and later Bernardino Bison. It will hardly be necessary, on the other hand, to reiterate that the aims of eighteenth century Venetian landscape are also fundamentally different from Tempesta in their picturesque grace, the sparkling painterly handling and, perhaps most of all, the colorful luminism, which was of no concern yet to the classical concept of Tempesta.

In Lombard landscape, it becomes more difficult to assess the effect of Tempesta's activity: the anonymous works are legion, the names minor, research is still almost completely lacking. The Brescian priest and self-trained painter Faustino Raineri, who lived from the late 17th century until 1755,

1. On Pedon, see mainly Delogu, in *Emporium* 1959, p. 200; Ricci Mostra, 1964, no. 7; Martini 1964, pp. 191, 198. Cf. also Precerutti Garberi, *Affreschi settecenteschi delle ville venete,* 1968, pl. 1, figs. 18 f. Ca' Borini was built in 1694, and the built-in pictures, still *in situ*, probably date from soon after. On Peruzzini, see exh. Florence 1969, p. 70.
2. A Rizzi, *Luca Carlevarijs*, Venice 1967, p. 95, figs. 9 f.

was 'a great imitator of Tempesta and adhered to his manner more than any other of Tempesta's followers' (Carboni, 1776, p. 20); we are given to understand that Raineri would also pass his works off as Tempesta's. But no works of either Raineri or of his once famous pupil and heir Agostino Bertelli (Brescia 1727–1776) can be traced at present. (For Bertelli, see the excerpts by Carboni-Maggi given here on p. 14). Bertelli derived his success mainly from the imitation of Tempesta, Berchem, and others, and was active for a few years in Genoa and Milan. Some of the imitations reproduced here may in fact be his.

From Tempesta's immediate pupils to Francesco Bassi in Cremona (414 f.), to Gaudenzio Botti and Giov. Giorgio Sanz in Brescia and Bergamo to G. Avellino, a Sicilian imitator of Rosa in Ferrara (by 1670), to his pupil Giuseppe Zola likewise in Ferrara, to the landscapes of Francesco Aviano in Vicenza and others, there are thus countless instances that reflect the radiation of our artist. The Cignaroli family of landscape painters in Verona and Turin is another example: two members seem to have been pupils of Tempesta; later, a striking survival of Tempesta appears in quite a few nocturnes and classical landscapes by the greatest of the Cignaroli, Vittorio Amadeo (1730–1800).[1]

No less important is Tempesta's action on another, hardly better known chapter of Lombard painting–the realism, in particular, animal painting. A study of the old inventories of collections from Milan to Venice reveals the enormous number of realist pictures from the eighteenth century with genre scenes, animals, still lives, and Bamboccesque subjects. Milan, Bergamo, Brescia, all were receptive to Tempesta's pastoral genre. Closest to his spirit among the animal painters is Angelo Maria Crivelli (Crivellone, dec. 1730), active mainly in Milan and considerably indebted also to Dutch animal painting. A specialist of 'basse-cour' animals, he could, if needed, elevate himself to boar hunts and similar themes. In Piacenza, his art is paralleled by his contemporary, Felice Boselli. Moments of Tempestism are felt in the widespread oeuvre of the Genoese Abate Cassana (437). In the first half of the 18th century, the foremost Brescian animalists were the brothers Giorgio and Faustino Duranti, who mainly excelled in poultry and birds.[2] The last figure to be mentioned here was also the greatest exponent of the genre–Francesco Londonio (1723–1783; fig. 438). His very personal style sums up a wide spectrum of precursors, including the Antwerp masters, Rosa da Tivoli, Castiglione. Tempesta stands at the beginning of this Lombard tradition that was to reach its fulfilment in Londonio. The fact that animalists are not the favorites of today's art market (a comeback is *eo ipso* certain) in no way lowers Tempesta's historic importance in this domain.

1. On Raineri, Bertelli, and Botti (1698–1775), see Calabi, 1935, pp. 65, 10, 14; on Raineri also Delogu, 1931, p. 168. On Zola (1672–1743), see Calabi, in *Riv. d'Arte*, vol. XII, 1934, p. 84, and Calabi, 1935, p. 85. On Aviani (act. 1701–1714), see Ballarin, in *Arte Veneta* 1956. On the Cignaroli, see L. Mallé, *Museo Civico di Torino, I Dipinti*, 1963, pl. 254 ff., and Donzelli, 1967, pp. 133, 138. On the Gallarati Scotti frescoes in Via Manzoni, see *Storia di Milano*, vol. XI, 1958, p. 223. On Deleidi, see L. Angelini, *L'avvento dell'arte neoclassica in Bergamo*, 1966, pp. 28, 140.
2. On Crivellone, see Delogu, 1931, pp. 171 ff., with catalog. On the Duranti (1683–1755 and 1695–1766), see *ibid.*, pp. 193 f., and Calabi, 1935, pp. 33 ff.

The Borromeo archives at the Isola Bella contain a copious dossier of correspondence with Tempesta, never hitherto mentioned. There are over forty letters by his own hand, dating from 1669 to 1689: one is from 1669, the bulk – 34 letters plus some scrap notes – are from prison in Genoa, 1679–1684, six letters are later. In addition, one letter, written in Parma in 1687, was published in 1855. Most of the artist's letters are addressed to Count Vitaliano Borromeo, miscellaneous ones to Cardinal Giberto Borromeo, Count Carlo Borromeo, to the Count's lawyer Carbonara, to Tempesta's brother-in-law, and to some other persons. By the artist's second wife are three letters addressed to the Count (1681, 1688). The archive preserves, furthermore, copies of the Count's answers and of his letters to Milanese, Genoese, Roman, Mantuan, and imperial dignitaries, pleading in favor of Tempesta's liberation.

A correspondence of this extent is particularly rare in the case of a Dutch artist. Indeed, from most Dutch artists no letters at all exist; there are seven by Rembrandt, but their content does not add significantly to our understanding of him (published by Gerson, 1961). The main reasons for this absence of epistolary documents were the fact that most Dutch painters had an oral contact with their patrons, and that the practice of isolated easel paintings did not involve lengthy discussions about the planning of the works.

The vital *raison d'être* of the letters was Tempesta's imprisonment, which left him no other means of communication with his protector. After his liberation, the exchange grew less regular, mainly because of the personal contact; moreover, the Count died in 1690. Only one letter to the Count dates from the two years that Tempesta spent in Venice, but we are told that he returned at intervals to Milan. Very likely not all of the artist's letters were kept after the Genoese years.

The prison situation explains both the interest and the limitation of the letters for us. They afford an immediate insight into Tempesta's personality and the particular problems of his existence in prison, the ups and downs from week to week, the alternation of hope and despair. All the letters from prison strike the same note: thanking the Count for his efforts, reporting the latest legal developments of the case, imploring the Count not to tire, suggesting steps to be taken and dignitaries to be contacted for petitions and help, assuring the nobleman of eternal devotion. Persons who were approached by the Count and whose names appear frequently in the letters include Emperor Leopold I (whose commissioner in Italy the Count was) and Empress Eleonora, the doges of Genoa (1679–1681: A. Spinola, 1681–1683: L. M. Invrea, 1683–1685: F. M. Imperiale Lercaro), members of the Genoese Grand Council and magistracy, the Duke of Massa, the Bishop of Sarzana, the Duke of Mantua, the Governor of Milan, etc. They all must have made their influence felt with the Genoese Grand Council. More informative about the artist are the reports about his existence, the failing health and declining eye-sight, the financial indebtedness, the constant tribulations. Never is there an allusion to the murder nor an admission of guilt.

As to painting, the letters yield very meager information. We learn that Tempesta was painting in prison, always being at the mercy of his guards. For some time, an airy room in a tower was conceded to him; then he was again placed into darkness where working proved almost impossible. Occasionally a painting is mentioned (only one by title: an Ark of Noah); he did a few works, apparently not many, for Borromeo. Others he had to do in order to bribe his guards and to please the noblemen of the Senate and Grand Council on whom his liberation depended (17 Dec. 1683). With all this, he hardly had a chance to work for a living. We get the impression that in prison he must have painted at irregular periods and that his production was uneven in quality. More than once, he speaks of several months' work for a picture.

Never do we find a hint of the artistic problems that must have occupied him when he was working. This is, to be sure, almost invariably the case with letters of painters. Few are those who, like Poussin, entered into the real questions of art in their letters. An exception in Tempesta's immediate surroundings are the sixty or so informative letters by Tavella, where matters of art hold the major place (see no. 376).

There is furthermore, at the end of the correspondence, the unedifying chapter of Tempesta's second wife Eleonora, who had mediated between the imprisoned artist and the Count and was on sufficiently familiar terms with the latter to display before him the chagrins of a betrayed spouse and to implore his help. There is, however, no indication that the Count's friendship for the artist grew cooler.

Tempesta's language complies with the verbose rhetoric proper to the time, and particularly to submissive petitions of the kind. Apart from this convention, the letters have the flavor of immediate spoken language, which the writer used with complete ease, except for the first letter, of 1669, where one still senses a foreign tone. On the whole, the letters cannot lay claim to literary refinements and a distinguished mode of expression. In this respect, the count's answers form a telling contrast.

It would have been pointless to print the entire correspondence, since much of it is repetitive and without interest. Relevant, factual material has been incorporated in the text chapters. I have thus limited myself to giving a few letters *in extenso,* and select passages pertaining to painting from other letters. A translation would have destroyed the live effect. Tempesta's handwriting is clearly legible only in a minority of letters. One of the neatest examples is reproduced on page 14. Others, often written in a minuscule script on scrap paper, cluttered and messy in appearance, cannot be fully deciphered. The spelling could hardly be less consistent; endings are mostly unclear, accents and capitalization arbitrary. I have transcribed as well as possible, omitting all accents, giving wrong endings where the text left no doubt, and omitting the formulas for address and greeting, except for a few cases.

1669, 7 September. Tempesta, Genoa, to Card. Giberto Borromeo, Rome.
Al Inmenentissimo Mr Cardinal Boromeo chi dio lo guardi, A Roma. Inmenentissimo Mr, non posso faer d'meno Come obligat.mo servitor di votra Inmenenza d'faer saper Come io foss stato qua à Genova 11 mese, et adesso son di rittorna per venier a Roma, é perche me trova tanto appresso di Milano et io non son stato altre volte, piliarò la mia strada per milano e parme se vostra inmenenza

me commandi o me trova bono di servier in qualche cosa, saro semper pronto a servier Come obligo mio Con tut'el core, se vostr inmenenza me fara gracie di scriver basta di scriver a pietro tempest pictor a Genova, me arrivera da Genova, per tanto me ricommando alla gracia di vostr inmenenz e ve baccio la mano e prego che mi scusa d'ardier che io la prego.
Genova al 7 d septebri 1669 voster obligatissimo servitor   Pietro tempest

1669, 14 September. Card. Giberto Borromeo, Rome, to his brother Count Vitaliano Borromeo, Milan.
Ill. mo Sig.re,
… A Pietro Tempesta pittore hollandese, che da Genova mi scrive di voler trasferirsi a Milano, io rispondo che si lasci costi veder da V. S; à cui ho voluto accennarle, perche sappia che egli è molto amorevole del Card. Homodei, e mio, e mi ha fatto qui di sua mano alcuna bagattella. Egli più che in altro, vale assai in dipinger Paesi con Marine, e laghi, e qui è stato solito di operar ad assai buon prezzo; sebene coll'essersi poi trattenuto in Genova può esser, che le doble Genovesi gli habbiano fatto mutar questo buon habito…

1679–1684. Letters by Tempesta from prison in Genoa.
1679, 18 May. Tempesta to Count Borromeo.
Al Ecc. mo Sig. re e P. rone Col. mo Sig. r Vitaliano Borromei, Milano. Gli Atheniesi soleano porgere sacrificij a un Dio ignoto che gli patrocinava: cosi io avisato, per quanto le strettezze di questi luoghi permettono, della cura, che V. E. s'è degnata pigliarsi di me, affinch'io goda la cara libertà, perche è un'effetto questo d'un Heroe che per ancor non conosco, porto–posso parimante dire–a un Nume ignoto i tributi della mia osservanza e l'offerta di me stesso. Intendo, in somma, che per togliermi da questi inferni ella impieghi il suo autorevole mezzo; e che per obligarmi alla valida sua Protezione, procuri estrahermi da si calamitosa miserie. Seguiti pure opera tanta meritoria, perche, oltra che null'altra azione hà piu del grande quanto quella di solevar altrui, le giuro, che chi mi torrà i lacci dai piedi, me gli ponerà al cuore, e chi mi farà godere aura di luce, sarà quella luce sola, a cui quasi a mia stella mi volgerò mai sempre: volarò alle sue piante, che imprimendo di continuo vestiggi di lodevoli azioni, meritano calcare i Troni e passeggiare i sentieri del Cielo, e confermatale con l'esibizion personale, quell'oferta che Le fo adesso in iscritto, Le darò il possesso attuale d'un vero suo servo, anzi d'un effettivo schiavo, per ricever da Lei quelle leggi, che si compiacerà prescrivermi e gli ordini com'io debba servirLa, poiche certo, si come mi spiace non havere habilità piu proporzionate al suo merito, cosi quale io sono, viverò continuamente soggetto a suoi stimatissimi commandi, e sarò sempre osservator riverente de Suoi cenni. Son'alcune settimane, che Dio m'hà favorito farmel'intendere, mà essendo qui dentro negato l'ingresso e l'uscita alle lettere, non hò potutu correre prima d'hora a far la confessione de miei oblighi a questo Nume ignoto, e attestarle la mia divozione, consecrandomela in perpetua. Adesso, che improvisa e furtiva occasione me lo permette, il fò, e la supplica, col dispensare alla qualità, e quantità della carta, gradire quest'alto e questa offerta, con quella generosità medesima con la quale ha intrapreso di aiutarmi, poiche riserbandomi farle conoscere per effetto, con servitù eterna, di quale catene m'havera legato beneficio cosi grande.

66

Affidandomi che non mi debba abbandonare Le auguro l'auge d'ogni maggior felicità, e le fo humilissima riverenza.

Dalla Torre di Genova li 18 Maggio 1679

Di V. Ecc. za   Humiliss. mo, Devot. mo, et ob. mo ser. re
                                                          Pietro Tempesta

1679, 6 August. Tempesta to Count Borromeo.

L'elezione del ser. mo Suo Zio a Doge di questa Real Rep. ca, mi porta a passarne seco quelli ufficij di congratulazione, a quali è tenuto un servitor vero, supplicando la benignità sua, gradire questo picciolo attestato della mia Divota osservanza; e perche sempre ho' tenuto V.S. Ill. ma, per l'auspice de miei solievi, pregola farmi godere adesso gli effetti della sua generosità, promovendo, in si favorevole congiuntura, tutto ciò, che può togliermi da queste miserie, affinchè poscia, io confessi, ch'ella è l'Idea della Gentilezza, e che chi è angosciato dai disfavori della sorte, non può riccorrere a soggetto chi più habbia del vero Cavalier di Lei, ne raccomandarsi a più benefico signore. In somma si compiaccia rendersi quell'arianna, che mi porga il filo per uscire, se non ha un labirinto, almeno da un mondano inferno; e s'assicuri che non vi sarà chi possa disponere di me, più dell'Illm. o Signor Bar. eo Dongho, nelle fortissime braccia della cui protezione rimettendomi, le auguro l'auge d'ogni felicità, e le fo humilissima riverenza.

Di Torre li 6. agosto 1679.

The Genoese Doge mentioned in the first line was Agostino Spinola, elected on 29 July.

1679, 14 December. Tempesta to Count Borromeo.

Troppo sarei reo di biasmevole colpa se nella vicinanza delle santissime feste con auguro di felicita non mi portassi a pagarle un tributo di vero e revirente devozione, che pero eccomi a pregarle dalla Liberalissima mano di Dio quelle allegrezze in questi santissimi giorni, che piu sono proprie per la Prosperita di V. Ecc. a e di tuta l'Ecc. ma sua Casa, e ad implorarle con le mie deboli preci la conseciazione di ogni suo desiderio, null'altro potendo fra tante obligazioni con le quali me La trovo legato, che pregar per essa continuamente, l'altissima quella generosa pieta, con la quale si è accinta a procurare nel mio solievo, quello d'un abbandonato straniero, che non ha altra speranza che nella pieta di V. Ecc. za, prego dunque a quella benignita cosi naturale del suo benignissimo cuore che non ha à sdegno abbassarsi è mitter l'occhio su le altrui calamità e confermarmele quel vero schiavo, che me Le son protestato, e che in effetto intendo di esserle, ma trovandome piu che mai sepolto nelle miserie di queste tombe, dove mi vedo consumare la Gioventù e la vita, con un intenso timore di havervi a lasciar le ossa prima che io possa travagliar qualche cosa per l'ecc. a v. a. Per carita dunque mi faccia degno del suo aiuto, e mi sia quell'ariadne, che col filo della sua pieta mi tolga da questo miserabile Laberinto, che nostro sig. r Iddio Gliene dia il merito, e io pregaro elli sempre per l'essaltazione di essa.

della carcere delle torre di geneva – al 14 di xmbr 1679.

1680, 21 January. Tempesta to Count Borromeo.

Fra le mie magg.ri pene che io provo di trovarmi in questo carcere è quella di dover mancare alle mie infinite obligacioni che devo all innata benignità d'un sig.re di tanta umanità come VS Ill.ma che veram.te lo devo tenere in luogo di Padre sebene ne sono indegno, non ostante la perdita da me fatta di chi mi fu Padre dell'anima di che confermerò l'obligacione sin doppo la morte come farò per il benig.mo patrocinio che VS Ill.ma se degna di havere di questo suo umile servitore…

The 'Padre dell'anima' must be the duke of Bracciano. In the following passages, Tempesta asks the count to intercede on his behalf with Senator Spinola di Gabella, as already the princess de Ligne (wife of the prince de Ligne, governor of Milan from 1674 to 1678) had done.

1680, 8 March. Tempesta to Count Borromeo.

Ieri fu da me, il Sig.r gio andrea Tassorella, secretario da qta Republica Ssma, e doppo molto discorso di scriti quadri che io faro per lei, contrasseme nel discorso di mia causa…

1680, 19 November. Tempesta to doctor Carbonaro.

1680, 22 October. Tempesta to Count Borromeo.

… senza un dinaro pieno di debiti, senza avere piu liberta, e questo è la causa che li quadri non ò potuto mandare a VS. Ill., adesso sono per mani due altri quadri per VS e vado facendo quanto posso e saranno meglio delli altri, spero in dio e subito che io posso le invigerò à VM, e prego di novo di perdonarmi mi misfatto, il quale venuto per causa di mia miseria e per esser stato ingannato di quel furbo di animella, al quale prego VS non dia orecchio perche è un falso huomo… e la prego per li cinque piaga di dio di non abandonarmi ma che abia pieta di mia miseria, e che si degna di impiegare sua efficace aiuto in mio pro, che so per sicuro se VS mi vuole aiutare, che io passero al palazzetto subito, che V Illm fara di mandare questa grazia, perche cosi mi à detto in confidenza il secretario tassorella, perche vien qualche volta parlare con meco…

1681, 17 March. Tempesta to Gio. Batt. Animella.

1681, 29 March. Tempesta to Count Borromeo.

Dentro una lettera de mons van merlo, io trovai un tesoro per me, ristretto in poco volume, dove è iscritto la clemenza e la carita che v.t ecc.lza va operando in service di un abandonato straniero…

1681, 9 July. Tempesta to Count Borromeo.

… Domenica matina che fu alle 6 del corente fu da me il sig. gio andrea tassorella secretario di qt ser.ma Republica e mi disse che due giorni passati, il ser.mo Duce lo fece chiamare, e li dice cosi, che il vesco di Sarzana suo fratello, li aveva scrito, che ieri aveva ricevuto Lettere da Roma del D.Livio, li quali facevano instanse grande per la liberazione del tempesta dove resta asai impegnato il vesco e che aveva scrito caldamente a lui… E adesso le dico che con il primo coriere mandero un quadretto piccolo fatto di me di buon gusto e con amore che un marinetta calma che ò mezo fato di veduta di naturale, e mandero per compagno qt primo une fortuna di mare, acio VS eccl vede un poco di roba di mia opera, e il compagno di quello che per Sig Tassorello che è di gran fattiga e fa molti mesi che è per le mani...

Don Livio is Prince Odescalchi, for whom Tempesta must have worked in Rome.

1681, 18 July. Scrap note by Tempesta to unknown adressee.

... Ieri vi ò inviato una cassetta con due quadri, uno di tre e quatro palmi per larghezza per spedire e uno d'arg.to in contante, il quadretto piccolo va al Eccl sigr Conte come trovarete avisato nella lettera sopra la posta, e VS mi face grazia di darli subito la lettera al Ill- conte con il quadretto, acio rest avisat del tutto...

1681, 19 July. Anna (-Eleonora) Tempesta, second wife of the artist, Milan, to Count Borromeo (absent from Milan).

... Questa mattina mi è pervenuto un quadretto inviatomi dal Tempesta, acciò lo porti à V.E., e alla Sua venuta gli lo portarò, quale scrive, che è apresso a far il compagno di quello che già V.E. tiene in sua casa; mi avvisa, che per mezzo del duce non ha havuto favore alcuno e che sono tutti mori bianchi, che con rigiri si vanno sottraendo dalle sue obligazioni, ne meno gli hanno letto il Processo, solo ogni giorno si và per Audienza, e sempre dà parole generali, hora resta serrata questa Strada. Solo se V.E. si vorrà compiacere ottenere la lettura dalla M.C. [Maestà Cattolica], che quella sarà la chiave della Prigione; e da tutti gli suoi amici gli viene dato questo Consiglio, sapendo quanto V.E. brama la libertà di questo provero huomo, che con il suo agiuto verso quella Corte, sarà il sollievo della sua libertà. Prego V.E. scusarmi del'incomodo, e me li dedico hum.a serva Milano li 19 Luglio 1681. Soggiongo, che inabsenza di V. Ecc. hò scritto all'Ill.mo Sig.r Donghe il modo da contenersi, con qualche ricordo a favore del Tempesta.

Devotis.a et obbendientis.a serva
Anna Tempesta

1681, 24 July. Anna (-Eleonora) Tempesta to Count Borromeo.

... Ho consiniato il quadreto al Sig. Cap.no Chocheti, et al Sig. Pietro lo ho fato instanza per il quadro companio di quello che V.E. tiene e fra breve spero sara qui, in questo prego V.E. scusarme del incomodo e qui per fine resto di augurarli ogni desirato suo bene. Milano li 24 luglio 1681.

1681, 4 August. Tempesta to Count Borromeo.

Viengo con lagrime di sangue, a dare Resa à V. eccl della mia disgrazia, e rovina, e do posta a V.E. che un mese passato viene qua a parlare con meco un Padre augustiniano scalzo che era venuto da Roma e che si dimando Padre Daniel, è luchese, un padre di garbo, e cosi mi mostro una lettera scritta da un altro Padre che sta a Roma, nel quale lettera conveneva cosi, che domenico di marche e tuti li suoi disiderano di sapere nova di me e essere pronti a farmi ugno piacere e darmi la pace se io

69

lo voglio. … Mi anno cercato da dipingere pero due giorno sono e non posso uscire di mia stanza e o paura che mi mettono soto in qualche tomba, dove non sapero novo da nisuno o bisogno che morire di fame e di meseria e qto innocentemente … quel traditore di animella mi a tradito, doppo avere mangiato tredici mesi mio sudore e sangue e li quatro quadri per regalare due al dom di marche e due per un Padre che mi scrisse che aveva fatto dare la pace … ma con il tempo si conossera mia innocenza, ma in tanto, non so come vivera e more di disgusto dove disidero la morte, trovandomi cosi tradito innocentemente e strappassato come un cano, dove mi viengo mittere alle piedi di v. eccl. con lagrime di sangue, che per li sinque piaga di dio v. ecl. mi aiuta adesso, per fare conossere mia innocenza e fare vedere che non proteggie un furbo, ma un povero virtuoso e huomo onorato…

1681, 20 September. Tempesta to Count Carlo Borromeo (nephew of Vitaliano), thanking him.

1681, 19 October. Tempesta to Count V. Borromeo.
Makes mention of letters in Tempesta's favor obtained or to be obtained from the Duke of Modena, the Empress, Balbi, Bart. Dongo.

1681, 25 November. Tempesta to Count Borromeo.

1681, 12 December. Tempesta to Count Borromeo.
… Li due quadri di V Eccl sono tirati avanti asai, e vado a lavorando qto posso, ma si come io vivo inqueto e mi anno levato molto commodita per di pingere acio io non posso aboccare cosi nisuno, mi fa perder le giornate, il gusto è il servello è non posso guadagnare con niente come devo guadanare e pur bisogna avere pacienza perche quel furbo di animella è causa di tuto questo male che dio le perdona.

1681, 17 December. Tempesta to Count Borromeo.
Christmas greetings.

1682, 22 January. Tempesta to Gio. Domenico Beltramo, husband of Tempesta's sister, Milan.
Mio sig.re, ò ricevuto la sua delle 17 del corente e ò tuto bene inteso. l'altro giorno mi anno levato la commodita da dipingere alla Campana, e animella è stato a risico di andare in prigione per queste spie che vanno dicendo che io scrivo per tuti, ma la causa principale è stat il comissario, sicome sa d'avere da me lire quatro cento, ò vedeva che io non lo pagavo, … e cosi sono tornato di alto e travaglio per lui e lui mi governa insino che sara pagato, VS considera in che stato mi trovo, adesso animella è incaldato con meco, perche à d'avere molti denari da me, et io non lo posso sodisfare adesso insino che non ò fatto al meno due quadri per il Comissario …

1682, 24 May. Tempesta to Count Borromeo.

Del Illmo Sig.r francisco massa paoli ò inteso una buona nova, il quale mi a fatto ritornare li spiriti e la sanita, si come era molti giorni che io sono meso amalato con un febre terzano, perche doppo che o visto che quando aveva trattato mia causa, e che non fece strada alcune, mi pilio tanto disgusto che dal l'ora in qua, non o piu gradito ora di buona sanità, ma quando o inteso che V.E. a d'operato tanto che la M. Del Imperatrice Leonora a fatto scrivere una lettera per Illm Sr Giulio Spinola, diretta al Ill. Colegio sono ritornato di morte alla vite, perche è la vera strada e non sara negato, cosi mi disse ancora Sr. Gio Andrea Tassorello l ultima volta che mi parla che pasà un mese, ma e piu di quindici giorni che le in leto lui ancore con dolori di fianchi è stato male asai, ma adesso sta meglio e lo spetto qt prima a parlare con meco …

1682, 23 July. Tempesta to Count Borromeo.

Già so che a V E sara stato scrito la mia disgrazia, e viengo solo pregare V.E. per li sinque piaga di dio, che abbimi misericordia di me, perche sono allo stato dove non si vede di mangiare senza lume e da dipingere con il lume non vedo piu, dove sono in miseria, e non o dinari … Di dipingere non vedo piu con il lume e pure besogna che fare qualche macchiette alla peggio, se non, besogno che mori di fame perche sono in debito con tuti e nisuno mi imprestarebe dieci soldi, e o perso la sanita e quasi la vista, e sono diventato quasi un cadavere, perche si come non ò avuto di caminare ugno die, mi sono con reverenza di v.E. gonfiato di … che non posso stare in piedi …

1682, 20 December. Tempesta to Count Borromeo.

Sono molto tempo che non ò scrito è V.E. per non infastidiarla … La prego per li sinque piaga di Dio di non stancarsi adesso intanto che non sia fornita tuta l'opera di mia tanta disiderata Liberta, e che posso venire alle piedi di V.E. e bacciarli le mani e servirli sino che saro vivo, a lei e se commandera ancora al Sre Massa Sarzano sono pronto a fare tuto quello che V E mi commandrà sempre … Cosi sara sicura mia Liberta la quale disidero con tutil cuore perche vado perdendo la vista del tuto, e la gioventù le forza, e divento un cadavere dallo disgusto e strappazzo di prigione dove non posso piu ò paura che al fino di perdere l'anima e il corpo se V E non mi aiuta …

1683, 9 January. Tempesta to Count Borromeo.

1683, 13 February. Tempesta to Count Borromeo.

Mi metto nelle braccie di V E, che lo face qto per la misericordia di Dio, e per Sua generosità, e che potra dire che avese riscattato un sciavo che non le manchera mai, e saro sempre a suoi commandi infine alla morte, e vedra quello che io so fare perche adesso non posso mostrarlo in cosa almeno perche adesso mi anno paltato per sempre sia IllS Gio Carlo Brignole al quale ò fatto un arco di noe che sono stato sinque mese a fare, e per compagno va il deluvio universale, e per eccl bernardo baliano ò tre quadri per mano che non sono … e adesso per Sr marcant. Doria fu fate due tele grande per farli di cosa asai, e qte sono tuti Sgri del magestrato dove besogna servirli e esser sciavo per sua virtù, per godere buone prigione e qualche arbitrio piu di altri, e non posso guadagnare tanto di mantenermi, sono scalzo e innudo come a V E sara ricontato presto di un prigionero che qui in torre, milanese, che qte prima andera in liberta, e si demanda Sgr Carlo Airoldo, il quale è stato molti mese con me e informato del tut. Del quadro di V E non mi riscio piu di parlare, ma adesso che li giornati comincono lungare un poco faro tut quello che posso per mandare il compagno a V E del quadro di palme tre e quatro ...

1683, 23 February. Tempesta to Count Borromeo.
... La vera strada sarebe qta che V E adoperasse tanto alla Corte del Imperatore che si contentasse il Magstr dell'Imperatore di fare scrivere due rige al G Con. Republica di Genova ...

1683, 14 April. Tempesta to Count Borromeo.
Havendo inteso che V E a visto il sbotzetto, e che la gustato a V E, e spero di mandarli il quadro qt presto si come Eccl et Srmi Sri del magistrato mi anno concesso la grazia di poter tornare a dipingere al Campanone, dove è carissimo e buon aria è cosi potro fare qualche cosa di piu che per il passato, è roba piu deligente e per serto questo estate V E avera il quadro. ora prego per amor di Dio che V E oprà tanto che vienga qta benedetta Lettera del Imperator ...

1683, 27 April and 30 April. Tempesta to Count Borromeo.

1683, 12 May. Tempesta to Carbonara.

1683, October to December. This document, probably prepared by Borromeo's lawyer, must have served in connection with petitions in favor of the artist addressed by the count to influential persons.
Sino del anno 1676 à 13 Genaro fu Carcerato nella Torre di Genova il celebre Pitore Pietro Tempesta olandese; Pretesto reo per la morte della q Lucia sua mollie, non essendosi mai aprovato la di lei morte sollo che l'Ecc.mo et Ill.mo magistrato delli inquisitori di stato li fecero sentenza di anni 20 di Torre che fu al li 27 7b.e l'anno 1679, sapendosi che d.ta Lucia sua mollie era adultera e dona publicha et in tempo che d.to sig.r Pietro fu lontano da lei diede a luce tre figlioli. Il magistrato fece la sentenza vigorosa per non essere in processo prove bastante che fosse il Tempesta che l'havese fatto ucidere e questo sollo per una semplice parola che d.ta Lucia dise prima di morir e che fu 'se non è stato mio marito non so chi possa essere che mi habia fatto ucidere'; trovasi che sono quatro anni che lui è sentenciato e non havere havuto la pace se devano levare anni dieci, che si trava che lui doverra stare à pregione ancora anni sei, ma prima della sentenza haveva soferto gia tre anni di torre secreta, che per simplice dito della deffonta non poteva patire tanta si rigorosa sentenza oltre haverla mantenuta in roma per detti otto anni a lire 100 il mese di moneta di Genova—acio non cometese adulterio, e che fuse adultera e notorio al Ecc.mo et Ill.mo magistrate come per lettere che tengono di suo fratelo, et essendo ragionevole che li fusero fatti boni li tre anni che ha soferto prima della sentenza che in tutto seriano ancora tre anni di prigionia, ne meno consta in processo che detto Tempesta sia

complice di d.ta morte non essendosi testimoni abanstanza che siano unicho contesta acio lo potesero piliare per convinto, et il suo servitore ha soferto una ora di corda che questo era abastanza liberarli tutti et la sentenza non fu datta ad formam statuti ma sollo di potenza et da tutti è statta biasimata detta sentenza.

1683, 17 December. Tempesta to Count Borromeo. Reproduced on p.74–75.

Ilus.mo et Eccel.m mio Sig.r e Patr.no Colend.mo.

Sono molte mese che non ò scrito à v.e. pche non mi sono risicato di incommodare piu, la cause lè che vede Crassiere ugne Die piu mio miserio, pche divento vecchio e vade perdendo mia vista asai asai, e mi sono rovinato con de cominsiare, da dipingere. Cosi deligente e fornito come ò fatt di due anni in quà, dove non posso guadagnare tanto che posso vivere, sè bene mi pagino piu di altra volte, ma p pagare mio stento besogne che mi pagassero tre volta altro tanto, p potere campare, o adesso tuti vogliono opra cosi deligente e con di roba asai, dove io more di nessessità, e si come sempre o quasi sempre io travaglio p li primi Sgri di qt. sità, besogne che faci alle meglio, pche ò di besogno di tuti, è intanto io mi vado distrugendo la vita e la robe, e qt le cause che non posso compire con nisuno, dove ò perso molti Patroni e amici e non posso remediare pche besogne che mio destino sia cusi, se Il Sr. Iddio non mi aiuta che lo remedia lui; non so piu che fare; solo posso pregare semp p quelli che me anno fatto di bene e che mi fanno di continuar, che il Sr Iddio le die sanita, e a me Liberta e sanità, acio possa ancora un Die mostrare l'inclinazione mio e fare qualche parte di mio debito e cosi qt. auguri a v.e. [per] le sant.m feste con ugne felicita da lei disiderato tanto spirituale come temporale e spero e pregero che il Sigr Iddio le concedera conferma, Io lo desidero di tutil cuore, e cosi qt. mi ricommando nelle grazie e carita di v.e e che il Sgr Iddio la inspiri di aiutarmi, a levarmi di qt miserie, e cosi qt.o mi inchino e face humil. Reverenza a v.e, e à tuti delle Eccl- Sua casa. D. v.e. semp

Al 17 di Xsmbris 1683

humil- e Dev.m et oblig- Sv.t
Petrus mulieribus
Aliter Tempesta

1684, 15 July. Tempesta to Count Borromeo.

Nel tempo che Genova fu sbarsagliato dalle bombe, é che io mi trovai con mile pericholo dalla morte, scrisse a V.E., due Lettere, il primo della quale io mandai, al Sig.r Secretario Tassorello, acio la mandasse a V.E., perche non sapevo a chi altro a mandarlo, perche a Genova tuti erano ritirati alle montagne per spavento, e se io mi avesse potuto ritirarlo mi sarei ritirato insino di la della montagne, perche chi non s'e trovato al presente di quella miseria non pa luo credere come era spaventevole, ma per quanto ò inteso della Sgra Leonora, V E non a rivecuto se ben il Sr Secretario Tassorello mi a scrito che a mandato a V E, ma il secondo che o mandato diretto alla Sgra Leonora per qt mi scrive à dato in mano di V E a gente da Milano, e per tuto Genova si dice delle grand'opera e carita che V E fa per me, perche qui per Genova si dice volgarmente che vado in liberta ora per ora ma si come io ò paura di restar piu presto prigionero per quel poco virtù che il Sr Dio mi à dato, che di esser com-

Ill.mo et Ecc.mo mio Sig.r è Patron Colend.mo

Sono molte mese che non ò scrito à v.e. è stato non mi
sono risicato di incommodare più. la cause te che uede
Crestiere ogne die più mio miserio, stato diuento uecchio
è uade perdendo mio uista asai asai, è mi sono rouinato
con de comintiare da dipingere cusi deligenti è fornite
come è fato di due anni in qua, doue non posso guadagna
tante che posso uiuere, se bene mi pagerio più di altri uolte
mi est pagare mio fronte bisogne che mi pagasseno tre uolta
altri tanti, st puterei campare. è adesso cusi uoglieno ogni
cusi deligente è con de roba asai, doue ce more di necessità.
è si come senza è quase senza io trauaglia st. li prime pro
di questi siti, bisogne che face alle meglio, stato è di bisogne
di subiti. è intante ci mi uade strengendo la uita è la robe,
è ogni le cause che non posso compire con nisuno, doue ò
perso molti Patroni è amice, è non posso remediare stato
bisogne che mio destini sea cusi, se per Dio mio non mi
aiuta che lo remedii lui, non so più che fare, solo posso
pregare è prego senza st. quelli che me anno fato de bene
è che mi fanno di continenti, che il Sig.r Dio lo die
sanità - è à mi libertà è sanità, acció possa ancora un die
mostrare l'inclinazione mio è fare quelche parte di mio debit,
è con questo auguse à v.e. le sant.me feste con ogni
felicità da lei disiderato tanto spirituale come temporale
è più. è prego che il Sig.r Dio li concederà con forma

Io la desidero di tutto cuore, e però ch. mi ricommando
nelle grazie e carità di v.e: e che il S. Iddio la inspire
di aiutarmi, e levarmi di qta. miseria. e però ch. mi
inchino e fare humilis. Reverenza a v.e e a tutti della
ecc.ta sua Casa.
D. v. e. serva

Il 17 di settembris
1653

Hum.ma S.ra e Da.ma et obl.ma Ser.
Di cani mulieribus
Aliter Tempesta

patito per aver da fare con molti cervelli, e si come io vedo che la cosa vano calmando a poco a poco e conosche la natura di qt clima, e l'Aria, non posso fare di meno de ritornare a pregare humilmente V E che non si stanca d'operare in mio solevo, se ben trovasse il tereno duro, perche se non si fa adesso non besogna sperare mai piu, e per qto prego v e per l amor di Dio, mentre già à operato per me, con tanta carita e amore da non stancarsi se non vede la mia liberta, acio io posso venire alli Piede di v e a pagare qualche poco tributo delle migliaie obligazione che o a v.e. e poter dire v e di avere comprato un sciavetto in me per sempre non avendo io altro desiderio che da morire in servitu del Illm, et Eccl- casa di Sri Borromeo alla quale sono stato sempre devoto, o morire per li gran obligo e benefici che ò rivecuti, e ugne dia prego nelli mie deboli orazioni il Sr Iddio, che concedi ugne felicità a v e.

1684, 19 October. Tempesta, four days after his liberation from prison, to Count Borromeo.
Do parte a v.e. che sabbatto sera a un ora de notte, per grazia di Dio, e d'v.e. la Sma Giunta me fece la grazia di mia Liberta, e a due ora di notte Im Sra marchesa Imperiale sorella del Principe di Monicha mi mando a dare la nova per suo maggior huomo, dove tuto questa notte stetto senza dormire e con mile pensieri fra il temore e la speranza, e cosi Domenica matina mi mando Illmo Sr Gio Carlo Brignole à dire che io ero libro e che le mandasse suo quadro che era quasi finito e che me aspettave in casa per finirlo e cosi lo credevo che era vero e subito doppo Im Sr marcantonio Doria mi manda a piliare suo quadro e mi mando a dire che non me impegnasse con nesuno, che me avesse parecchiato un partamento e la sua vatola e sua carozza in ugne tempo … et io lo ringrazio di tanto favore contro mio merito ma che io non poteva disporre di me, perche sono stato dimandato dal Sr Ambastor di Spagna per ordine del Im Sr Conte di Melgardo Governator del stato di milano per sua grazia, dove conveniva d andare per lo primo in casa del Sr Ambastor de Spagna e opservare suo commando, e qt escuso fece con tuti per non aver gusto di andare in casa di nesuno, e cosi doppo pranzo il Sr secretario Tassorello me porto la mia relassita e me dise quanto aveva operato come la verita, che senza lui non se sarebe mai fatto quello che s e fatto, perche forse piu del meta di cavalieri di Genova disgustati per avermi liberato, per esser fora di speranza d aver mai piu di mia opera a modo sua, e questo se à visto perche martedi matina Illm magestrato di suprema se misse insieme per anullare quello che aveva fatto la Sm Giunta, pretendendo che non à tanto autorita di fare, e cosi per buona sorte Il Sr Consigliere del magestrato di suprema era malato … Il secretario tassorella me disse che io andasse in casa del Sr Ambastor di Spagna e che io facesse tuto quello che mi commandavo, e cosi mi pilio una cadrega con la roba di camera perche vestito no aveva, e me scusai con ugne cortesia e volto molto allegro, e doppo che ero venuto per offerire mia vita a lui e ringraziarlo e per opservare suo commando e le bacio le mani e cosi mi disse che non era lui che mi aveva fatto liberare e che a lui non è obligo nesuno, ma che io vadi domatina a buon ora in casa della Sigr marchesa Imperiale, e che conosce tuto quel bene che ò ricevuto da lei, perche ad instanza di lei e stato fatto tuto e che opservavo tutto quello che mi commandasse, e cosi ieri matina a bon ora me piliai una cadrega e me ne ando in roba di camera in casa della Sra marchesa e spettai che fose levata e subito me fece tiamare, e cosi fece quello che Sr Ambasator mi aveva comisso, e mi riceve con tanta

grazia e allegrezza e se rallegra di vedermi di nova e che stavo bene e che ero diventato piu giovane che ero prima, e che quello che a fatto a fat per carita e per mia virtu; avevo ditto che io non faro un niente per nesuno quando saro fori, ma che andavo subito a Milano per fare mio obligo al Ecc Sr Governator di Milano e a V. e., ... e cosi fece la marchesa subito tiamara il suo sarto e mi pilio le mesuri e me a fatto vistire da capo a piede d cavalier. ... E per qte feste di Natale saro alle piede di vostra Ecza e faro mia offerta della vita, e con qto mi inchino e face hu- Reverenza a v.e. e al Ecc Sr Carlo suo Sr nepote e a tuti della Ill- sua casa.

Il 19 di 8tobris 1684.

1684, 22 October. Tempesta to Count Borromeo.
Spero che v.e. avera ricevuto la mia lettera che lo scrito giovedi passato dove contiene tuto come e andato a mia bramata liberta. venerdi matina andai de nova a ringraziar Sr Ambastor d'Spagna conforma me aveva ordenato Il. Sra marchesa Imperiale, e cosi mi vide vestito tut in altro mode e ne ebbie gusto e me disse che sua casa era a mio commando ... E qto natale saro d v.e. a fare quello che o sempre ditto di offerirle a servirla del restanti di mia vita ...

1684, 10 December. Tempesta to Count Borromeo.
Ieri matina o inviato una cassa a milano dove è dentro mio studio cioè disegno e qualche pictura ancora, e libri di pictori qualche d'uno e si come non ò a casa che nesuno mitte dentro le mano ò pigliato l'ardore di mettere il sopra scritto al v ecza acio vada sicuro e che nesuno dia fastidio ... La Sra Anna pagera li la postatura e prego v. Ecza me scusa del'audace, e che si compiace di farli consegnare alla Sra Anna mia Sra ... e innansi la festa di natale saro alle piedi di v. eza.

1686, 26 October. Tempesta, Milan, to Count Borromeo.
Sono arrivato à Casà d V.E. per le lettere per Modena e per Parma, e o trovato che V.E. era partito per Isola dove viengo a Pregarla di farme grazia di mandarme qua subito, perche mia partenza sarà pl Giorno doppo StCarlo e la prego d mandarme una o due per modena e una o due per Parma, a Sig.ri Grandi della Corte, ò a chi pare V.E. faranno piu eficatie e validi e per esser servitor sempre d'v.e. prego d farlo Come fosse per un amico suo Caro et à mio ritorno ricontero à V.E. il seguito, et operaro ancora il Le penelli Con affetto e me inchino e faci hu-Reverenza.

Milano All 26 d'8-bris 1686.

1686, 9 November. Tempesta, Milan, to Count Borromeo.
Rendo infinita grazia à V.E. della Lettera che mi à mandato diretta al Il. marchese Montecucoli, ma si come per il tempo cattivo non si puo passare per lie agre, non posso partire ancora per molto giorni, dove d'nuovo io viento in fastidire V.E. con pregarli per un altra Lettera à qualche Cavaglier d'garbo alla Corti del I.m Duca di Parma, perche là non ò nessun'introduction, e me sarebe caro di esser intraduto in quella Corte con qualche Lettere onorevole di V.E. sapendo molto bene che V.E. in quella Corte à di autorita asai, dove di nuove suplico di farme q.t grazia e di mandarmi

quanto Prima e staro attendendo la grazia di V.E. e à mia venuta mi riardero dal Isola bella, e à V.E. me inchino a fare hu.a Reverenza.

Milano All 9 di 9vmbris 1686.

1687, 15 March. Tempesta, Venice, to Mons. Angelo Maria Arcioni, Abbot of the monastery of S. Giovanni Evang. in Parma. This letter, which I have not been able to find in Parma, is the only one by Tempesta to have been published so far; it appeared in Campori, 1855, p.319. At that time, the letter was kept in the library of the monastery of S. Giovanni in Parma. Abbot Arcioni, aged 83, was a friend of the arts.

Ill.mo et Molto Rev.do mio Sig.re e Patron Col.mo.

Non ò scritto prima a V.S.M.R. perchè credevo a mio ritorno di venire a reverire a bocca, ma si come adesso io ò stabelito di fermarmi qualche tempo qua, perchè ò preso Casa per un Anno, perchè l'aria confà molto a mia sig.ra Consorta e a me ancora è veramente una Città di godere perchè ve sempre qualche cosa di nova di vedere a piena sempre di forestieri, dove non manca mai di saper nova de tuta l'europa e anco ... Il cl. Sig. Nicolò Contarini il quale mi aveva invitato qua à trattato veramente di vero Cavagliere e non se po far di più, ma adesso come ò scrito di sopra ò preso Casa per me, sopra la fondamente nove vicina li jesuiti, dove si vede di cosa bella di vedute, perchè se vede da lontano le montagni di Germania e il mare d'altra banda, e qua è stato gradito di molte delettanti e Cavaglieri mio venuto in q.ta Città, perchè di Pittori di figure cie ne asai, ma di Paesi e marine e animaletti non ci è, o quelli che sono, sono di poco, dove non manca di far per Dei Grazia, e quando arivai a Modena vendei quelli due quadri che V.S.M.R. à visto a Principe foresto di Modena per 255 doppie, e adesso face quatro altri per Modena della stessa grandezza, et il Marchese Gio. Battista Montecuccoli al quale ci aveva una lettera, e mi à fatto mile Grazia e onore, e ò visto di quadri superba a Modena d' ... valanthomenij, e qua a Venetia non mancano di quadri bellissimo di vedere ugno di in Casa di Particolari dove vado passando il tempo qualche volta virtuosamente e con grandissimo gusto. io aveva impermisso di scrivere a quel Cavagliere che era in Convento con V.S.M.R. ma ne scordato suo nome me pare che dicevano Cavaglieri bovi o bosi non so giusto e per questo prego a V.S.M.R. me face la Grazia di mostrargli questa lettera e di salutare di tut il Cuore di mia parte perchè è veramente Cavagliero di vaglia e amator di virtuosi e degno di lode, e se V.S.M.R. averà occasione di vedere quel S.r Bressano Pictor di Bataglie prego di farme grazia di salutarlo da mia parte e se io qua posso servire V.S.M.R. e quel Cavagliero bovj o altri in qualche cosa prego onorarmi di suoi Commandi, troveranno sempre in me un vero servitor e per non più tedoarlo mi fermo e face hum. Reverenza Di V.R.M.P., ò ricevuto Lettera da Genova del S.Gio. Batta. Merano e suo felice arrivo, ma me scrive che sta più volontiera fora di Genova che a Genova. Venetia 15 di Marzo 1687, Humil.mo devot.mo et obblig.mo serv. Petrus Mulieribus aliter Tempesti.

'Sr. Bressano' is Francesco Monti, called il Brescianino, battle painter (Brescia 1646–Parma 1712); Cavalier Bovj cannot be identified; Gio. Batt. Merano is a Genoese painter of religious subjects (1632–1698, after 1668 in Parma; long Vita by Ratti).

1688, 1 May. (Anna-) Leonora Tempesta, second wife of the artist, Venice, to Count Borromeo.

L'Infelice Leonora Tempesta ricorre à solevarsi l'anima con essagerationi à V.E. Pietro Tempesta cosi infamamente mi tratta che mi pare d'esser in un Inferno. Le villanie i strappazzi, e le ingiurie che mi fà non le sopporterebbe Giobbe. E questo per causa che lui s'attrova inamorato in una Giovine quivi in Millano di modo che mi vorebbe morta overo fuor del mondo per sposarla; once io penso che ne seguirà poco bene perche io non posso più star cosi. Volesse Dio che io havessi fatto à modo di V.E. e del Sig. Dino Molis, e della Principessa Trivulcia et altri che tutti mi persuadevano lasciarlo morir in priggione. L'essermi io amogliata con lui, è stata una falsa invention sua di dire che fosse morto il primo marito perche si come è poco catolico è anco molto infame et hora che mi ha presto presto ridotta à mendicar doppo consumatomi quasi tutto barbaramente ancora mi tratta per verdermi fuor del mondo. Io m'attrovo disperata con questo Ingrato che è come V.E. sà qui sempre à millano et à tutti propaga che io sia una matta, e m'infama per venir su li suoi diritti; once io non sò piu che rissolvere vendendomi disperata. Hà anco villaneggiata la mia persona oppresso l'ecc.mo Nicolo Micheli Nob. Veneto e li fà credere tutto con le sue false e traditorie forme di operare; onde si pensi V.E. come la posso passare se Iddio non vi mette la sua mano.

Intanto perche questo Tempesta và dicendo che non li hò data dote, e perche V.E. è stata quella che hà levato il dinaro dal banco di S.Giorgio di Genova per portarli in dotte hò scritto al Sig. Ant. o Camoglie che non dia dinari ad'altri che à V.E., onde la supplico riceverli, e trattenerli acciò non mi vadino alla malhora ancor questi perche bisognerebbe poi che io andassi à cercar la elemosina. Dalla presenti non mi faccia risposta alcuna mà giovi solamente al mio solievo perche lui và intracciando ogni passo che io faccio per impedire ogni mio solievo.

V.E. vedda se è falsa questa persona, che fà che quel certo Animela scriva lettere infame contro di me per mostrarle alla Nobiltà à mio dishonore; e questa è la mercede di 9 anni che hò strusciato per acinarlo, e cavarlo si può dir dalla forca. Io son infelice al piu alto segno perche non hà altra mira che di disfarsi di me, mà teme di dovermi dar la dote indietro, e per questo mi infama. Direi d'avantaggio mà non voglio tediar VE. Li porto le mie riverenze e mi conf.mo.

pmo maggio 88. Ven.a

1689, 17 December. Tempesta, Venice, to Count Borromeo.
Personal accusations against Tempesta's second wife.

CATALOG OF ILLUSTRATED WORKS

The medium, where not otherwise specified, is oil on canvas. Most paintings in private collections had to be measured within the frame.
'Isola Bella' refers to the collection of Prince Borromeo, Isola Bella, Lago Maggiore.

1–45 PRECURSORS

The arrangement of this section is not chronological, but reflects the order in which the artists discussed here became influential for Tempesta: school of Antwerp; Roman school: Claude, Gaspard, Rosa, Mola; Bassano; Genoese animalists, Castiglione; Lauri.

1–3 FLEMISH ANIMAL PAINTERS
Tempesta's large animal pieces from his early Antwerp year of c.1656 (188f.) derive from Rubens, Snyders, P.de Vos, and above all Fyt. This heritage is still felt in Tempesta's later animal pieces (312ff.)
LIT. The respective entries in E.Greindl, *Les peintres fla-mands de nature morte au XVIIe siècle*, Brussels 1957, and exh. Brussels 1965. The works reproduced here are not mentioned in these two texts.

1 JAN FYT
Antwerp 1611–1661.
BUZZARD AND POULTRY
MADRID, PRADO, no.1527.
95 × 134 cm. A copy was formerly in the Novak collection, Prague. Composition and handling are particularly close to Tempesta's no. 189.

2 PAUL DE VOS
Hulst 1596–Antwerp 1678.
EAGLES AND WOLF
VIENNA, CZERNIN COLLECTION, as Snyders.
160 × 240 cm. There is a pendant in the same collection. To my mind by P.de Vos or an immediate follower of his.
LIT. Catalog of the collection, by K.Wilczek, 1936, no. 93, as Snyders.

3 PAUL DE VOS
BOAR HUNT
PARIS, LOUVRE, no.2144.
232 × 348 cm. According to Houbraken, also Tempesta 'excelled especially in painting boar hunts in the manner of Frans Snyders,' but none of these pictures are known today.
LIT. Louvre catalog, by Lafenestre, 1907, no.2144, as Snyders, with former attribution (in the Musée Napoléon) to M. (*sic*) de Vos.

4,5 JACQUES D'ARTHOIS
Brussels 1613–c.1686.
During his early sojourn in Antwerp, Tempesta must have become acquainted with many works by d'Arthois, who was the leader of the Brussels landscape school. The two may also have met. Judging from Tempesta's later production, the contact with the Flemish master left a lasting impact on the Dutchman. Despite the difference of age and school, one feels a general affinity of temperament between them. Both share a similar taste for monumentality, for rich settings, and for surface-filling forms.
LIT. Thiéry, 1953, p.136. Laes, in *Misc. L.v.Puyvelde*, 1949, p.166. Exh. Brussels 1965, p.7.

4 LANDSCAPE
STOCKHOLM, NATIONAL MUSEUM, no.1183.
85 × 110 cm. Signed at the bottom left. Compare Tempesta's no.297.

5 LANDSCAPE
VIENNA, KUNSTHISTORISCHES MUSEUM, no.1167.
173 × 218 cm. Compare Tempesta's nos.251, 254.

6 NICOLAS POUSSIN
Les Andelys 1594–Rome 1665.
LANDSCAPE
MADRID, PRADO, no. 2310.
120 × 187 cm. The style of this masterpiece, datable c. 1651, inspired certain particularly crystalline paintings from Tempesta's late phase (300 f.).
LIT. Gnudi, in *Nicolas Poussin (Colloque)*, ed. A. Chastel, Vol. I, Paris 1960, p. 235. A. Blunt, *The Paintings of Nicolas Poussin, A Critical Catalogue*, London 1966, no. 216, with further lit.

7 CLAUDE LORRAIN
Lorraine 1600–Rome 1682.
COAST VIEW
NEW YORK, WILDENSTEIN & CO.
73.5 × 96.5 cm. An example of a picture type favored by Claude in the late 1630's. It influenced Tempesta during his Roman years, in particular at the stage of the Colonna frescoes (176, 181).
LIT. My *Claude Lorrain*, New Haven 1961, no. 26, with further lit.

8 CLAUDE LORRAIN
VIEW OF THE CRESCENZA
ENGLISH PRIVATE COLLECTION
39 × 58.5 cm. Green and brown tones; the castle brown, the sky pale yellow at the horizon. This fine painting, identified by me only recently, shows a site of which Claude must have been fond. The same country house recurs in several of his nature drawings, some of which he inscribed *Crescenza*, which refers to the ancient *casale* a few miles north of Rome, off Via Flaminia. The inscription by Payne Knight (dec. 1824) on the back of the frame, 'Castellum Gensianum Colonnensium villa maritima a Claudio Gillée Lotharingensi depicta ex eorum aedibus Romae,' gives therefore an erroneous identification of the site (Genzano) and may or may not be correct as regards the Colonna provenance. The painting is recorded in the *Liber Veritatis* as number 118, which places it into the year 1650. The poetic, lyrical character of this work anticipates many classical landscapes of future generations: Tempesta (290), Tavella (385), Orizzonte (444).
COLL. Downton Castle, Herefordshire. LIT. My *Aggiunte a Claude*, in *Paragone* 233, 1969, p. 54.

9–16 GASPARD DUGHET
Rome 1615–1675.
During his Roman phase, the young Tempesta was principally influenced by Gaspard, whom he must have known personally. Under the impact of Gaspard, his style changed from Dutch and Flemish to Italian. See also Gaspard's fresco no. 170.
LIT. The following titles conspicuously point out the need for a comprehensive study of Gaspard. Sutton, in *GBA* 1962, p. 269. Arcangeli, in exh. catalog, Bologna 1962 (so far the best study). Friedlaender and Blunt, *The Drawings of Nicolas Poussin*, vol. IV, London 1963 (Shearman, on Gaspard; unsatisfactory). Waddingham, in *Paragone* 161, 1963, p. 37. Harris, in *Burl. Mag.* 1964, pp. 58, 115 (on the S. Martino frescoes). Chiarini, in *Burl. Mag.* 1969, p. 750.

9 LANDSCAPE WITH THE FLIGHT INTO EGYPT
ROME, GALLERIA DORIA PAMPHILJ
86 × 136 cm. Datable around 1650. Stormy landscapes occur frequently in Gaspard's younger and middle years (compare also the Tempest of the Mahon collection, exh. Bologna 1962, no. 107). They exercised a deep influence on the late Nicolas Poussin, Tempesta (235, 255), Orizzonte (440 f.), and others.
LIT. Doria catalog, of 1816, as Gaspard, with figures by N. Poussin. Sestieri, 1942, no. 436. Modern Doria catalogs, no. 350. Buscaroli, 1935, p. 83. Waddingham, in *Paragone* 161, 1963, p. 42.

10 LANDSCAPE
ROME, GALLERIA DORIA PAMPHILJ
275 × 385 cm. Tempera. Grey-green tones. Compare Tempesta's no. 287.
LIT. Doria catalog, of 1816, as Gaspard. Waterhouse, *Baroque Painting in Rome*, London 1937, p. 62, as Gaspard. Sestieri, 1942, no. 584, as anonymous, 18th century, of limited merit. Modern Doria catalogs, no. 81, as Gaspard.

11 LANDSCAPE
CHANTILLY, MUSEE CONDE
37 × 48 cm. This type of small, tightly filled and densely painted landscape must have inspired many paintings by Tempesta (287), whose compositions are, however, less classical.
COLL. Reiset. LIT. Catalog of the museum, of 1899, no. 78 (pendant: no. 79).

12 LANDSCAPE
PARIS, LOUVRE, no. 1903, as J. F. van Bloemen.
72 × 96 cm. Though traditionally considered a work by Orizzonte, this picture seems to me typical of Gaspard on account of the composition, the refined handling, and the figures. Compare the preceding and, for the large tree, Poussin (6).

13 LANDSCAPE
BAVARIAN PRIVATE COLLECTION
50 × 66 cm. The painterly quality of this small, densely packed composition justifies the traditional attribution to Gaspard. It compares with the larger landscape of the Molinari-Pradelli collection (*GBA* 1962, p. 272, fig. 3) and is datable in the 1630's. The setting anticipates many similar, yet more rigid works from Tempesta (294) to Orizzonte (443).

14 LANDSCAPE WITH ST. JOHN
MILAN, BRERA, no. 709.
228 × 335 cm. The figure by Mola. Ordered in 1661 in Rome by the Milanese Cardinal Luigi Alessandro Homodei (who also patronized Tempesta) for Sta. Maria della Vittoria in Milan, together with a pendant showing St. Paul in a landscape, by Rosa (Brera no. 607) and a painting for the high altar showing the Assumption of the Madonna, likewise by Rosa (now Paris, Notre-Dame). The two landscapes go ultimately back to Titian's St. Peter Martyr. Compare Tempesta's no. 263. Homodei furthermore ordered for a different Milanese church Rosa's Madonna del Suffragio (now in the Brera; see Salerno, 1963, p. 55).
LIT. Latuada, *Descrizione di Milano*, vol. III, 1737. Sutton, in *GBA* 1962, p. 290.

15 VIEW WITH TREE TRUNK
ROME, GALLERIA DORIA PAMPHILJ
217 × 49 cm. This and the following work belong to a series of tall, decorative canvases of the same size (another is reproduced by Sutton, in *GBA* 1962, p. 283). They compare with Tempesta's smaller nos. 221, 226 f.
LIT. (Pair) Doria catalog, of 1816, as Gaspard. Sestieri, 1942, nos. 62, 30, as poor school works. Modern Doria catalogs, nos. 398, 74, as Gaspard.

16 ROCKY VIEW
ROME, GALLERIA DORIA PAMPHILJ
217 × 63 cm. See the preceding.

17 SCHOOL OF GASPARD
LANDSCAPE
ROME, GALLERIA DORIA PAMPHILJ
280 × 113 cm. A decorative, large work from the vicinity of Gaspard. Compare Tempesta's nos. 226 f. See also the Farnesina frescoes nos. 171 f.
LIT. Doria catalog, of 1816, as Gaspard. Sestieri, 1942, no. 77, as Rosa. Modern Doria catalogs, no. 73, as Graziani (on whom cf. no. 417).

18, 19 PIETRO TESTA (IL LUCCHESINO)
Lucca 1611 – Rome 1650.
Working in the orbit of Mola, Cortona, and Poussin, Testa's painted and engraved landscapes anticipate solutions by Tempesta.
LIT. Lopresti, in *L'Arte* 1921, pp. 10, 74. Marabottini, in *Commentari* 1954, pp. 116, 217; Harris, in *Paragone* 213, 1967, p. 35.

18 VIEW WITH LARGE TREES
PARIS, LOUVRE, CABINET DES DESSINS, no. 1915.
Drawing, 217 × 275 mm. Pen, brown wash. Many equally rich landscape drawings by Testa exist. The closest stylistic parallels are in Gaspard and Mola. Tempesta may have known such drawings in Rome. A comparable layout occurs in his painting no. 251.
COLL. Mariette. LIT. Chiarini, in *Paragone* 187, 1965, p. 64. EXH. Louvre, Cabinet des Dessins, *Mariette*, 1967, no. 137.

19 THE PRODIGAL SON TENDING THE PIGS
Engraving, 210 × 315 mm. Signed in this first state 'P Testa in. fec. Roma' and, in the second state, 'H Mauperche excud.' Compare Tempesta's nos. 206, 313.

20–23 SALVATOR ROSA
Arenella (Naples) 1615 – Rome 1673.
The impact of Rosa's art on Tempesta is second only to that of Gaspard. The three artists were active in Rome during the same years. It is above all Rosa's painterly handling which left its mark on the Dutchman.
LIT. Salerno, 1963.

20 COAST VIEW
MADRID, PRADO, no. 324 ('Gulf of Salerno').
170 × 260 cm. Monogrammed at the bottom center. Painted about 1640. A large, stately example of a type of image which was dear to Rosa and proved influential for Tempesta (271 ff.).

ENGR. Parboni. LIT. Prado catalogs, no. 324. Voss, 1924, p. 571. Salerno, 1963, p. 144, with further lit. A. Pérez Sánchez, *Pintura italiana del s.* XVII *en España*, Madrid 1965, p. 435.

21 ESTUARY VIEW WITH ROCK ARCH
ROME, GALLERIA DORIA PAMPHILJ

66 × 150 cm. From the late forties. There are several comparable compositions by Rosa, large ones as well as small ones (a tiny, signed one is in Palazzo Pitti, Florence; repr. Cipriani, *La Galleria Palatina*, Florence 1966, p. 154). They form the prototypes for many of Tempesta's river views (277).
LIT. Doria catalog, of 1816, as Rosa. Ozzola, *Salvatore Rosa*, 1908, p. 256 as not by Rosa. Pettorelli, *Salvatore Rosa*, 1924, p. 46, as not by Rosa. Sestieri, 1942, no. 440, as Rosa. Modern Doria catalogs, no. 349. Salerno, 1963, p. 146, as Rosa.

22 LANDSCAPE WITH TOBIAS AND THE ANGEL
PRIVATE COLLECTION

72 × 106 cm. Painted soon after 1650. Compare Tempesta's no. 296.
LIT. Salerno, 1963, no. 51, with further lit.

23 LANDSCAPE WITH THE BAPTISM OF CHRIST
GLASGOW, ART GALLERY AND MUSEUM

173 × 260 cm. Pendant to St. John in the desert, in the same museum (Salerno, 1963, pl. XVI). According to Baldinucci (*Notizie ...,* ed. 1847, vol. V, p. 457), the pair was painted for Marchese Guadagni. After 1650. Compare Tempesta's no. 297.
LIT. Salerno, 1963, p. 142.

24 SCHOOL OF ROSA
LANDSCAPE
LONDON, NATIONAL GALLERY, no. 1206.

73 × 109 cm. A similar composition from the school of Rosa is at the museum of Valence, France, no. 148.
LIT. Buscaroli, 1935, pl. 48, as F. d'Angeli. *Summary Catalogue* of the museum, 1958, no. 1206, as style of Rosa.

25 BARTOLOMEO TORREGIANI
?Naples–Rome 1675?
LANDSCAPE
BAMBERG, CIVIC MUSEUM, no. 310.

98 × 133 cm. Too little is as yet known about this artist active in the orbit of Rosa to define his personality.

Judging from the few certified works in the Doria and Pallavicini collections, Rome (cf. Zeri, *La Galleria Spada in Roma,* Florence 1954, no. 165), the traditional attribution to him of this work and of its pendant in the same museum is plausible on account of the basic dependence from Rosa, the motives of wilderness, the unlikely setting, the flickering handling. The picture anticipates, in a more romantic flavor, some of Tempesta's mountainous landscapes (257, 338). Also the pendant, with two bent trees in the center, offers a comparison with Tempesta and, more even, with Marco Ricci (410). On Torregiani as a draftsman, see Chiarini in *Paragone* 183, 1965, p. 61.
COLL. Hemmerlein, 1838. LIT. Catalogs of the museum, of 1874, no. 102, and 1927, no. 310, both as Torregiani.

26 PIER FRANCESCO MOLA
Mendrisio (Ticino) 1612–Rome 1666.
ELIJAH AND THE WIDOW OF ZAREPATH
SARASOTA, FLA., THE JOHN AND MABLE
RINGLING MUSEUM OF ART

66 × 49 cm. The same museum has a compositionally and thematically corresponding pendant (no. 139, repr. in the catalog of 1949). The influence of Mola on Tempesta–who may have known him in Rome–is comparable to that of Cortona. Mola's rich handling, his saturated compositions, and the classical tenor of his art must have appealed to Tempesta; compare his nos. 220 ff.
LIT. Catalog of the museum, of 1949, no. 138.

27 SCHOOL OF MOLA
LANDSCAPE WITH THE REST ON THE FLIGHT
ENGLISH PRIVATE COLLECTION, as Mola.

Panel, 23 × 28 cm. Datable around 1650. From the immediate vicinity of Mola, and ipso facto also related to Domenichino, Albani, Grimaldi. Compare Mola's Riposo in London, National Gallery, and a painting by Frans de Neve listed under no. 431.
EXH. London, Burlington Fine Arts Club, 1925, no. 3, as Mola.

28 PIETRO DA CORTONA
Cortona 1596–Rome 1669.
LANDSCAPE
ROME, PINACOTECA CAPITOLINA

Panel, 17 × 27 cm. There is a pendant, representing a harbor scene. Painted about 1625. Tempesta must have sensed a deep affinity with the rich personality of Cor-

tona, the abundance of his compositions, the substantial quality of his brushwork. Though the pure landscape is rare in Cortona's oeuvre, landscape holds an important place in many of his frescoes and history paintings.
LIT. G. Briganti, *Pietro da Cortona,* Florence 1962, p. 171. EXH. Bologna 1962, no. 131.

29 PIER FRANCESCO CITTADINI
Milan 1616–Bologna 1681.
LANDSCAPE WITH TOBIAS AND THE ANGEL
ISOLA BELLA
Canvas, 19 cm., circular. A few holes. The pendant, in the same collection, shows a landscape with the Flight into Egypt. The traditional attribution to Cittadini is convincing. Compare Tempesta's equally small tondi nos. 229 ff. The presence of this pair in the Borromeo collection suggests that Tempesta may have been familiar with Cittadini's work. Landscapes are rather rare in Cittadini's oeuvre; two other examples are in Dresden (Loth; Hagar and the Angel). He was active for most of his life in Bologna. His repertoire consists mainly of religious paintings, portraits, and still lives (flowers). See on him Riccomini, in *Arte antica e moderna* 1961, p. 362 (four landscapes reproduced). Exh. Naples 1964, p. 100 Three dozen drawings by him are at Windsor Castle (Kurz, *Bolognese Drawings ... at Windsor Castle,* London 1955, nos. 151 ff.).

30–32 BASSANO
Tempesta's animal pieces and religious paintings with large animal groups in the foreground are picture types ultimately created by the Bassano. Jacopo da Ponte's sons and their imitators propagated such broadly painted images in countless examples until well into the seventeenth century. For the purpose of demonstrating the influence on Tempesta, it does not matter that the question of authenticity is, within the school of the Bassano, often an insoluble one. Compare Tempesta's nos. 313, 316, 323 (with Bassanesque farm houses).
LIT. Arslan, 1960.

30 JACOPO DA PONTE (BASSANO)
Bassano 1517/18–1592.
PARABLE OF THE SOWER
LUGANO, THYSSEN-BORNEMISZA COLLECTION
138 × 127 cm. Compare Tempesta's no. 316.
LIT. Catalog of the Schloss Rohoncz collection, by R. Heinemann, Lugano 1958, no. 22. Arslan, 1960, p. 170, with further lit.

31 FRANCESCO DA PONTE (BASSANO)
Bassano 1549–Venice 1592.
LANDSCAPE (MAY AND JUNE, WITH THE SACRIFICE OF ISAAC)
VIENNA, KUNSTHISTORISCHES MUSEUM, no. 296. 82 × 114 cm. One of a series of six works by Francesco da Ponte and assistants.
LIT. Arslan, 1960, p. 381. Older catalogs of the museum, no. 296.

32 GEROLAMO DA PONTE (BASSANO)
Bassano 1566–Venice 1621.
AUTUMN
MILAN, CASTELLO SFORZESCO, no. 72, as Jacopo da Ponte.
79 × 110 cm.
LIT. Arslan, 1960, p. 289, as Gerolamo da Ponte.

33 CIRCLE OF AGOSTINO TASSI
Rome c. 1580–1644.
ENTRY INTO THE ARK OF NOAH
BAGNAIA, VILLA LANTE
Fresco, done about 1613, in the Stanza della Fama of the Casino Montalto; it is part of an Old Testament cycle painted in the lunettes of the vault. The type of image goes back to Tassi's teacher Paul Bril and to Flemish engravings of the sixteenth century (Marten de Vos). Compare later Tempesta's menagerie pictures of the same or related subjects (240 ff.).
LIT. On Villa Lante, see last Salerno, in *Connoisseur* 1960, p. 157, and A. Cantoni, *La Villa Lante di Bagnaia,* Milan 1961.

34–36 SINIBALDO SCORZA
Voltaggio 1589–Genoa 1631.
Scorza, of noble birth, was the first Genoese representative of animal painting, a specialty brought to full bloom by Castiglione and Vassallo. Influenced by Tassi and Snyders, Scorza's small animal scenes form the Italian counterpart to R. Savery and the Velvet Brueghel (who during the 1590's had stayed in Italy for several years). Scorza also produced street, battle, and genre scenes in the manner of the Bamboccianti. He worked mainly in Genoa, with sojourns in Turin and Rome.
LIT. M. Bonzi, *Sinibaldo Scorza-Antonio Travi,* Genoa 1964 (unsatisfactory). EXH. Naples 1964, p. 107. Genoa 1969, p. 77.

34 ORPHEUS
PRIVATE COLLECTION, GENOA
74 × 98 cm. Grey-green tints. In the distance, the women approaching to kill Orpheus. One of Scorza's most refined late works. The subject occurs at least half a dozen times in his oeuvre (another version is reproduced in *Genoese Masters*, exh. Dayton, Ohio, Art Institute, 1962, no. 48).
LIT. Griseri, in *Studies … Dedicated to William E. Suida*, London 1959, p. 317. EXH. Genoa 1969, no. 32 (as unpublished).

35 CIRCE
GENOA, PALAZZO BIANCO, no. 343.
43 × 69 cm. Compare Tempesta's no. 313. The subject occurs often in Genoa (Castiglione, Vassallo, J. Roos).
LIT. Delogu, 1931, p. 39.

36 ORPHEUS
GENOA, PALAZZO BIANCO, no. 1728.
101 × 128 cm.
COLL. Bequest Ricci.

37 SCHOOL OF SCORZA
ANIMALS AFTER THE DELUGE
PRIVATE COLLECTION, GENOA
48 × 59 cm. Above, the Ark and the sacrificial altar. Close to Scorza. Compare Castiglione's no. 40 for a less conventional rendering of the subject.

38–40 GIOVANNI BATTISTA CASTIGLIONE (GRECHETTO)
Genoa c. 1600/10–Mantua 1665.
Trained under the animal painters Scorza and Jan Roos (active in Genoa from 1616 to 1638, pupil of Snyders). Worked in Genoa, Florence, Rome, Naples, Venice, again Genoa, then for many years as court painter in Mantua. His rich animal pieces made a deep influence on Tempesta.
LIT. Delogu, 1928. A. Blunt, *The Drawings of … Castiglione … at Windsor Castle*, London 1954. Exh. Genoa 1969, p. 169.

38 ANIMALS AND FIGURES
ROUEN, MUSEE DES BEAUX-ARTS
193 × 284 cm. From the early years. Compare Tempesta's nos. 312, 314.
COLL. Came to the museum in 1837, as Castiglione.

LIT. Blunt, *loc. cit.*, p. 5. P. Rosenberg, *Invent. des coll. publ. françaises, Rouen, tableaux français …*, Paris 1966, p. 182.

39 EXODUS SCENE
PRIVATE COLLECTION, GENOA
94 × 141 cm. Brownish tones. As in the case of other famous compositions by Castiglione, there exist several versions of this composition; best known are the larger and more elongated ones in the Pitti, Florence (no. 4351) and in the Brera, Milan (no. 592; repr. *Mantova, Le Arti*, vol. III, Mantua 1965, fig. 333). This type of Old Testament Exodus scenes was a specialty of Castiglione. It was first propagated by the Bassano and became the model for Exodus scenes by Tempesta. (259–267).

40 SACRIFICE OF NOAH
PRIVATE COLLECTION, GENOA
127 × 180 cm. Silvery grey tones. Compare Tempesta's nos. 240–242.

41 SCHOOL OF CASTIGLIONE
PASTORAL SCENE
TOURS, MUSEE DES BEAUX-ARTS
94.5 × 145 cm. From the orbit of Castiglione (compare his no. 38), with a classical note reminiscent of Bourdon.
COLL. Bequest Luzarche d'Azay, 1962. LIT. Lossky, in *Revue des Arts* 1964, p. 192.

42–45 FILIPPO LAURI
Rome 1623–1694.
Lauri's father and teacher was the landscape painter Balthasar Lauwers (Baldassare Lauri), a native of Antwerp who settled in Rome, became a pupil of Bril, and died in Rome in 1641. Filippo achieved widespread fame by his small pictures with religious or mythological figures placed into a landscape. His style belongs to the general trend of Cortonism. It has close affinities with Mola and Albani and anticipates in turn the art of Francesco Trevisani. The refined handling of Lauri's work is part of his Flemish heritage. In the earlier years, he occasionally collaborated with Cortona and Gaspard; there are also some altar pictures and frescoes by him. Tempesta, who may have known Lauri in Rome, became receptive for the suavity of his figures. In the small works, Tempesta shows a basic affinity with Lauri; this influence is felt particularly in the group of pictures by Tempesta at Burghley (327 ff.; the same collection

comprises one of the largest groups of works by Lauri).
Lit. Voss, 1924, p. 574. B. Riccio, in *Commentari* 1959, p. 3.

42 The Voyage of Jacob
British Royal Collection, Hampton Court, no. 84.
91.5 × 138.5 cm. One of the artist's largest works (aside from a few altarpieces and frescoes), and one of his masterpieces. Painted, according to Pascoli, for marquess Pallavicini. The landscape betrays the influence of Rosa (23). Compare Tempesta's somewhat larger Old Testament voyage no. 265 and his Flight no. 237, which this work by Lauri in all probability precedes.
Engr. T. Major, 1754, in-fol., as Jacob's Departure.
Lit. Voss, 1924, p. 575. M. Levey, *The Later Italian Pictures in the Collection of … The Queen*, London 1964, no. 531.

43 Erminia and the Shepherds
Burghley House, Marquess of Exeter, no. 143.
Copper, 30 × 41 cm. Signed on the stone at the bottom right 'F.L.' and inscribed on the verso Lauro. Compare the large pastoral by Tempesta no. 322 and his small tondi nos. 229 ff.
Lit. This and the following work, as well as several other Lauris at Burghley, are mentioned in the various old guidebooks of the collection, for which see the reference under no. 213.

44 The Judgment of Midas
Burghley House, Marquess of Exeter, no. 25.
Copper, 13 × 22 cm. Signed and dated 1681 on the reverse. Pendant to a Flaying of Marsyas in the same collection (no. 26; signed 'F.L.' at the bottom center and dated 1681 on the reverse). Compare Tempesta's no. 209, which must date from several years later.
Lit. See the preceding.

45 Baptism of Christ
Losely Park, J. R. More-Molyneux Coll.
Octagonal copper, 37 × 37 cm. Signed at the bottom 'F.L.' Compare Tempesta's no. 328.

46–135 MARINES

46–65 PIETER MULIER THE ELDER
Haarlem c. 1610–1670.

46 Stormy Sea
Greenwich, National Maritime Museum
Panel, 39.5 × 58.5 cm. Monogram on floating plank.
Coll. Palmer, mimeographed list of the National Maritime Museum, 1962, no. 25.

47 Stormy Sea
Leningrad, Hermitage, no. 3482.
Panel, 52.5 × 63.5 cm. Monogram on floating plank on the left. Not mentioned in any catalog.

48 Stormy Sea
Greenwich, National Maritime Museum
Panel, 38 × 58.5 cm. Less fine than others, but probably nevertheless genuine.

49 Seascape
Prague, National Gallery, no. 0. 2739.
Canvas, 111 × 163.5 cm. Larger by far than most other works of the artist. The composition compares with no. 56.
Lit. J. Sip, *Prague, National Gallery, Dutch Paintings* (in Czech), 1965, no. 69.

50 Seascape
Private Collection
Panel, 51 × 81 cm.

51 Seascape
Formerly in a Leningrad Collection
Panel, size unknown. Monogram on floating plank on the left.

52 Seascape
Private Collection
Panel, 52.5 × 84 cm. Monogram on floating plank in the center right.
Exh. Dordrecht, *Goede onbekenden*, 1959, no. 58. Arnhem, *17de e. meesters uit Gelders bezit*, no. 51, wrongly as J. Porcellis. (The monogram is clearly that of Mulier.)

53 SEASCAPE
PRIVATE COLLECTION
Panel, 41 × 61 cm. Monogram on leeboard of left hand vessel.

54 SEASCAPE
FORMERLY IN A LENINGRAD COLLECTION
Panel, size unknown. Compare no. 58.

55 SEASCAPE
MUNICH, BAVARIAN STATE COLLECTIONS, no. 5257.
Panel, 46 × 63 cm. Monogram on floating plank on the right.

56 SEASCAPE
PRAGUE, NATIONAL GALLERY, no. DO. 4343.
Panel, 47 × 63.5 cm. Monogram on floating plank.
LIT. Catalog of the museum, 1955, no. 413. Sip, *loc. cit.*, no. 68.

57 SEASCAPE
KARLSRUHE, STAATLICHE KUNSTHALLE
Canvas, 42.5 × 38.5 cm. Monogram on floating plank on the left.
LIT. Catalog of the museum, by Lauts, 1966, no. 1875.

58 SEASCAPE
AMSTERDAM, RIJKSMUSEUM
Panel, 38.5 × 60 cm. Monogram on the left hand side of the boat.
LIT. Catalog of the museum, of 1934, no. 1684a.

59 SEASCAPE
GREENWICH, NATIONAL MARITIME MUSEUM
Panel, 32 × 56 cm. Monogram on floating plank.
COLL. Palmer, 1962, no. 24.

60 COAST VIEW
PRAGUE, NATIONAL GALLERY, no. O. 2356.
Panel, 35.5 × 45.5 cm. Monogram on the balustrade at the right. Compare Tempesta's drawing no. 150.
LIT. *Umeni*, vol. 13, 1940/41, p. 383. Sip, *loc. cit.*, no. 70.

61 COAST VIEW
UNKNOWN LOCATION
Panel, 52 × 83 cm. Monogram on plank at the bottom left, below the small boat. One of Mulier's finest and largest works. Compare similar motives in the two following pictures.
COLL. Cologne, Wallraf-Richartz Museum, no. 1632, until 1934, when it was sold on the art market.

62 COAST VIEW
KARLSRUHE, STAATLICHE KUNSTHALLE
Panel, 46 × 80.5 cm.
LIT. Catalog of the museum, by Lauts, 1966, no. 1848.

63 COAST VIEW
PRIVATE COLLECTION
Panel, 37 × 48 cm. Monogram at the bottom left.
COLL. Sale Munich, Weinmüller, 14 Dec. 1955, lot 956.

64 SEASCAPE
GREENWICH, NATIONAL MARITIME MUSEUM
Panel, 39.5 × 53 cm. Monogram on top of the rock.
COLL. Palmer, 1962, no. 26.

65 COAST VIEW
GREENWICH, NATIONAL MARITIME MUSEUM
Panel, 39.5 × 51 cm. Monogram on the extreme left, at half height.
COLL. Palmer, 1962, no. 23.

A SELECTION OF OTHER MONOGRAMMED
PANELS BY MULIER THE ELDER

COX COLLECTION, AMSTERDAM. 41 × 61 cm.
DRESDEN, STATE COLLECTIONS. 54 × 84 cm. COLL. Bt. 1940. LIT. *Holländ. und vläm. Meister des 17. Jhs.*, Dresden 1962, no. 27, repr., wrongly as monogrammist L. Me. Clearly by Mulier.
FORMERLY DRESDEN, MUSEUM, no. 1378, now destroyed. Square, 34.5 cm. LIT. First in the catalog of 1835. Bernt, no. 568. Ebert, *Kriegsverluste der Dresdener Gemäldegalerie*, 1963, p. 123, repr.
THE HAGUE, MAURITSHUIS, lent to the Arnhem museum. 40 × 61 cm. LIT. Catalog of the Mauritshuis, 1949, no. 549. Catalog of the Arnhem museum, 1956, pl. 28.
KIEV, STATE MUSEUM. 77.5 × 102 cm. COLL. Khanenko, Kiev. LIT. Catalogs of the museum, 1931, no. 385, and 1961, no. 127, repr., wrongly as Tempesta.
FORMERLY KIEV, KHANENKO COLLECTION. 35 × 53 cm. Not monogrammed. Facsimile in the catalog.
LEIPZIG, MUSEUM. 42 × 63 cm. LIT. Catalog of the museum, 1929, no. 1044.

PRIVATE COLLECTION. 43 × 37 cm. EXH. Utrecht, *Kunstbezit der Reünisten*, 1956, no. 20.

VIENNA, SALE DOROTHEUM, 5 Dec. 1961, lot 83, repr. 40 × 61 cm.

ART MARKET (Preston Gallery, London, 1967). Beach View. 24 × 27 cm. COLL. Verrijn Stuart, Heemstede. EXH. Dordrecht, *Zee- Rivier- en Oevergezichten*, 1964, no. 56, repr.

66–85 PRECURSORS OF TEMPESTA

66 PAUL BRIL
Antwerp 1554–Rome 1626.
EXPULSION OF JONAH
CRACOW, WAWEL, no. 2393.
128 × 175.5 cm. A famous composition, known first from Bril's fresco at the Scala Santa, of c. 1589 (Mayer, *Das Leben und die Werke der Brüder Bril*, 1910, pl. 16b). Another, small version with minor differences is at the Ca' d'Oro, Venice, to my mind an inferior copy (46 × 63 cm. Repr. Faggin, in *Paragone* 185, 1965, pl. 15, as Bril). There is, moreover, a drawing of this composition in the British Museum (catalog Hind, vol. V, p. 137, no. 1, pl. XLV). On Bril, see last Faggin, *loc. cit.* This type of a seastorm stands at the beginning of an evolution which leads to Tempesta (117).
COLL. Stanislas Podczaski.

67 CORNELIS DE WAEL
Antwerp 1592–Rome 1667.
NAVAL BATTLE
PEGLI (GENOA), MARITIME MUSEUM, no. 2253.
124 × 159 cm. In great need of cleaning; has suffered and is obscured by varnishes. With over forty years spent in Genoa, De Wael is essentially a member of the Genoese school, although his art never loses his original Flemish idiom. He lived in the Ligurian capital from 1613 to 1656, then until his death in Rome. He always was a protector of Flemish artists. The outstanding artistic quality and wide subject range of his important oeuvre have not been sufficiently pointed out and still await an adequate study. Numerous paintings survive, widely scattered (I note, as one of the finest series, a group of six landscapes with genre scenes in Venice, deposited in the Prefettura). His principal domains were the landscape, seascape, harbor scenes, genre subjects, and battle pieces.

Least known are the marines, yet he must have produced many of them, especially in Genoa, where he was in fact their first great promoter. His example in this field was immediately followed by his countrymen van Eertvelt and G. van Eyck, both of whom were his pupils in Genoa during the 1630's. Probably the Spaniard Juan de Toledo (1611–65) also learned from him. De Wael's importance for Genoese marine painting thus prepared the ground for Tempesta's success. The two artists must almost certainly have known each other during the span of ten years in which they both lived in Rome. De Wael's death inventory contains a sea storm by Tempesta (see here p. 136). For lack of certified tempests by De Wael, it is not yet possible to evaluate exactly Tempesta's debt to him, but De Wael's Flemish heritage, his Italianate grandeur, and his broad, colorful handling represent a striking anticipation of the manner of Tempesta. The naval battle reproduced here, probably an imaginary scene, is unusually large. The same museum conserves another large marine by De Wael–a southern harbor scene with ships and figures (no. 2356; 95 × 147 cm.)–as well as several works from his circle (nos. 2317, 2341, etc.). On this artist, see above all M. Vaes, in *Bull. inst. hist. belge de Rome*, 1925, p. 80 (excellent historic account, but no study of the oeuvre).

68–70 JAN BLANCKERHOFF
Alkmaar 1628–Amsterdam 1669.
The three examples given here will acknowledge the refined mastery of this insufficiently known marine painter, whose typically Dutch art opens the way for the sea storms of Tempesta. He was a pupil of C. van Everdingen, became a master at Alkmaar in 1649, was a seaman, and sojourned three times in Rome, where his Bent name was Janmaat. The documented oeuvre is still small, but comprises several tempests similar to our first example. In accordance with Dutch tradition–and by contrast with Tempesta–the coloring is kept in greyish tones, the compositions are pointedly delicate, the handling is very stylish. Tempesta may have known him in Holland or in Rome.

68 SEA STORM
KARLSRUHE, STAATLICHE KUNSTHALLE
48.5 × 59.5 cm. Monogram 'BH' at the bottom right.
COLL. Count Lucchesi, 1803. Castle of Mannheim. LIT. Catalog of the museum, by J. Lauts, 1966, no. 1869.

69 ROUGH SEA AND COAST
ROME, GALLERIA DORIA PAMPHILJ
50 × 69 cm. Monogram 'BH' on the small boat. In all probability done in Rome. The motives on the right are clearly Italianate. The type of image anticipates Manglard (134).
LIT. Doria catalog of 1816, as Manglard. Sestieri, 1942, no. 534, as school of Tempesta. Modern Doria catalogs, no. 246, as Blanckerhoff.

70 ROUGH SEA
COPENHAGEN, STATE MUSEUM
56 × 72 cm.
LIT. Catalog of the museum, of 1946 and 1951, no. 61.

71 AERNOUT SMIT
1641/42–Amsterdam 1710.
ROUGH SEA
KARLSRUHE, STAATLICHE KUNSTHALLE
89.5 × 147 cm. Signed on the plank at the lower right 'A Smit.' Grey tones. A pupil of Blanckerhoff and contemporary of Tempesta, Smit practiced various types of marines. The certified oeuvre is small, but has a personal quality. It became increasingly colorful. The idiom is purely Dutch. No Italian sojourn is known.
COLL. Count Lucchesi, 1803. Castle of Mannheim. LIT. Catalog of the museum, by J. Lauts, 1966, no. 1877.

72 LUDOLF BAKHUYSEN
Emden 1631–Amsterdam 1708.
SEA STORM
DUTCH PRIVATE COLLECTION
76.5 × 104.5 cm. Rough sea storms, always more favored in Flanders than in Holland, are not often encountered in the Dutch marine painters of the generation of Tempesta. Two of the finest examples by Bakhuysen are here offered for comparison with Tempesta's contemporary production. Bakhuysen's compositions are more restrained, his coloring is monochromatic, the principal emphasis lies on atmospheric values, which Bakhuysen developed with unsurpassed mastery.

73 LUDOLF BAKHUYSEN
SEA STORM
BRUSSELS, ROYAL MUSEUM (lent to the embassy at The Hague).
173.5 × 341 cm. Signed at the bottom right 'L Backhu.' One of the artist's largest works. See the preceding.

COLL. Bt. at the Baillie sale, Antwerp 1862. LIT. Catalog of the museum, of 1949, no. 19.

74–80 MATHIEU VAN PLATTENBERG
Antwerp 1608–Paris 1660.
Pupil of van Eertvelt, for a short time in Italy. From before 1630 until his death in Paris, *peintre du Roy pour les mers*. The details of Plattenberg's personality and the development of his art are still shrouded in darkness, but several dozen widely scattered paintings of sea storms traditionally attributed to him (none signed) form a reasonably consistent stylistic group, combining Flemish types with a broad painterly treatment. The latter reminds one of Rosa (compare Rosa's Coast View, in Naples), but as Plattenberg left Italy before Rosa began to paint, the influence, if any, went from the Fleming to Rosa. Plattenberg's paintings come closer to Tempesta's early sea storms than those of any other artist. Tempesta must then have seen works by him in Italy. There exist also three dozen rather modest engravings by Plattenberg signed 'Mathieu Monta(i)gne'–sea storms, Italianate harbors, and landscapes in the taste of d'Arthois. See also the remarks under Monsù Montagna (84).

74 ESTUARY VIEW
GREENWICH, NATIONAL MARITIME MUSEUM
62 × 90.5 cm. Brown-grey tones. If by Plattenberg, probably from the Flemish phase.
COLL. Palmer, mimeographed list of the National Maritime Museum, 1962, no. 18.

75 ROUGH SEA
GREENWICH, NATIONAL MARITIME MUSEUM
68 × 95 cm. Warm tones. Compare no. 65, by Mulier the elder.
COLL. Palmer, 1962, no. 19.

76 SEA STORM
POMMERSFELDEN, COUNT VON SCHÖNBORN
110 × 150 cm. An important point of reference for Plattenberg because of the early record.
COLL. Schönborn family, by 1721. LIT. Schloss Weissenstein catalog, 1721, no. 7. Pommersfelden catalog, 1845, no. 65. Schönborn-Wiesentheid catalog, by Frimmel, 1894, no. 415. EXH. Solingen, Deutsches Klingenmuseum, 1965, no. 36.

77 SEA STORM
GREENWICH, NATIONAL MARITIME MUSEUM
100 × 141 cm. Grey tints.
COLL. Palmer, 1962, no. 21.

78 SEA STORM
GREENWICH, NATIONAL MARITIME MUSEUM
58.5 × 93 cm.
COLL. Palmer, 1962, no. 20.

79 SEA STORM
MUNICH, BAVARIAN STATE COLLECTIONS, no.
5193.
139 × 212 cm. Exceptionally large.

80 SEA STORM
WÜRZBURG, UNIVERSITY MUSEUM, no. 365.
88 × 147 cm.
LIT. Catalog of the museum, of 1914, no. 365. *Münchner Jahrbuch*, 1914/15, p. 30.

81 MATHIEU VAN PLATTENBERG?
SEA STORM
GRAZ, ALTE GALERIE JOANNEUM, as Rosa.
74 × 98 cm. Certainly not Rosa, but most probably van Plattenberg by comparison with other works of his.
COLL. Paris art market. LIT. Catalog of the museum, of 1923, no. 266, as Rosa.

82 MATHIEU VAN PLATTENBERG?
SEA STORM
ANTWERP, ROYAL MUSEUM, no. 5038, as van Eertvelt.
67 × 90 cm. The style and the greyish coloring of this picture resemble van Plattenberg (77) much more than van Eertvelt, but the handling differs somewhat from the bulk of van Plattenberg's work.
COLL. Elsen, 1948. EXH. Antwerp, Scaldis, 1956, no. 559, as Plattenberg.

83 MATHIEU VAN PLATTENBERG?
SEA STORM
ANTWERP, ROYAL MUSEUM, no. 714, as manner of Tempesta.
50 × 79 cm. Illegible monogram on a plank. By a Netherlandish artist in the vicinity of van Plattenberg and Tempesta.
LIT. Catalog of the museum, of 1948, no. 714.

84 MONSU MONTAGNA?
SEA STORM
BRESCIA, PINACOTECA, no. 159, as van Plattenberg.
116 × 188 cm. Water dark green, rocks brown. A large picture of excellent quality. It is finer and more colorful than the bulk of the works attributed to van Plattenberg. The Italian provenance, while not conclusive, casts some doubt on the attribution. Might this instead be a work by the renowned Monsù Montagna, who is known to have worked in Brescia and who died in 1644? (See no. 85.) It is, at any rate, conceivable that the picture precedes Tempesta's late phase, in which case it would be a prototype for his late sea storms of the kind of no. 116. See also the pair nos. 127f., characterized by an even more incisive style.
COLL. Count Tosio Martinengo. LIT. Catalog of the museum, of 1927, p. 63. C. Panazza, *La Pinacoteca e i musei di Brescia*, Bergamo 1968, p. 148, both as Plattenberg.

85 MONSU MONTAGNA?
COAST VIEW
ANGERS, MUSEUM, no. 261, as unknown French, 18th century.
22 × 47 cm. Pendant of no. 260, a coast view with rocks on the right, a barge and a tower on the left. This pair, of rather modest merit, comes from the collection of the marquess of Livois, Angers, 18th century, and figured as Rinaldo de la Montagne in the catalogs of the museum of 1805, 1820, and later; this attribution was changed to the present one in the catalogs of 1870 and 1881 (by H. Jouin, nos. 300, 299). Setting and style derive directly from Rosa (20) and conform to the standards of his school (compare nos. 424ff.), pointing *eo ipso* forward to the eighteenth century. Already Ticozzi (1832, vol. III, p. 161) reports that van Plattenberg was often confused both with Tempesta and with Rinaldo della Montagna; speaking of the latter (*ibid.*, vol. II, p. 470), he reiterates how Montagna's works were confused with those of Tempesta. The most frequent confusion was between van Plattenberg and Rinaldo della Montagna, alias Renaud de la Montagne, or Montagne de Venise (Félibien, *Entretiens*), or, most commonly, Monsù Montagna, a Dutch painter (born Reinier van Bergen?) of marines and sea storms who settled early in Italy and remained there. Félibien implies that he was Dutch; Lanzi calls him *olandese*. The always well-informed Lanzi has him working especially in Florence and Rome, does not

speak of Venice, but gives for the first time the date of his death, Padua 1644; he also says that in Rome he was often confused with Tempesta, but that his skies are more open than Tempesta's. Lanzi speaks of him immediately after Tempesta. Félibien mentions both van Plattenberg and Montagne in very similar terms (*Nicolas de Plate-Montagne faisoit fort bien des Mers et du Paisage. – Montagne de Venise a parfaitement peint des mers et des naufrages*). If the death date is correct, Monsù Montagna did indeed anticipate Tempesta's manner and may have paved the way for him.

Sea storms by Montagna are encountered frequently in old inventories of Venetian and Brescian collections. Some examples: Venice, G. B. Tirabosco, 1655: *Una copia Tempesta di Mare del Montagna.* Venice, Renieri, 1666: *Due quadri di mano del Montagna, ove si vedono due Fortune di Mare longhi quarte 8, larghi quarte 6 in circa.* Venice, Bergonzi, 1709: five sea storms by Montagna. See S. Savini-Branca, *Il collezionismo veneziano nel '600,* Padua 1964, pp. 104, 125, 172, 174. In Brescia, 1760: *due burrasche notturne, di monsu montagna;* see here p. 137.

I have found only six extant tempests under his name: the two at Angers; two at the Uffizi, darkened beyond recognition; and two at Montpellier, Musée Fabre, one of them repr. by Donzelli, 1967, p. 295, fig. 322; however, the Montpellier pictures were given to the museum in 1825 by Fabre as anonymous and were called 'Niccolo Montagna' (confusion with Nicolas, portrait painter, brother of M. van Plattenberg?) only in 1830 and later catalogs. See also a sea storm ascribed to Montagna by Voss in *Cicerone,* vol. 20, 1928, p. 612, repr. In conclusion, pictures called Montagna in Italy are likely to be by him and not by van Plattenberg. Judging from the sources, I would have expected pictures by Montagna to resemble nos. 76-83 rather than the small Angers pair.

86–118 TEMPESTA

86 COAST VIEW
STOCKHOLM, NATIONAL MUSEUM

99 × 136 cm. A work of little merit, but possibly from Tempesta's earliest years. The style is close to Mulier the elder (64 f.). For the central rocks, see also Tempesta's no. 111. The framing rock on the right is a device often found in Dutch Italianate masters such as Cuylenborgh or van Troyen.
LIT. Catalog of the museum, of 1958, no. 527, as Tempesta.

Another picture attributed to Tempesta in the museum (no. 563, formerly as 'J. Peeters?') is of uncertain authorship.

87 NOCTURNAL COAST VIEW
SENS, MUSEUM, no. 113.

51 × 67 cm. Inscribed on the back in pen 'Tempesta pinxit. Romae.' Very dark. With its fantastic forms and loaded atmospheric effect, this is not a very attractive work, but it belongs to the very few seascapes which on account of an inscription or provenance can convincingly be ascribed to Tempesta's Roman years. If the flashy side of the artist's personality is already present here, the artistic mastery is not yet that of the Colonna frescoes. The date of the painting may thus be close to 1660. The rock arch recurs in other coast views, especially in the early no. 109.

88 SEA STORM
ROME, GALLERIA DORIA PAMPHILJ

90 × 131 cm. Dark tints; yellow clouds. Probably the kind of image which Tempesta produced in his first Roman years.
LIT. See no. 89. Sestieri, 1942, no. 400, as anonymous, 17th century. Not in the modern Doria catalogs.

89 SEA STORM
ROME, GALLERIA DORIA PAMPHILJ

50 × 67 cm. Very dark grey tones. From the Roman years, about 1660. Not a work of much merit. The style compares with no. 90, in the same collection, thus supporting the attribution to Tempesta's Roman phase.
LIT. This work and no. 88 must be the *Marina del Tempesta* and the *Burrasca del Tempesta* listed in the Doria catalog of 1794, pp. 61, 142. Sestieri, 1942, no. 391, as anonymous, end of the 17th century. Modern Doria catalogs, no. 309, as Tempesta.

90 SEA STORM
ROME, GALLERIA DORIA PAMPHILJ

290 × 383 cm. Dark grey tones. The style supports the traditional attribution of this painting to Tempesta, although it stands quite alone in its size. It is his largest canvas altogether and compares today only with the sea storm of his Colonna frescoes (178); the date must likewise be in the later sixties. Despite the darkened appearance, the composition and such details as the opening in the sky, with what must be the sun, are characteristic of

the artist. This kind of picture must have established his reputation. It can be assumed that he did many other, similar works, from which a great number of Italian sea storms of the later seventeenth century were in turn to derive.

LIT. Must be the *Grande Tempesta del Cav. Tempesta* mentioned in the Doria catalog of 1794, p. 67. Doria catalog of 1816. Sestieri, 1942, no. 104. Modern Doria catalogs, no. 84; all as Tempesta.

91 SEA STORM
PRIVATE COLLECTION, GORIZIA

82 × 120 cm. Greenish tints. The flickering handling of this impressive painting differs notably from Tempesta's Lombard marines. But by comparison with the following, less refined works from the Genoese years, the painting may nonetheless be by Tempesta and date from his Genoese phase.

COLL. Count Segrè-Sartorio, Triest. LIT. Quoted in Fiocco, *Venetian Painting of the Seicento and the Settecento*, n.d., p. 84.

92, 93 SEA STORMS
MAINZ, MUSEUM, nos. 247, 248.

50 × 66 cm. A pair. Blue-grey tones. Similar to the following pair and to some works by van Plattenberg. Probably by Tempesta, dating from his Genoese years.

94, 95 SEA STORMS
GENOA, PALAZZO ROSSO, nos. 334, 337, as anonymous.

90 × 115 cm. A pair. Dark grey tones. These and the following works at the Maritime Museum, Pegli, are in reality better, darker, and less flickering in the contrasts than the reproductions suggest. They all come from Genoese collections; most of them are traditionally ascribed to Tempesta. Though this attribution may in one or two cases give rise to doubts, everything indicates that this was indeed the type of sea storms produced by the artist under great stress during the eight years of his prison term.

Differences of handling from one work to the next may be credited to these circumstances. The type and the style derive from van Plattenberg, particularly in the present pair, and, apparently, from Monsù Montagna. The pictures are done in a broad and flashy manner, aiming at superficial, spectacular effects, with little concern for painterly refinements. The legibility is often impaired by the darkening of large portions.

COLL. Bequest Duchess of Galliera.

96, 97 SEA STORMS
PEGLI (GENOA), MARITIME MUSEUM, nos. 2412, 2413.

38 × 60.5 cm. A pair. Dark grey tones, blue skies, some orange for the clouds. See no. 94. The same museum has a few other, similar sea storms, very likely by the same hand: nos. 2358 (without coastal view) and pendant 2359 (with coastal rocks on the right); 2316 (with coastal rocks on the right; or is this by Tavella?).

98 SEA STORM
PEGLI (GENOA), MARITIME MUSEUM, no. 2357.

40 × 66 cm. Dark bluish-grey tones, with brown rocks. See no. 94.

99 SEA STORM
PEGLI (GENOA), MARITIME MUSEUM, no. 2343.

74 × 96 cm. Cold green-blue tones with much white. See no. 94. For the oddly shaped rock, compare nos. 111, 116. The handling compares with the small no. 108, but seems coarser than in no. 98, in fact almost incompatible with it. However, eight years of work in prison may account for very different results, and it seems best to respect the traditional attributions.

COLL. Gift Ed. Isnardi.

A similar composition by Tempesta in a Genoese private collection was reproduced in *Liguria*, Nov. 1957, p. 7.

100 SEA STORM
PRIVATE COLLECTION, COMO

72 × 94 cm. Several figures on the cliff at the lower left. Vivid blue-green, brown (rocks), and yellow tints (opening in the clouds).

Despite its rough handling, the picture is in effect better than the reproduction suggests. If, as likely, by Tempesta, it probably dates from the Genoese or Roman years.

101 SEA STORM
MILAN, CASTELLO SFORZESCO

119 × 150 cm. Very probably by Tempesta, from the Roman or Genoese phase, but impossible to judge in its actual dirty state. The handling of the clouds and the waves compares with the small nos. 104, 108.

COLL. Bequest Bolognini. LIT. Catalog of the museum, c. 1920, no. 247, as manner of Tempesta.

102 TEMPEST WITH THE APPARITION OF CHRIST PARMA, PINACOTECA STUARD, no. 94, as manner of Veronese or of Tempesta.

57.5 × 183 cm. For the condition and the provenance, see no. 196. A large and unusual work, certainly by Tempesta, dating from the late years.

Format and subject must be accounted for by a special commission. On the left, a boat carrying the Apostles. The subject is not explicit; only Christ's apparition to the Apostles (John 21: 1-8) applies, although the scene is not represented in the traditional way (see also no. 107). The sweeping handling reflects the influence of Tintoretto; see in particular Tintoretto's Christ at Lake Galilee (figure on the left). For the present figure, compare no. 328.

103 SEA STORM WITH JONAH THROWN OVERBOARD
MODENA, COLLECTION PROF. NANNINI

160 × 230 cm. An unusually large work, showing a frightful whale in the center. Darkened and in need of cleaning, it can hardly be appreciated in its present condition, but is no doubt genuine and must date from the Lombard years (1686/87?). The ancestry of the picture reaches as far back as M. de Vos' painting of the same subject, of 1589 (destroyed; formerly Berlin; cf. Judson, in *Misc. I. Q. van Regteren Altena*, 1969, p. 294, repr.).

COLL. From the ducal palace of Sassuolo, Modena; can be traced after the Este sale of 1798 over various owners to the Count d'Espagnac, Sassuolo, who sold the picture many years ago to the present owner.

104-107 SEA STORMS WITH JONAH THROWN OVERBOARD, JONAH EXPELLED BY THE WHALE, CHRIST SLEEPING DURING THE STORM, AND THE MIRACULOUS DRAUGHT. MODENA, GALLERIA ESTENSE, nos. 271, 272, 284, 285.

28 × 48 cm. A set of four small works, with related subjects. Genuine, but sunken and much obscured by varnish. The fourth work can represent either the calling of Peter and Andrew (Matth. 4: 18-20) or Christ's apparition to the Apostles (John 21: 1-8). Together with no. 102, these are Tempesta's only known seascapes with religious subjects. The execution seems less refined than in the artist's large sea storms from the late years.

Whether or not the pictures are the four works done for Modena in 1687 as cited in Tempesta's letter of 15 March 1687 (see here p. 78) remains a question. They may indeed date from the Lombard years.

LIT. Catalogs of the museum, of 1854, by Castellani Tarabini; of 1925, by Ricci; and of 1933, by Zocca; all as Tempesta; of 1945, by Pallucchini, nos. 597-600, as school works on account of weak quality.

A picture from the surrounding of Tempesta, similar to no. 104, exists in two larger variants, one at Buckingham Palace (formerly Windsor Castle, no. 396), the other at Stourhead, National Trust, both as Gaspard. See also Tavella's no. 122.

108 SEA STORM
ISOLA BELLA

37 × 30.5 cm. Dark, with orange clouds. This work and the following pair, which shows an equally rough handling, probably date from the Genoese years.

109 COAST VIEW
ISOLA BELLA

47.5 × 47.5 cm. Despite its darkish brown tints, the picture represents a sunset. There is a pendant, too dark to be reproduced, which is a contrastingly composed coast view with the moon breaking through heavy clouds, and a hill on the right. Both pictures depend heavily on Rosa and are painted as circular images on a square canvas (the dark ground also covers the corners). Probably from the Genoese years.

110 STORMY COAST VIEW
ISOLA BELLA

30 × 36 cm. A small work of fine quality. Grey-blue tints. Similar motives as in the following. The rocks emerging in the foreground compare with Mulier the elder (64). Probably from the Lombard years.

111 STORMY COAST VIEW
ISOLA BELLA

38 × 50 cm. See the preceding.

112 STORMY COAST VIEW
GREENWICH, NATIONAL MARITIME MUSEUM

41 × 72.5 cm. Rather dark, with grey sky. Late.
COLL. Ingram, no. 36. LIT. *Concise Catalogue of Paintings* of the museum, 1958, p. 85.

113 ROUGH SEA
GREENWICH, NATIONAL MARITIME MUSEUM
70 × 170 cm. A splendid, large work of late date, representing a picture type unusual for Tempesta. The clouds are violet, the sea is green and white.
COLL. Ingram, no.18. LIT. *Concise Catalogue of Paintings* of the museum, 1958, p.85.

114 SEA STORM (color plate IV)
ISOLA BELLA
87 × 123 cm. Pendant to the landscape no.294. Sky mainly grey-violet, with yellowish-white clouds above the large ship, the sea greenish. See the following.

115 SEA STORM
PRIVATE COLLECTION, GENOA
118 × 168 cm. Signed on the rock at the bottom right 'Cav. P.Tempesta' (faint). Greyish tints, dark on the left; orange in the sky. The largest of Tempesta's late tempests and, together with the preceding, the finest work of the kind.
COLL. From a recent Roman auction.

116 SEA STORM (color plate III)
GENEVA, MUSEE D'ART ET D'HISTOIRE
113 × 165.5 cm. Pendant to the landscape no.322, dated 1696; this date applies therefore here, too. Tempesta's only battle scene. A large work of highest quality and colorful appearance, with dominating bluish tones. The composition recalls B.Peeters (e.g., Shipwreck, 1647, Vaduz), the painterly style is indebted to Venetian art (especially the clouds), the galleys recall G.van Eyck.
COLL. Gift G.Revilliod.

117 SEA STORM
AMIENS, MUSEE DE PICARDIE
105 × 142 cm. In need of cleaning. Compare the following works, as well as P.Bril (66).
COLL. Bought 1846. LIT. Catalog of the museum, of 1899, no.209.

118 SEA STORM
LOST. FORMERLY BRESLAU, MUSEUM, no.291.
43.5 × 59 cm. Signed on the rock to the left of the figures 'Gavaglier 1701 Pietro Tempest. fec.' Has disappeared during the last war. A small example of Tempesta's favorite subject, apparently of fine quality.

119–135 SCHOOL WORKS

119, 120 TEMPESTINO
See notice under no.364.
SEA STORMS
VALENCIA, MUSEO PROVINCIAL
Metal, 25 × 35 cm. (The second reproduction slightly cut.) Without forming a contrasting pair, both works show the same style. By subject and support, they differ from the few landscapes ascribed to Tempestino, yet are not incompatible with them. The traditional attribution to Tempestino is convincing for intrinsic reasons: the type of image conforms closely to Tempesta's Roman and Genoese sea storms; for the rock arch, compare no.87. They are thus datable in the 1660's. The painterly handling has a personal touch which is brought out by the small format. It also recalls Cornelis de Wael.
COLL. Bequest Francisco Martinez Blanch, former Spanish consul in Nizza, 1835, nos.25f., as Tempestino. Late 19th century catalogs of the museum also enumerate as by Tempestino three landscapes, which can no longer be identified.

121–123 CARLO ANTONIO TAVELLA
Milan 1668–Genoa 1738. See notice under no.376.
The few examples given here are almost the only marines of Tavella known to me, though he must have produced more of them in his early years. It seems that he eventually abandoned the type. In this genre too, Tavella proves a faithful follower of Tempesta. A rare example from Tavella's early maturity belongs to A. Costa, Genoa (Sea storm with Christ and the Apostles, c.1710's. EXH. Genoa 1969, no.133).

121 SEA STORM WITH JONAH THROWN OVERBOARD
GENOA, PALAZZO ROSSO, no.3300 (lent to the Maritime Museum, Pegli).
Pen drawing, 510 × 380 mm. Inscribed by the artist at the top 'Galera che corre in fil di meta con grosso tempo. Di Pal. 5 e Pal 7. Finito 9 Novem. 1710 Per l'Ill.o Sig. Gio. Batta. Torre Genova,' and numbered 22. Discussed in the following entry. For Tavella's drawings, see also no.391. The penmanship of this drawing calls to mind the drawing by Tavella's teacher Solfarolo, no.131.
COLL. Bertolli. Orlandini. Bought in 1933.

122 SEA STORM WITH JONAH THROWN
OVERBOARD
GREENWICH, NATIONAL MARITIME MUSEUM,
as Tempesta.

58.5 × 84 cm. The sails yellow-brown, the sky grey and
light orange. The coast line appears on the extreme left
and right. Compare Tempesta's no.106. An attribution
of the painting to Tempesta must be ruled out on account
of the coloring and the harder handling. The composition corresponds exactly to the center of Tavella's drawing listed in the preceding entry. Tavella did the drawing
in 1710 after a now unknown painting of his which
measured 161 × 115 cm. (7 × 5 palms). The Greenwich
picture is too small to be a cut-down piece of that original work. Judging from the handling, it is an authentic
replica by Tavella.
COLL. Palmer, 1962, no.22, as Tempesta.

123 SEA STORM
CREMONA, PINACOTECA, no.266, as Tavella.

100 × 122 cm. In the museum called a pendant to a copy
(here no.361) of the same size after Tempesta's no.255
(which has a different pendant of its own). Whether or
not the two Cremona pictures are by the same hand is
doubtful; the shipwreck is better and is done on a finer
canvas than the landscape. The composition is so entirely
in the spirit of Tempesta that the picture may well be a
copy of a lost Tempesta. Handling and coloring support
the attribution to Tavella, probably 1700-1710.
COLL. (Pair) Bequest Marquess Ponzone, 1836, as anonymous works. LIT. A.Puerari, *La Pinacoteca di Cremona*,
1951, nos.265, 266, as early Tavellas.

124 TAVELLA?
SEA STORM
PRIVATE COLLECTION, BRESCIA

94 × 141 cm. Of excellent quality, vividly colored. The
setting is so much in the spirit of Tempesta that the picture could be ascribed to this artist, were it not for a
somewhat more polished execution which is reminiscent
of Tavella's no.122. This is, therefore, very probably an
example of Tavella's early marines done in imitation of
Tempesta.

125 UNKNOWN ARTIST
STORMY COAST VIEW
PRIVATE COLLECTION, BERGAMO

120 × 180 cm. A large work of good quality, done under
the immediate impact of Tempesta's late shipwrecks.

126 UNKNOWN ARTIST
STORMY COAST VIEW
PADUA, MUSEO CIVICO, no.1584.

82 × 116 cm. The handling and several compositional
features not common to Tempesta place this work into
the artist's immediate following, close to the sea storms
of the early Marco Ricci and of Bartolomeo Pedon. It
is the kind of picture which the early Pedon could be
expected to have done (see p.62).
COLL. Inventory of the museum, of 1900, as 'Tempesta?' LIT. Haumann, 1927, fig.93. Delogu, 1931, fig.71;
both as Tempesta. Catalog of the museum, by Grossato,
1957, no.188, as Riccesque.

127, 128 UNKNOWN ARTIST
STORMY COAST VIEWS
PIACENZA, MUSEO CIVICO (lent to the Municipio).

186 × 282 cm. A pair. Water green-grey, rocks and hills
yellowish, skies grey and pink, sails yellow. These remarkable, large pictures belong to the best examples of
Italian seascape painting. Despite a very personal and incisive style, a convincing attribution has so far not been
possible.
Datable in the later seventeenth century, the pictures
were probably influenced to some degree by Tempesta
(114). Francesco Monti, to whom they have been attributed, and who is known to have painted sea storms, has
a more painterly style.
COLL. Ducal Farnese collection, Piacenza. LIT. Catalog
of the museum, by F.Arisi, 1960, nos.435, 436. Arisi, *La
quadreria e l'arredamento del Palazzo Farnese di Piacenza*,
1965, nos.435, 436; both times as 'F.Monti?'

129-131 GIOVANNI GREVENBROECK, CALLED
IL SOLFAROLO
Notices from 1667 to 1695.

129, 130 SEAPORTS
ALENÇON, MUSEE DE PEINTURE, nos. MNR698, 697
(lent by the Musées Nationaux).

Copper, 32 × 52 cm. A pair. The first is inscribed on the
pedestal of the statue '1690 GIO. GREVEMBROECK.' Vivid
colors.
Giovanni Fangrefenbruch is first listed in the Roman
Stati d'anime from 1667 to 1669, as living together with
the landscape painter Adriaen Honich, alias Lossenbruy
(Bertolotti, *Artisti belgi ed olandesi a Roma*, Florence 1880,
p.169). Next, we hear of him in Milan, according to

Ratti's *Life* of Tavella (1769): having been apprenticed until the age of thirteen with Gius. Merati, Milan, the young Tavella spent the next seven years (1680-1687) with Grevenbroeck; 'there flourished in those days in Milan another painter of the name of Giovanni Gruembroech, commonly called il Solfarolo (the Sulfurous) because of a particular genius he had in painting views of landscapes that looked as if they were burning. Enthused by his manner, the young Tavella tried to be admitted to his school, which he achieved easily. Under the tutelage of this second teacher, the ingenious disciple applied himself to a more demanding and fervent study. He copied various works by his teacher and by others. Then he turned to representing in color and with the pen, which he handled with ease, the extended views of the most beautiful scenes which presented themselves to him, often painting therein different fires and burnt villages. In such studies he continued until his twentieth year.' The last mention of Jan van Grevenbroeck dates from 1695, by which time he had returned to Holland and was a member of a Dordrecht corporation. It is not possible to trace Solfarolo's influence on the young Tavella, for the earliest paintings by Tavella, dating from 1690/92 (376), show a Gaspardesque classicism which must already represent a radical departure from Solfarolo's lesson; and Tavella's next, post-Gaspardesque phase is determined by the influence of Tempesta. None of Solfarolo's landscapes is known today, but we have by him the two signed seaports of 1690 reproduced here, which show spectacular effects of sunrise and sunset and are done in an unmistakably Dutch idiom of miniature-like refinement on copper. Their type of image goes ultimately back to Tassi and Claude, their handling brings to mind the small marines by Verschuier.

These two pictures also determine the manner of two other Grevenbroecks who seem to have been the sons of Giovanni. One is Orazio, said by Zani to have been born in 1678. Five paintings signed 'Oratio Grevenbroeck,' without dates, are identical in style with the two of Giovanni–small seaports on copper with miniature-like handling; four of these were published by Bodkin in *Procedings of the Royal Irish Academy*, vol. 62, Section C, Feb. 1934, pl. 2 (exh. Birmingham, 1950, nos. 19–22; sold at Sotheby's, 11 Nov. 1959); another was sold at Christie's, 18 May 1951, lot 156. A set of landscapes and seaports on copper strikingly similar to those of Jan and Orazio, but signed by an otherwise unknown Joseph Ruiz, was sold at Christie's, 23 June 1967, lot 113, two

repr. The other Grevenbroeck is Alessandro, recorded in the early eighteenth century, mainly in Venice. See on him Fiocco, in *Boll. del Museo Civico di Padova*, 1959, p. 28, and Delogu, in *Boll. dei Musei Civici Veneziani*, 1963, no. 1, p. 1. A further, large canvas by him, signed 'Alessandro Grevenbroeck Anno 1724 in Venezia,' was at the sale of the Hungarian Museum of Applied Art, Budapest, 21 Feb. 1921, lot 205, repr.

Lastly, there are two Grevenbroecks of the eighteenth century: the marine and landscape painter Charles-Léopold, perhaps the son of Orazio, said to have come from Milan, active in Paris around 1731, and deceased in Naples in 1758/59 (many of his works survive in France); and Jan II, painter of intimate genre pieces, probably the son of Alessandro, born in Venice in 1731 and deceased there in 1807.

131 SEAPORT
LONDON, BRITISH MUSEUM, no. 1946-7-22-1, as Tempesta.

Drawing, 310 × 472 mm. Black chalk, part of the lower section drawn out in pen. On account of the similarity with the signed Grevenbroeck paintings, this drawing can be ascribed to Jan I (or, less likely, to Orazio or Alessandro) Grevenbroeck. The drawing clearly served as the detailed model for a painting which probably had the same size. The attribution (of uncertain date) to Tempesta is untenable, but may point to some contact between the artists. I have seen a few other drawings of this style in various collections, partly attributed to Tassi (e.g., Hert sale, New York, Parke-Bernet, 25 Nov. 1949, lot 95, repr., seaport, as Claude).

132 UNKNOWN ARTIST
SEASCAPE
PEGLI (GENOA), MARITIME MUSEUM, no. 2360, as anonymous.

115 × 95 cm. Dutch flag. Probably Genoese, late seventeenth century, from the surrounding of Tempesta. The upright oval format is common with decorative Italian marines.

133 UNKNOWN ARTIST
COAST VIEW
PRIVATE COLLECTION, FLORENCE

99 × 73 cm. There is a pendant with a similar setting. Italian, early eighteenth century.

134 ADRIEN MANGLARD
Lyon 1695–Rome 1760. See notice under no. 185.
COAST VIEW WITH SHIPWRECK
PRIVATE COLLECTION
60 × 88 cm. A fine example of this precursor of Claude-Joseph Vernet. Despite the difference in time, it owes an immediate debt to Tempesta's pictures of the same type (178), but has a generally lighter character and a more streamlined composition. Paintings by Manglard were formerly kept in great number in the Rospigliosi and the Doria collections (see for the latter the Doria catalog of 1794).
COLL. Rospigliosi, Rome.

135 CLAUDE-JOSEPH VERNET
Avignon 1714–Paris 1789.
NOCTURNAL COAST VIEW
PARIS, LOUVRE
66 × 98 cm. Pendant to a sunset. From 1734 to 1752, Vernet was active in Rome, where he must have seen coast views of Tempesta. The basic type of Vernet's coast views and such effects as the startling moonlight can be followed back over Manglard to Tempesta (269–280) and Claude. The same holds true for Vernet's pupil Charles Lacroix.
LIT. Catalog of the museum, French School, by Brière, 1924, no. 930. F. Ingersoll-Smouse, *Joseph Vernet*, Paris 1926, no. 443.

136–169 DRAWINGS

136–139 PIETER MOLIJN
London 1595–Haarlem 1666.
Molijn's drawings are very numerous and show a consistent stylistic unity. They form the point of departure for Tempesta's draftsmanship. By far the greatest part of Molijn's dated sheets range from 1653 to 1659; earlier dates are rather rare (examples: 1625–De Boer coll.; 1626–Brussels, no. 2569; 1629–Berlin, no. 4330, and Amsterdam, Fodor; 1634–Dresden).

136 LANDSCAPE WITH RUIN
PARIS, ECOLE DES BEAUX-ARTS
149 × 194 mm. Chalk, light brown wash. Signed at the upper right 'PMolyn 1653.' The setting is distinctly northern, whereas the ruin, a variant of Minerva Medica in Rome, is directly taken over from a now lost painting by Breenbergh engraved by Bachely. Molijn is not known to have been in Italy; sufficient other Dutch views by him from the same year are known to make a Roman sojourn unlikely. One other sheet from 1653 shows a Roman view–Ripa Grande (at Düsseldorf; unpublished). Molijn was probably the brother of Willem Molijn, who is recorded as an artist in Rome from 1616 to 1628 (no works known). Tempesta must have left Haarlem in 1654 for Flanders and Italy.
COLL. Masson. LIT. Catalog of the museum, by Lugt, 1950, no. 393.

137 LANDSCAPE WITH RUIN
HAMBURG, KUNSTHALLE
145 × 191 mm. Chalk, brown wash. Signed at the upper right 'P Molyn 1654.' A characteristic example of Molijn's refined draftsmanship in the fifties. Ruined towers of this kind were first made popular by Lastman, Moeyaert, S. Ruysdael, van Goyen.

138 LANDSCAPE
WEST BERLIN, PRINT ROOM, as Molijn.
212 × 352 mm. Chalk, brown wash.
LIT. Bock-Rosenberg, 1930, no. 5406, as Molijn. Review by Lugt in *Preuss. Jahrbuch*, 1931, p. 54, as Tempesta.

139 LANDSCAPE
HAMBURG, KUNSTHALLE, no. 22189.
154 × 203 mm. Chalk, brown wash. An example of a number of drawings by Molijn which are in a somewhat broader style than usual, coming thereby particularly close to Tempesta's Dutch sheets (cf. no. 162).

140–158 TEMPESTA: CERTIFIED DRAWINGS
A selection of sheets bearing Tempesta's signature or old attributions to him.

140 VILLAGE SCENE
CAPE TOWN, NATIONAL GALLERY OF SOUTH AFRICA
209 × 369 mm. Chalk, brown wash. Inscribed on the verso

by a later hand 'P. Mulier.' Picture type and style of this and the following sheet bring to mind the manner of Adriaen van Ostade. Also Barend van Gael and occasionally Herman Saftleven worked in this manner. The drawing furthermore strengthens the attribution to Tempesta of nos. 161 f.

COLL. Michaelis bequest, no. 321.

141 ROAD WITH HOUSES
PARIS, ECOLE DES BEAUX-ARTS

146 × 188 mm. Chalk, brown wash. Inscribed on the verso by a later hand 'Molier.' The handling recalls Adriaen van Ostade and van Goyen, but is looser. A comparable sheet is in the Groningen Museum (catalog by Bolten, 1967, no. 53, repr.).

COLL. Masson. LIT. Catalog of the museum, by Lugt, 1950, no. 419. The other drawing given there to Tempesta, an upright view of houses across an archway (Lugt 420), may be by him too, but this is less certain.

142 VIEW OF LEEREDAM
AMSTERDAM, RIJKSMUSEUM, no. A 221.

258 × 405 mm. Chalk, brown wash. Inscribed on the verso by a later hand 'S waterpoort to Leerdam. P. Mulier ft.' View of Leerdam near Gouda, from outside the walls. Nearly identical with the following drawing, which represents an insoluble problem: is it by Mulier, or was it his model by Berchem, or is it an imitator's repetition after the Amsterdam sheet?

LIT. Knab, in *Misc. I. Q. van Regteren Altena*, 1969, pp. 136, 138, as 'J. van Ruisdael?' (unconvincing; no mention of the inscription and of the Weimar sheet).

143 VIEW OF LEEREDAM
WEIMAR, SCHLOSSMUSEUM, no. KK 4782.

223 × 380 mm. Chalk, brown wash. Formerly attributed to Berchem. See the preceding.

144 RIVER VIEW
FLORENCE, UFFIZI

232 × 357 mm. Chalk, grey and brown wash. Signed at the upper right 'PMLIER f. Ao. 1657' (1654?). The last digit is unclear; the date resembles the date 1657 on the following sheet. The fact that the drawing is in Italy might suggest that it was done there. But subject and style are entirely Dutch, in the manner of Molijn. Very possibly it was done from nature in Holland, in which case Mulier may have carried the sheet to Italy. None of the drawings dated from the Roman years is so entirely Dutch in character.

COLL. Santarelli, catalog of 1870, p. 586. EXH. Uffizi, *Disegni fiamminghi e olandesi*, 1964, no. 80.

145 LANDSCAPE
LONDON, WITT LIBRARY, no. 4084.

188 × 300 mm. Chalk, grey wash. Signed at the upper right 'PML fc. 1657.' This and the following drawing, done in the same year, are Tempesta's earliest clearly dated works from Rome, where he must have arrived a year earlier. Layout and handling of this sheet are however not Italian, but continue to belong to the orbit of Molijn. Only in the small, Italianate fortress and in the distance is there an allusion to Dutch Italianizing artists. Within this basically Dutch language one can, on closer view, notice some compositional links with Gaspard (9).

146 LANDSCAPE
BRUSSELS, ROYAL MUSEUM, PRINT ROOM

228 × 353 mm. Chalk, brown wash. Signed at the upper left 'PMLIER f. 1657.' See the preceding. A stately drawing in the manner of Dutch Italianizing artists such as Berchem. Especially the figure group reveals the influence of Berchem's drawings. The scenery, a sort of romanticized Rhine valley, is imaginary and more northern than Italian in character.

COLL. Jolles. De Grez. LIT. Catalog of the museum, De Grez coll., 1913, no. 2662.

147 LANDSCAPE WITH BUILDINGS
VIENNA, ALBERTINA, no. 8703.

285 × 372 mm. Chalk, brown wash. Inscribed by a later hand at the bottom right 'P. Molier.' The delicate handling corresponds to that of the two preceding sheets of 1657, but the scenery is now distinctly Italianate, in the taste of Berchem and Dujardin. Probably from the Roman years, late 1650's.

EXH. Albertina, *Claude Lorrain*, 1964, no. 363.

148 LANDSCAPE
WEST BERLIN, PRINT ROOM

118 × 166 mm. Chalk, brown wash, heightening. Signed at the upper right 'PML Alias Tempesta fc. Roma A. 1659.' (This is the earliest occurrence of the surname Tempesta.) The style grows out of the stage of 1657 (145), but both the scenery and the handling are firmer. The drawing stands halfway between Molijn and Gaspard/Mola.

LIT. Bock-Rosenberg, 1930, no. 13471.

149 LANDSCAPE
WEST BERLIN, PRINT ROOM
98 × 139 mm. Chalk, grey wash. Signed at the upper right 'pieter Mulier fec. Ao 165-' (last digit illegible; 1658?) ... (month; Agos?) *29*. This and the three following sheets of the same size at Berlin may come from a sketchbook (all were first in the collection of Frederic William I of Prussia and are numbered by a later hand at the top center).
The setting is characteristic of Dutch Italianate landscapes such as those of Berchem or Schellincks.
LIT. Bock-Rosenberg, 1930, no. 13473, as 1653.

150 COAST VIEW
WEST BERLIN, PRINT ROOM
98 × 139 mm. Chalk, grey wash. Signed at the upper left 'PMLIER fec. A 1658' (?). The last digit is subject to doubt; 1654? The horizontal scribble is the common form of an 8. Subject and style of this sheet are completely Dutch, in the manner of Mulier the elder's paintings (see no. 60 and a lost picture from Dresden, no. 1378, monogrammed *PML*, repr. in Bernt, no. 568). There must have existed pictures of this type by Tempesta, too.
LIT. Bock-Rosenberg, 1930, no. 13472, as 1652 (which is surely incorrect).

151 ITALIAN LANDSCAPE
WEST BERLIN, PRINT ROOM
96 × 140 mm. Pen, brown wash. Signed at the bottom left 'Mlier 1662.' This reading is the most satisfactory (in Tempesta's handwriting, a 5 differs from the third digit in this date). This and the following sheet, signed in the same way, are firmer than the preceding on account of the penwork. The sceneries are now entirely Italian. The style alludes to certain of Claude's drawings from the forties.
LIT. Bock-Rosenberg, 1930, no. 13475, as '1652 (1682?)'.

152 LANDSCAPE
WEST BERLIN, PRINT ROOM
98 × 138 mm. Pen, brown wash. Signed at the bottom left 'MLier.' See the preceding. Probably dates from 1662 as well.
LIT. Bock-Rosenberg, 1930, no. 13474.

153 SHEEP
VIENNA, ALBERTINA, no. 8705.
58 × 155 mm. Red chalk. Inscribed by a later hand 'Cav. de Mulierib.' This and the two following sheets are the only known animal drawings by Tempesta. They would seem to be from the late years, but there is as yet no evidence for a precise dating. Judging from Pascoli, Tempesta must have done a great number of such sheets.

154 DONKEY
VIENNA, ALBERTINA, no. 8704.
180 × 130 mm. Red chalk. Inscribed by a later hand 'Cav. de Mulierib.' See the preceding.

155 CAMEL
MONTPELLIER, MUSEE FABRE
120 × 180 mm. Black chalk, pen lines at the bottom. Inscribed by a later hand 'Ant. Tempesta.' Although ascribed to Antonio Tempesta, this drawing is almost certainly by Pietro. It compares with the two preceding, whereas Antonio's style is different. Camels rarely occur in Pietro's paintings (240).
COLL. Gift Bonnet-Mel. LIT. *Invent. gén. des richesses d'art de la France, province, monum. civils*, vol. I, 1878, p. 357, no. 1198, as 'Molyn-Tempesta.' (The other two drawings listed there in the same way are by or after A. Tempesta.)

156 ROCKS AND SHRUBS
COLOGNE, WALLRAF-RICHARTZ MUSEUM, no. 2913.
280 × 374 mm. Blue paper, pen, water color, chalks, heightening. Inscribed at the bottom right 'Pitro Tempesta.' A fine nature drawing, exceptional for its color effect. It stands directly in the tradition of Claude and Gaspard and probably dates from Tempesta's Roman years. Similar passages occur in several of Tempesta's paintings (215, 255, 276, 297).
Apparently by the same hand is a drawing of very similar subject and style in the British Museum, no. Pp. 4-77, given to Gaspard (267 × 407 mm. On grey paper. From Rogers and Knight. See Hind, catalog of Claude drawings of the British Museum, 1926, no. 378, and Sutton, in *GBA* 1962, p. 284, repr., both as Gaspard).

157 ROCKS AND TORRENT
PRIVATE COLLECTION
236 × 285 mm. Grey paper, pen, brown wash, heightened. Inscribed at the lower left 'Tempt fec.' Subject and style compare with the preceding (and, again, with Claude and Gaspard). Similar passages occur in several paintings (204, 235).
COLL. Colnaghi's, London, 1964.

158 WOODED VIEW
LONDON, BRITISH MUSEUM
218 × 307 mm. Pen, brown wash. Inscribed at the bottom right 'C.Pe.ro Temp.ta 1712.' Tempesta died in 1701. Either the drawing is genuine and the inscription was added later, or it was done by an imitator in 1712 after a drawing by Tempesta. The second hypothesis is less likely. Despite the absence of close parallels, the drawing may convincingly be a genuine work and presumably date from the late years. The handling is not incompatible with no.156, the type of image compares with the painting no.287. The style, characterized by colorful contrasts of light and shade, derives from Gaspard's drawings of similar subjects done in the same media (see Friedlaender-Blunt, *The Drawings of N.Poussin*, vol.IV, 1963, pl.230). At the same time, the style points towards the eighteenth century. Marco Ricci occasionally produced similar drawings in his early years (e.g., a sheet in Oxford; see Pilo, in *Paragone 165*, 1963, fig.28).
COLL. Knight. LIT. Hind, *Cat. of Drawings by Dutch and Flemish Artists*, vol.3, 1926, p.150.

159–169 TEMPESTA: ATTRIBUTED DRAWINGS
A selection of sheets which may be ascribed to Tempesta on stylistic grounds or which bear a traditional attribution to him.

159 TREES AND BUILDINGS BY A RIVER
AMSTERDAM, MUSEUM FODOR
195 × 296 mm. Chalk, brown wash. A fine sheet, certainly representing a Dutch view. Seems to be by the same hand as the view of Leeredam (142). The same motif recurs in another, similar drawing of the Albertina originally attributed to J. van Ruisdael (Knab, *loc. cit.,* fig.19).
LIT. Catalog of the Fodor collection, Amsterdam 1863, no.111, as Mulier. Knab, in *Misc. I.Q. van Regteren Altena*, 1969, pp.136, 329, as Berchem, which does not convince me.

160 LANDSCAPE
BESANÇON, MUSEE DES BEAUX-ARTS, no.2744, as Roghman.
207 × 318 mm. Chalk, brown wash. Certainly not by Roghman. The close stylistic resemblance with no.140 points to the Dutch phase of Tempesta.
COLL. Gasc.

161 DUTCH HOUSES
HAARLEM, TEYLER MUSEUM, no.R.75.
175 × 228 mm. Chalk, brown wash. The place identified by an old inscription on the verso as *te bolswart*. Compares with no.140.
LIT. Catalog of the museum, by Scholten, 1904, p.226. Bolten, *Groninger Museum voor Stad en Lande, Dutch Drawings …*, 1967, p.88, as Mulier.

162 MOLIJN OR TEMPESTA
A DUTCH HOUSE
HAMBURG, KUNSTHALLE, no.22192, as Molijn.
172 × 240 mm. Chalk, brown wash. On the borderline between the two artists. Compare the preceding.

163 VIEW WITH HOUSES
HAARLEM, TEYLER MUSEUM, no.R.76.
255 × 285 mm. Pen, brown wash. The same Dutch site as in the following. Both sheets are conceivably by the same hand, this one worked out more carefully.
LIT. Catalog of the museum, by Scholten, 1904, p.266, as Mulier.

164 VIEW WITH HOUSES
LEIDEN, PRINT ROOM
275 × 390 mm. Pen, brown wash. See the preceding.
COLL. Welcker, no.208. EXH. Amsterdam, Fodor museum, 1934, no.74.
The same collection contains three other sheets attributed to Tempesta (nos.2489, 3149, Welcker 4774), but those are more questionable.

165 VIEW OF STA.COSTANZA IN ROME
LEIDEN, PRINT ROOM
212 × 356 mm. Pen, brown wash. Inscribed on the verso *Tempio di Baccho*.
COLL. Welcker, no.687, as Mulier.

166 LANDSCAPE
VIENNA, ALBERTINA, no.46835.
140 × 212 mm. Chalk, greyish wash. Inscribed at the lower left, by a 19th c. hand, 'Pietro Molijn.' An imaginary view of Dutch-Italianate character. The delicate manner and the type of image are very plausible for Tempesta's early Roman years (compare also no.147), although no close parallels among the paintings exist. Certainly not by Molijn.

167 BROOK WITH ROCKS
PRIVATE COLLECTION
90 × 225 mm. Pen, brown wash. Compare nos. 156f., which are of superior quality. This type of drawing derives from the circle of Claude in the 1630's (see my *Claude Lorrain, The Drawings*, Berkeley 1968, nos. 1134 f.).

168 ITALIAN GATEWAY
LEIDEN, PRINT ROOM, no. 2269.
313 × 204 mm. Chalk, grey wash.

169 A TREE
LEIDEN, PRINT ROOM
330 × 205 mm. Grey paper, red chalk. The origin of the attribution is unknown. No other drawing compares

closely. If by Tempesta, presumably from the early phase, since the entire character of the drawing is Dutch. Weathered trees occasionally occur in Tempesta's later paintings (228).
COLL. Welcker, no. 1310.

Other drawings given to Tempesta include an upright design for a book illustration, repr. in the Houthakker catalog, Amsterdam 1966, no. 33. Not convincing are: two drawings in the Louvre, attributed to Tempesta by Lugt (Louvre catalog), and a wooded landscape repr. in the 1966 catalog of Prouté, Paris, no. 21, and in the 1966 catalog of Zeitlin, Los Angeles, no. 52 (the 'signature' at the bottom left reads at best '...esta ft').

170–185 FRESCOES

This section contains a few examples of entire room decorations from the circle of Gaspard, preceding Tempesta's frescoes by a short time; Tempesta's Colonna frescoes; and a few later examples. For a discussion, see p. 37.

170 GASPARD DUGHET
Rome 1615–1675. See notice under no. 9.
ROME, PALAZZO COLONNA
Fresco decoration of the salon adjacent to that of Tempesta. Both rooms are the same size. Here, the landscapes are by Gaspard and date from the early 1650's (see p. 40). The painted space continues the real one in a perfect illusion. The continuous landscapes are seen across a painted loggia supported by an inner and an outer row of columns. The basic scheme of this decoration is prefigured in the Renaissance–above all in Peruzzi's Farnesina frescoes and, closer to Gaspard, in Genga's decoration of a room in Villa Imperiale at Pesaro (A.R. Turner, *The Vision of Landscape in Renaissance Italy*, Princeton 1966, fig. 147). In the latter, each bay shows a self-contained landscape.

171, 172 SCHOOL OF GASPARD
ROME, FARNESINA, SALA DI GALATEA
Fresco, c. 300 × 200 cm. These two examples belong to the wall decoration of the Sala di Galatea, which comprises, besides Raphael's Galatea, five upright and seven smaller, oblong landscape frescoes, all by one hand. They

form a most impressive ensemble. The frescoes are separated from each other by painted pilasters or windows. All have the same mood and green tonality, but each forms an independent composition. They have never been studied, and no documents relating to them are known. The old guide books do not mention them. Only recently has a name–that of Gaspard–been given to them, although neither Baldinucci, Pascoli, nor any other source cite the frescoes. As to the date, it can be regarded as almost certain that they belong to the first extensive restoration of the Farnesina around 1650; this date is inscribed on one of the pilasters. Since then, the frescoes have been restored several times. While these later and apparently extensive repaints all but facilitate the attribution, the Gaspardesque character of the frescoes is beyond doubt; compare, e.g., the layout of no. 171 with the painting no. 10. On the other hand, the details of the composition, the handling, and a certain monotony of the whole are, in my estimate, incompatible with Gaspard himself and point to a follower. There is some affinity with the few works known from Graziani. If the suggested date proves correct, this decoration would be an important prototype for Tempesta (226f.), Onofri, and for many minor landscape frescoes from the second half of the seventeenth century.
LIT. For the brief mentions of the frescoes, see R. Förster, *Farnesina Studien*, 1880, p. 47. Buscaroli, 1935, p. 201. E. Gerlini, *La Villa Farnesina in Roma*, 1949, p. 21

(two other frescoes repr. in figs. 18 f.). C. Frommel, *Die Farnesina und Peruzzis architektonisches Frühwerk*, 1961, p. 19. E. Börsch-Supan, *Garten-, Landschafts- und Paradiesmotive . . .*, 1967, p. 280.

173–181 TEMPESTA
ROME, PALAZZO COLONNA
Each image measures 315 × 220 cm. Datable shortly before 1668. Discussed on p. 37.

182 SCHOOL OF GASPARD
ROME, PALAZZO IN CORSO UMBERTO
A room with fresco decorations simulating a colonnaded loggia opening towards a park. Above, a painted frieze in the antique taste. From the surroundings of Gaspard. Not of outstanding quality, but an interesting and by now very rare example of a type of room decoration which must have been fairly popular at the time. An exact date is hard to establish; possibly preceding Tempesta's Colonna frescoes.

183, 184 CRESCENZIO ONOFRI?
Rome 1632?–Florence, after 1712. See notice under no. 417.
ROME, PALAZZO ROSPIGLIOSI-PALLAVICINI
Each image measures about 300 × 300 cm. This is part of an entire fresco decoration, now transferred on canvas, of the *Sala degli Arazzi* on the ground floor of this richly adorned palace. Putti open the draperies, giving access to pleasant, imaginary landscapes done in vivid green tones. The painted buildings include some extant ones (here the Tomb of Cecilia Metella and Villa Aldobrandini, at Frascati). The style is so close to Onofri's Theodoli frescoes at San Vito Romano, to his Colonna frescoes quoted on p. 40, and to his paintings discussed under no. 417, that his name may tentatively be considered for these frescoes too, although no documentary evidence exists.

185 ADRIEN MANGLARD
Lyon 1695–Rome 1760.
ROME, PALAZZO CHIGI
Three views of the large *Camera delle Marine* on the second floor of the palace, decorated in fresco with continuous marines and tempests by Manglard, who is documented to have been paid for this work in 1748. (Adjacent to it is a room with contemporary landscape frescoes in an architectural framework, by an unknown artist.) These frescoes represent one of the finest examples of such decorations dating from the 18th century. Despite the difference of eighty years, there is a striking basic affinity with Tempesta's frescoes in Palazzo Colonna, a palace in which Manglard has likewise been working. He lived in Rome from about 1710 until his death, sought after by local (Rospigliosi) and international collectors. A continuator of Claude and Rosa, he became in turn the model for Claude-Joseph Vernet. He is mainly known for his marines and coast views (for an example on canvas, see no. 134), but he also did a number of landscapes and portraits; some of his landscape engravings are directly derived from Gaspard (a few are reproduced in A. Busiri Vici, *Giov. Batt. Busiri*, Rome 1966, figs. 234 ff.). His art still awaits critical study; the only bibliographic item is an article by A. Rostand in *GBA*, Dec. 1934, p. 263.
LIT. *Via del Corso*, Rome, Cassa di Risparmio di Roma, 1961, pp. 188, 193.

186–349 PAINTINGS BY TEMPESTA

Separately listed are his Marines (86–118) and his frescoes (173–181).

186, 187 PORTRAIT OF TEMPESTA'S SECOND WIFE ELEONORA BELTRAMI AS MINERVA
SELF-PORTRAIT
ISOLA BELLA
69 × 52 cm., rectangular canvases with oval image. A pair, the heads facing each other. He has bushy hair and wears a fur cap; she wears a bluish dress, the shield is dark red, the background a dark sky. The coloring of both, especially in the flesh, is vivid. The location of the pictures at the Isola Bella suggests *eo ipso* a post-Roman date. Also for matters of age, it is impossible to assume that the woman might be the artist's first wife, whom he abandoned by 1670, when he was 33 years old: here, he looks older. The woman is represented as Minerva, protectress of the arts, with breast-plates, shield, and lance. But she also has a definite portrait character and has, in the Borromeo collection, traditionally been

known as Tempesta's wife. She became his second wife in 1679, during his imprisonment. In 1687/88, their marriage broke apart (see the letters). A likely date for the portraits is thus 1685, shortly after his liberation from prison. The pictures were probably done as a tribute to Count Borromeo for his decisive help in liberating Tempesta. The artist was then aged 48, which is compatible with the painted effigy. These are the only known portraits done by Tempesta. As unique and not overly ravishing works, they are not linked to a specific artistic situation, but conform generally to Italian idealizing portraiture of the late seventeenth century, drawing both from the style of Maratta (faces) and Baciccio (dress of the woman), with an undertone of a northern feeling about them. (The late portraits of Maes represent the Dutch equivalent.) The art of Justus Sustermans (dec. 1681) provides the nearest stylistic parallel. In northern Italy, the more personal portrait art of P.F. Cittadini (dec. 1681) may be compared, too. An identical, likewise genuine version of the self-portrait exists in the Uffizi's collection of self-portraits (no. 1659; 72.5 × 56.5 cm.; damages around the head). An engraving of it by P.A. Pazzi (1752/62) figures, with a short *Life*, in Gori's *Musæum Florentinum*, Florence 1763, a line engraving by P. Lasinio is in *R. Galleria di Firenze Illustrata*, Ser. III, *Ritratti di Pittori*, vol. IV, 1833, p. 69. Soprani mentions in the *Life* of Tavella two now unknown portraits representing Tempesta by Enrico Waymer, a portraitist active in Genoa (1665–1738).

188, 189 WILD DUCKS ATTACKED BY A DOG
WILD DUCKS ATTACKED BY A FALCON
WEIMAR, SCHLOSSMUSEUM, nos. 73, 74.
121 × 170 cm. A pair, with contrasting compositions. Datable in the Antwerp sojourn, c. 1655, and thus until now the earliest known pictures of the artist. Compare Flemish models (1–3).
LIT. First mentioned in the inventory of 1824. Catalog of the museum, of 1913, nos. 248, 249, as Tempesta.

190 LANDSCAPE
MILAN, CASTELLO SFORZESCO, no. 852.
49 × 65 cm. If the convincing traditional attribution to Tempesta is correct, this must be an early work. It is strongly influenced by Gaspard. For equally surface-filling works by the latter, compare no. 11 and a view of Tivoli in the Molinari-Pradelli collection (exh. Bologna 1962, no. 115).
COLL. Bequest Carozzi, 1941.

191 STORMY LANDSCAPE
PRIVATE COLLECTION, ROME
40 × 63 cm. Style and composition are rather unusual for Tempesta, but not incompatible with him. The pronounced Gaspardism of this work, together with the traditional attribution to Tempesta at Villa Lante, suggest that this may be a landscape from his Roman years.
COLL. From Villa Lante, Bagnaia.

192 LANDSCAPE
GENOA, PALAZZO ROSSO, no. 1084.
69 × 95.5 cm. Dark, stormy atmosphere. Traditionally called a pendant to no. 272; but the two do not form an evident pair. Still Gaspardesque, and thus probably from the Genoese years.

193 PASTORAL LANDSCAPE
PRIVATE COLLECTION
40 × 51 cm. Dark green tints; the animals reddish. The type of image derives from Gaspard (e.g., his small picture in London, National Gallery, no. 68) and, to a lesser extent, from Castiglione; compare the following. Probably from the Genoese years.

194 PASTORAL LANDSCAPE
PRIVATE COLLECTION, MILAN
47 × 60 cm. Probably from the Genoese phase. Theme and execution reflect the manner of Castiglione's Exodus scenes (38), where motives such as the monument on the right of this picture appear. The closest parallels in Tempesta's oeuvre are nos. 193 and 313; in the latter, the female figure is strikingly similar to the one on the left of this work. The picture type, represented in Holland by Berchem and his numerous followers, continues in the art of Michel Carrée (1657–1727) and of Simon van der Does (dec. after 1718).

195 PASTORAL LANDSCAPE
PRIVATE COLLECTION
28 × 34 cm. A minor work of Gaspardesque character, probably from Tempesta's early Italian phase. Compare the larger and far more refined stormy landscape no. 255.
LIT. Nicodemi, in *L'Arte* 1958, p. 443.

196, 197 LANDSCAPES
PARMA, PINACOTECA STUARD, nos. 81, 82, as 'Tempesta?'
Circular, 37 cm. A pair. Green tints, the skies blue and

white. The compositions derive in essence from Gaspard. See also Cittadini's tondo (29) and Tempesta's highly refined tondi on copper (229). This and six other works in the same museum, listed hereafter and under no. 102, were collected by Gius. Stuard (Parma 1791–1834). They are summarily listed in the short catalogs of the gallery of 1925 and 1961, the two tondi as 'Tempesta?', four others as school of Rosa, one as school of Tempesta. They are, however, by the same hand and reveal the same style. All are done rather crudely (least so the small tondi) and are moreover disfigured by heavy layers of varnish. Only the announced cleaning might allow us to decide if these works were essentially done by studio hands. The dating is uncertain; Tempesta's presence at Parma in 1686/87 does not provide a safe guideline, as his four splendid pictures at the Pinacoteca Nazionale come likewise from old Parmesan collections, but are of far superior quality. By comparison, the Stuard pictures seem to be earlier (Genoese?), or studio works.

198 LANDSCAPE WITH FISHERMAN
PARMA, PINACOTECA STUARD, no. 88, as school of Rosa.
54.5 × 74 cm. For the condition and provenance, see no. 196. The yellow clouds and blue mountains may be later overpaints. The composition resembles no. 204, which is larger, more detailed, and of finer execution. There is a pendant (Stuard, no. 90), too dark to be reproduced, which shows a coast view with rabbits in the foreground and a burning house in what seems to be a heavy sunset atmosphere, the composition resembling to some extent no. 272.

199, 200 MOUNTAINOUS LANDSCAPE. VIEW WITH BRIDGE
PARMA, PINACOTECA STUARD, nos. 89, 91, as school of Rosa.
55 × 73.5 cm. A pair, daylight scenes. For the condition and provenance, see no. 196. The mountainous landscape is a rather conventional composition, characteristic of the school of Gaspard; compare the large, refined no. 257 and, later, Roncelli's no. 408. The view with the bridge goes back to a type of image occurring in the first half of the century. Dominating arches of bridges are found, e.g., in Poelenburgh, Breenbergh, Gaspard; in Tempesta, compare nos. 233 and 267, the latter of 1701.

201 LANDSCAPE WITH ANIMALS AND THE SACRIFICE OF NOAH
PRIVATE COLLECTION, GENOA
90 × 110 cm. Dark green and reddish-brown tones; rubbed in portions of the sky. In the center distance appears a small, sacrificing figure which must be Noah. Although not the most engaging by its appearance, this picture is of considerable interest. It is made up by large surface areas of the animals, the clouds, and the symmetrically flanking trees. This arrangement still betrays its origin in the mannerist tradition of the Bassano (30). The intentional simplification in the layout is paralleled by the flickering, summary handling–a brushwork found also in a number of other works by Tempesta such as the small nos. 108 f. or the large nos. 202, 259. The picture differs moreover from Tempesta's late, more complex, and more refined Noah pictures (240 f.) in which an additional Flemish influence is present. All this entitles us to ascribe this work and those of similar character to Tempesta's Genoese phase. The influence of Castiglione (38) is felt in the realistic rendering of the animals no less than in the composition and the technique.
COLL. Said to come from an old Genoese collection.

202 LANDSCAPE WITH THE RAPE OF EUROPA
NEW YORK, COLL. MR. AND MRS. J. O'CONNER LYNCH
173 × 123 cm. The sky blue and white. Traces of suffering in some portions of the center. Compare for the subject no. 281. This is an impressive, large work, painted with considerable verve and bold contrasts of color, thus probably dating from the Genoese years (see also the preceding). There is a strong effect of recession from the spectators of the foreground over the figures enacting the myth to the distant landscape.
COLL. Bt. a generation ago at a New York sale. EXH. Binghamton, N.Y., *Lynch Coll.*, 1969, no. 45.

203 STORMY LANDSCAPE
LENINGRAD, HERMITAGE, no. 3224.
59 × 75 cm. A complex, interesting, and unusual composition, still strongly influenced by Gaspard, and presumably dating from the pre-Lombard years.

204 LANDSCAPE WITH FISHERMEN
MILAN, CASTELLO SFORZESCO, no. 246.
73 × 98 cm. An elaborate composition, of which the smaller painting no. 198 is a simpler variant. Style and

provenance suggest a date in the Lombard phase. To my mind very likely genuine; for the style, compare also no. 215.

COLL. Bequest Mira. LIT. Catalog of the museum, c. 1920, no. 246, as manner of Tempesta.

205, 206 PASTORAL LANDSCAPE. LANDSCAPE WITH ST. JOHN
DRESDEN, STATE COLLECTIONS, nos. 1520 (destroyed), 1519.

35 × 48 cm. Traditionally regarded as a pair. The compositions are contrasting. The second work has been considerably damaged and rubbed; compare for its composition Claude's lost painting of the same subject, *Lib. Ver.* 97.

COLL. From Vienna or Regensburg. LIT. Catalogs of the museum, of 1912 and 1930. No. 205 only: Ebert, *Kriegsverluste der Dresdener Gemäldegalerie*, 1963, p. 123.

207 ISOLA BELLA, PALAZZO BORROMEO
A view into the 'Salone del Tempesta', in which over fifty paintings by Tempesta are now hung.

208 PASTORAL LANDSCAPE
ISOLA BELLA

40 × 56 cm. In the foreground, the frequently occurring motive of a herdsman driving his flocks.

209 LANDSCAPE WITH THE JUDGMENT OF MIDAS
ISOLA BELLA

59.5 × 74 cm. Midas presiding over the contest between Pan and Apollo. Brightly colored figures. The subject was not only dear to Italian classical landscape, but also occurs in Flemish landscape of the early seventeenth century (e.g., Coninxloo, at Dresden; Thiéry, 1953, pl. 4). Compare also Lauri's no. 44.

210 PASTORAL LANDSCAPE
ISOLA BELLA

45 × 154 cm. The classical composition borrows elements from Gaspard and Domenichino. There is a contrasting pendant, too dark to be reproduced, which represents a mountainous landscape with rocks and a cascade on the left half, trees on the right, a pastoral group and a distant view in the center. The pair must have served as sopraporte.

211, 212 PASTORAL LANDSCAPES
BUDAPEST, MUSEUM, nos. 271, 269.

27 × 32.5 cm. Heavily cracked. A pair, of good quality. The composition of the first work echoes certain pastorals by Claude produced at the time of Tempesta's Roman sojourn (e.g., *Lib. Ver.* 163, 166); cf. also the larger no. 248. The density of the handling and the idyllic character of the two pictures anticipate the eighteenth century; compare especially Orizzonte (442–444).

COLL. Esterhàzy, catalog of 1812. LIT. Catalogs of the museum, of 1954 and 1968 (by Pigler), nos. 271, 269.

213, 214 NOCTURNAL PASTORAL LANDSCAPE. PASTORAL LANDSCAPE
BURGHLEY HOUSE, MARQUESS OF EXETER, nos. 496, 488.

48 × 75 cm. A pair, darkened. Both have many motives in common with other pictures by Tempesta. The first compares above all with the upright no. 223, which shows basically the same composition, likewise in nocturnal illumination; compare also no. 249 (small bridge). In the second work, the tower and bridge, alluding to the Plautian tomb with Ponte Lucano, add to the Gaspardesque character of the picture; compare no. 283 and Gaspard's huge Ponte Lucano in the Doria gallery (*GBA* 1962, p. 282, repr.).

At Burghley, eight pictures are traditionally ascribed to Tempesta (this pair; no. 327; and five small pictures, nos. 328 ff.), four large ones traditionally ascribed to Tempestino (364 ff.). All have suffered and darkened. The five small Tempestas form a group of their own and show an unusual facet of the artist – religious figure pieces. These go in turn together with the large religious work no. 327. The latter, and almost certainly the five small Tempestas, date from the Lombard years, whereas the Tempestinos must have come from Rome. The origin of the pictures is not known, but some may have been acquired with the bulk of the baroque pictures by the fifth earl at the end of the seventeenth century (cf. Waterhouse in *Burl. Mag.* 1960, p. 57). The first mention is in *A History ... of Burghley House*, 1797, pp. 74, 81 (nos. 213, 214, 329 only), repeated in *A Guide to Burleigh House*, 1815; among the three listed works is one which forms a pendant to a work listed only in later catalogs (330), which suggests that the collection already comprised more than three works. All twelve figure summarily in *Burghley*, by W. Charlton, 1847, eight as 'Molyn-Tempesta', four as 'Tempesta or D. Tempestino'.

One, no. 327, came from Signor Gabiani in Florence (not listed in the book of 1797).

215 PASTORAL LANDSCAPE
VIENNA, KUNSTHISTORISCHES MUSEUM, no. 1328.
60 × 76.5 cm. A fine, unconventional work. The composition brings to mind some pastorals of Claude (e.g., *Lib. Ver.* 109, in New York).
COLL. First recorded in the collection in 1824. LIT. Catalog of the museum, of 1938, no. 1328.

216 LANDSCAPE
ISOLA BELLA
73 × 60 cm. Pink tints in the sky. There is a dark pendant showing buildings and trees on the left, the moon, clouds, and water in the center, a rock with tree on the right. Weathered tree trunks of the kind seen here–a motive especially dear to Dutch landscape–occur not infrequently in Tempesta (226, 228, 295, 301).

217 LANDSCAPE
ISOLA BELLA
46 × 37 cm. There is a pendant, too dark to be reproduced, with tall trees on either side and a sleeping nymph surprised by a faun at the lower left.

218 LANDSCAPE
CAMBRIDGE, MASS., FOGG ART MUSEUM, no. 1961.55, as anonymous.
65 × 52.5 cm. This composition is known in two versions, one at Cambridge, the other, larger one at Agnew's, London (1968; 84 × 71 cm.; from Italy). In the latter, the ducks and the tiny figures below the pyramid are absent. The composition is no doubt by Tempesta, and both versions may be genuine. Compare no. 219. Almost the same group of washerwomen appears in no. 222 (see also no. 298). The Cambridge version is the only painting by Tempesta at present in an American museum.
COLL. Entered the museum in 1961.

219 LANDSCAPE WITH THE REST ON THE FLIGHT
ISOLA BELLA
72 × 62 cm. At first, the figures may have been placed in the left half of the foreground. Owing to the emphasis on verticals and horizontals, this Gaspardesque composition has a particularly classical bearing.

220, 221 PASTORAL LANDSCAPES
ISOLA BELLA
38 × 28 cm. A pair, with tall, flanking trees on opposite sides. The first has a Venetian quality due to the romantic setting with distant mountains, the layout determined by several diagonals, and the coloring dominated by the yellow tints of the clouds. The second is darkish; spatial diagonals are not emphasized here.

222, 223 NOCTURNAL PASTORAL LANDSCAPES
ISOLA BELLA
56 × 42 cm. Illegible signatures on stones at the bottom? A pair, both rendered as moonlight scenes (however unlikely the nocturnal laundrying is), with dark brownish tints and tall, slender trees on opposite sides. In the first work, a distant house is seen in flames. Compare no. 218 for the figures. The pendant compares with the slightly larger no. 213, which shows a very similar setting in the oblong format.

224, 225 PASTORAL LANDSCAPE. NOCTURNAL PASTORAL LANDSCAPE
ISOLA BELLA
83 × 71 cm. Companion pieces, both with pastoral scenes and water in the foreground, trees on opposite sides. The first shows daylight in dark yellowish tints, the second moonlight in bluish tints. For the layout, compare the larger and therefore more complex pair nos. 263 f.

226, 227 LANDSCAPES
ISOLA BELLA
74.5 × 38 cm. A pair with tall trees in the foreground on opposite sides. The sky is pink in the first, slightly pinkish at the horizon in the second. The weathered tree trunks are characteristic of Tempesta (compare no. 216). The compositions, rooted in the tradition of Gaspard (15) and of Mola (26), lead to the eighteenth century. Especially the evocative coloring points into the future. There is, for instance, a striking similarity with an upright pair of landscapes by Paolo Monaldi (active in Rome, mid-eighteenth century; see Heim Gallery, London, *Baroque Paintings*, 1968, figs. 59 f.).

228 LANDSCAPE
BRITISH PRIVATE COLLECTION
60 × 48 cm. At its appearance on the art market, the picture had a pendant, which is not known to me. For the

motives of the weathered tree trunks, see no. 216. The style comes very close to Tavella (384).
COLL. London art market, c. 1964 (pair).

229–231　LANDSCAPE WITH THE FLIGHT INTO EGYPT. LANDSCAPE WITH THE REST ON THE FLIGHT. LANDSCAPE WITH CHRIST IN THE DESERT
ISOLA BELLA
Copper, circular, 22 cm. Tempesta's smallest paintings. Green tints. The last represents Christ in the desert, driving away the tempter (on the left) and being served by angels (Matth. 4:11). Like several other small works listed hereafter, these three tondi, which rank among Tempesta's best paintings, show a miniature-like refinement. The compositions and the intense painterly execution have a distinctly northern character; they stand in the tradition of the Frankenthal masters, Elsheimer, Bril, the Velvet Brueghel. Also to mind come the early coppers by Claude, such as the Westminster Riposo. In Italy, F. Lauri and F. Albani are closest, and there may be an echo of Scorza's miniatures, with which Tempesta was probably familiar in Genoa.

232　PASTORAL LANDSCAPE
ISOLA BELLA
43 × 63 cm. Signed 'Cavaglier P. Tempesta fecit' on the bridge. Hangs as pendant to no. 311. The sun in the yellow sky. An idyllic view with Dutch reminiscences (on the right). The type of image points towards the eighteenth century.

233　PASTORAL LANDSCAPE
BRESCIA, PINACOTECA, no. 204.
43 × 31 cm. The sky yellowish on the right. Similar in character to the following, larger work. Both come from old Brescian collection, which makes it likely that they date from the Lombard years. They differ from the set of upright pictures at the Isola Bella (220 ff.) by more decorative compositions which anticipate the taste of the rococo; compare similar bridge motives in nos. 232 and 267 (1701).
COLL. Tosio Martinengo. LIT. Catalog of the museum, of 1927, no. 204. Calabi, 1935, p. 102.

234　PASTORAL LANDSCAPE
BRESCIA, PINACOTECA, no. 210.
84 × 67 cm. Sky grey, blue, and violet. See the preceding.
COLL. Bequest L. Cicogna. LIT. Calabi, 1935, p. 102.

235　LANDSCAPE
MILAN, BRERA
151 × 225 cm. Traces of a signature on a rock at the bottom right? This large work is one of the artist's most singular and romantic compositions. While still recalling works by the young Gaspard (9) and by Rosa (23), it anticipates Tavella (384), Marco Ricci (Mostra 1964, no. 72, repr.), and certain examples of Venetian eighteenth century painting (see Martini, 1964, fig. 239, for an astonishing parallel as late as Antonio Diziani).
LIT. Catalog of the museum by Malaguzzi Valeri, 1908, no. 626.

236　STORMY LANDSCAPE
DESTROYED. FORMERLY DRESDEN, STATE COLLECTIONS, no. 1516.
73 × 99 cm. According to the descriptions, had grey stripes of rain on the right and heavy clouds in a golden illumination from the left.
COLL. 1741 from Venice. Destroyed in 1945. LIT. Catalogs of the museum, of 1912 and 1930. Haumann, 1927, p. 15. Ebert, *Kriegsverluste der Dresdener Gemäldegalerie*, 1963, p. 44.

237　LANDSCAPE WITH THE FLIGHT INTO EGYPT
ISOLA BELLA
43 × 62 cm. Yellowish tints. Belongs to the type of fanciful variations on the theme of the Flight, with bridge, boat, angels, and the like – a type much in favor at the time, based on innovations of the Carracci, Testa, and Albani. The same spirit prevails in the Burghley pictures, nos. 327 ff.
COLL. 1744 from Senago, another Borromeo property (inscription on the back).

238　LANDSCAPE WITH THE FLIGHT INTO EGYPT
ISOLA BELLA
43 × 62 cm. A fine picture, in brown-yellowish tints. Compare the preceding.

239　STORMY LANDSCAPE
DRESDEN, STATE COLLECTIONS, no. 1518.
35.5 × 59.5 cm. In the foreground, a donkey killed by a stroke of lightning; the motive is like a profane equivalent of the conversion of St. Paul.
COLL. 1741 from Venice. LIT. Catalogs of the museum, of 1912 and 1930. Bernt, 1962, vol. 4, no. 204.

240 LANDSCAPE WITH THE SACRIFICE OF NOAH
MILAN, AMBROSIANA

122 × 178.5 cm. This and the two following, somewhat smaller works are closely connected with each other. They date from the late years. For the subject of Noah, see first no. 201. The encyclopedic display of animals represents a type based on Flemish as well as Italian precursors (Savery, Jan Brueghel, Bassano, Ant. Tempesta, Scorza, Castiglione); some of these prototypes are here grouped under nos. 33 ff. While the execution of this picture owes more to the Italians, Tempesta clearly used engravings by and after Savery for the composition. Many details of the arrangements of the animals cannot be explained without such a direct contact; suffice it to compare Savery's painting of the entry into the Ark at Dresden (1620; Thiéry, 1953, pl. 19), where the horse, the camel, and the elephant are placed in the same way.
COLL. Gift 1934. LIT. Galbiati, *Itinerario … Ambrosiana*, 1951, p. 122, wrongly as 'manner of Mulier.'

241 LANDSCAPE WITH THE SACRIFICE OF NOAH
KASSEL, MUSEUM, no. 414.

121 × 172 cm. A masterpiece of refined execution, somewhat smaller than the preceding. On account of the provenance probably from the Venetian phase, 1687–1690. A pendant representing the entry into the Ark, presently unknown, was likewise engraved by Monaco.
COLL. Counts Algarotti, Venice; engraved with this mention by Pietro Monaco (b. 1710). In Kassel by 1749, inventory of Landgraf Wilhelm VIII, no. 704. Not in the 1783 catalog. From 1807 to 1815 in Paris.
LIT. Catalog of the museum, of 1958, no. 414. Bernt, 1962, vol. 4, no. 203.

242 LANDSCAPE WITH ORPHEUS
PRIVATE COLLECTION, PIACENZA

105 × 160 cm. A masterpiece of very refined execution. See no. 240. The painting shares numerous details with the two preceding works (horse, peacock on a tree stump in the center foreground, camel, elephant, etc.).
COLL. By descent. EXH. Piacenza, 1868, as Tempesta (cf. A. Bonora, *Belle Arti e Commercio*, Piacenza 1868, p. 37).

243 PASTORAL LANDSCAPE
ISOLA BELLA

31 × 40 cm. Signed on the stone between the two figures 'Cavagliere Pietro Tempesta.' Bright greenish tints, blue sky. The type of the castellated building, recurring in other works of the artist, can be traced back to Bril, Carracci, and Domenichino.

244 WOODED LANDSCAPE
ISOLA BELLA

29 × 36 cm. Hangs as pendant to the following. Executed with ravishing refinement. While the intimate, surface-filling density of the view still echoes the taste of the Frankenthal masters, the composition is clearly organized by verticals and horizontals; the forest fills the left half; the distant view occupies the upper right quarter.

245 LANDSCAPE
ISOLA BELLA

29 × 36 cm. Pink sky. Three washerwomen in the foreground; in the distance, two fires. The layout compares with no. 248. Hangs as pendant to the preceding.

246 PASTORAL LANDSCAPE
ISOLA BELLA

29.5 × 36 cm. Green tints, fine handling.

247 WOODED LANDSCAPE
ISOLA BELLA

25.5 × 29.5 cm. One of the finest examples of the intimate, miniature-like type of small pictures which still reflect the influence of the filled, wooded views of Coninxloo and Bril (compare, e.g., Thiéry, 1953, pl. 7, 22).

248 PASTORAL LANDSCAPE
ISOLA BELLA

59.5 × 74 cm. Illegibly signed on a stone at the bottom right. Smoke emerges from the houses on the right (a kiln, rather than a fire).

249 PASTORAL LANDSCAPE
ISOLA BELLA

100 × 150 cm. Dark green, brown, and pinkish tints. An important, late work. In accordance with the large size, the composition is complex. The same layout, and partly the same details, recur in the following. The composition shares the central tree, the group of buildings on the left, and the carriage drawn by oxen with a lost landscape by Poussin known from Chatillon's engraving (Blunt, *The Paintings of Nicolas Poussin*, 1966, no. 217). Compare also Tavella (384) and Panfi (418).

250 PASTORAL LANDSCAPE
PRIVATE COLLECTION
62 × 88 cm. The composition corresponds essentially to no.249, which is larger and contains a few more details. This smaller version is known to me only from the photograph. So far as one can judge, it seems likewise genuine. If so, it would be almost the only extant case of a faithful repetition by the artist.
COLL. Sale Aarau (Switzerland), Hufschmied, 28 Nov. 1958, lot 161, then untraceable in private hands.

251 LANDSCAPE
ISOLA BELLA
81 × 117 cm. Green tints. Compare J.d'Arthois (5) and P.Testa (18).

252 STORMY LANDSCAPE
ISOLA BELLA
84.5 × 130.5 cm. Hangs as pendant to the coast view no. 273. Dark green tints, the sky dark blue. The left and right halves clearly separated, the horizon at half height. The forest passage evokes strong Flemish memories ranging from Bril to Rubens.

253, 254 PASTORAL LANDSCAPES
ISOLA BELLA
73 × 97 cm. An important pair, of refined handling. Green tints, the first also with brown tones for the animals and the foliage. The large round tower and adjacent buildings in the first picture are Tempesta's only 'Giorgionesque' structures–a type that later recurs in Marco Ricci and Roncelli (403). The layout of the second work compares with the large no.430, by J.-B. Forest; there are, moreover, parallels in Flemish art from d'Arthois (4) to Huysmans (432).

255, 256 STORMY LANDSCAPE. WINTER
LANDSCAPE
STUTTGART, STATE GALLERY, nos.249, 256.
62 × 72.5 cm. A pair, of excellent quality. On account of the provenance probably from the Venetian years, 1687/90. The surface-filling, stormy landscape compares with no.276 and derives ultimately from similar scenes by Gaspard (compare his stormy landscape of the Mahon coll., exh. Bologna 1962, no.107). There are two copies of Tempesta's picture, listed here as nos.360f. The winter landscape–not a very winterly one at that–is, surprisingly enough, the only known example by Tempesta of a

type of image which was so much in favor with Dutch landscape painters, but hardly found in Italy. (A strange example is by Filippo Napoletano, at Poggio Reale, Florence; see exh. Florence 1969, fig.23.) Marco Ricci and Tavella (see for both no.382) continued this type of winter landscapes, which one can later follow over Pedon, Diziani, and Bison to Deleidi in Bergamo (L. Angelini, *L'avvento dell'arte neoclassica in Bergamo*, 1966, p.140, repr.).
COLL. Bought in 1852 from Barbini-Breganze, Venice.
LIT. Catalog of the museum, of 1962, nos.249, 256.

257, 258 MOUNTAINOUS LANDSCAPE.
LANDSCAPE
ROTHESAY, SCOTLAND, MARQUESS OF BUTE
146 × 198 cm. An important pair, done for a patron in Padua (see below), and thus dating from the Lombard years. The tight filling of the surface with massive forms places the pictures among the artist's most heroic creations. In accordance with the large dimensions, the compositions are complex, comprising numerous planes. The mountainous landscape, flanked by huge fortresses, is of exceptional design, whereas the pendant compares with several other, less grandiose works (294, 297, 300). The figure group seems to be purely pastoral.
COLL. Probably bought with the bulk of the collection by the third earl of Bute (1713–1792) for Luton Hoo. In the Luton Hoo MS. by the first marquess, c.1799: 'The works of Tempesta are little known or sought after in England, in Italy they are exceedingly prized. These (a pair) were painted for a particular family in Padua and taken off the first nails on which they were hung to be placed here' (i.e., at Luton Hoo). EXH. British Institution, 1847, nos.62f., as 'Dom. Tempesta' (the 'Domenico', must perforce be a wrong identification). LIT. Waagen, *Treasures of Art in Great Britain*, vol.III, 1854, p.484 (first publ. 1838), as Tempesta.

259, 260 PASTORAL LANDSCAPE. LANDSCAPE
WITH THE HOLY FAMILY
PRIVATE COLLECTION, GENOA
100 × 100 cm. A pair, of outstanding importance. The atmospheres are not contrasting. The influence of Castiglione is particularly pronounced in the entire layout and in individual motives such as the woman on the white horse; compare, e.g., Castiglione's Old Testament pastoral in the Manning coll., New York (Dayton, Art Institute, *Genoese Masters*, 1962, no.22, repr.; the composition

engraved by Chasteau, 1635–1683, as Journey of Abraham and his wife into Egypt). As in comparable works by the Bassani and Castiglione, the subjects of this pair, though primarily pastoral, can also be understood in a religious context: the first may be an Old Testament journey (Rebekah?; cf. no. 265), the other probably shows the Holy Family (the child seems to be too old for the Flight; on the other hand, there is a donkey at the extreme right).

LIT. Bonzi, in *Liguria*, July 1960, p. 12.

261 PASTORAL LANDSCAPE
PRIVATE COLLECTION
98 × 104 cm. Sunset atmosphere. A masterpiece from the later years, comparable in layout and character with no. 260.

262 PASTORAL LANDSCAPE
WESTON PARK, EARL OF BRADFORD, as attributed to Bout and Baudewyns.
74 × 66 cm. To my mind very likely a late work by Tempesta. Compare no. 260 and Tempestino's no. 365.

263, 264 LANDSCAPE WITH OLD TESTAMENT JOURNEYS
PRIVATE COLLECTIONS, GENOA
160 × 127 cm. The second is signed, above the dog, 'Cavaglier P. T.' The other, known to me only from a photograph, is probably signed too. An important, large pair with contrasting compositions, which still echo the lesson of Rosa in the layout and in the design of the tall, flanking trees. As is the case in many works of Castiglione, the figures are not merely pastoral, but have an Old Testament character, without referring clearly to a specific event; the first might be interpreted as the journey of Rebekah (an angel is closing the cortege), the other as the journey of Abraham. For other, similar groups in Tempesta, see nos. 259–267. In importance, this pair compares with a pair of equally refined, large landscapes done in 1704/11 by Onofri in a more classical vein (Florentine galleries; exh. Florence 1969, figs. 84f.). See also no. 416, from the circle of the early Ricci.

LIT. Bonzi, in *L'Arte* 1937, p. 306, as journeys of Abraham and of Tobias; reprinted in his *Galleria Genovese immaginaria*, Genoa 1968, p. 59.

265 LANDSCAPE WITH THE JOURNEY OF REBEKAH
NEW YORK, WALTER P. CHRYSLER COLLECTION
(color plate II)
121 × 163 cm. A famous masterpiece. On account of the provenance, it probably dates from the Venetian phase, 1687–1690. In accordance with the large size, the layout is complex. As in many pictures by Castiglione, the subject, though apparently purely pastoral, is in fact meant as an Old Testament scene; Rebekah, riding on a camel, is crossing the bridge in the middle distance. Compare similarly nos. 264, 267. The theme is common throughout the seventeenth century. I am not struck by the stylistic similarities with a group of six smaller landscapes from the early eighteenth century in the Pallavicini collection pointed out by Zeri (Zeri, *La Galleria Pallavicini in Roma*, 1959, no. 394).

COLL. Consul Smith, Venice; engraved with this mention by G. Leonardis (1710–c. 1782). O. Morley Leigh, England. Colnaghi. EXH. Portland, Art Museum, *Paintings of the Coll. of Walter P. Chrysler*, 1956, no. 42. Norfolk, Va., Museum, 1968.

A larger copy, reminiscent of Roncelli in the broad brushwork and the coloring, is in a Milanese collection (140 × 190 cm.). A smaller copy was a few years ago on the Genoese art market.

266 PASTORAL LANDSCAPE
PRIVATE COLLECTION, GENOA
85 × 117 cm. The sky violet and blue, the animals brown. In the foreground, a lamb is being slaughtered. An important late work, of classical character.

267 LANDSCAPE WITH THE JOURNEY OF REBEKAH
PRIVATE COLLECTION, MILAN
115 × 160 cm. Signed on the rock at the bottom center 'Cav. P. Tempesta 1701.' An important late work. For the subject, see nos. 264f.

LIT. Nicodemi, in *L'Arte* 1958, p. 443.

268, 269 STORMY LANDSCAPE. NOCTURNAL ESTUARY VIEW
PRIVATE COLLECTION, MILAN
Oval, 94 × 118 cm. A pair. Compare the following pair.

270, 271 LANDSCAPE (color plate VI). NOCTURNAL COAST VIEW
ISOLA BELLA
30 × 48 cm. A pair. The landscape, lightly painted in

green tints, with blue mountains and a yellow-blue sky, has an extraordinarily fresh, 'natural' look. The small size may have contributed to the absence of the obvious constructive schemes found in most other pictures. For a basically similar layout in a more formal work, see no. 205. There is a Flemish note in the design of the foreground and the motive of the oxen (compare Huysman's no. 432). One is further reminded of the plein-airism of François Desportes (1644–1736). The coast view, done in dark grey-violet tints, is more conventional. Its layout compares closely with the larger nos. 272f.

272 NOCTURNAL ESTUARY VIEW
GENOA, PALAZZO ROSSO, no. 1083.

69.5 × 95 cm. Dark tints. For the composition and the handling, compare no. 271. The rather perfunctory execution is not far from no. 108, which probably dates from the Genoese phase; also this work, which has a Genoese provenance, might thus belong to those years. Cf. no. 192.

273 COAST VIEW (color plate VII)
ISOLA BELLA

84.5 × 130.5 cm. Possibly signed at the lower left, but illegible. Hangs as pendant to the stormy landscape no. 252. The bottom of a ship is being coated with tar. This is one of the most impressive versions of a subject dear to Tempesta; compare the following and no. 277. The coloring is light and gay, suggesting daylight, despite a somewhat unusual appearance of the sun. The compositional prototypes are provided by early works of Claude (*Liber Veritatis* 17, 19, 31, and others) and by Rosa (20), but the airiness of the decorative color scale in Tempesta's work points much more towards the future (C.-J. Vernet; no. 135).

274 NOCTURNAL COAST VIEW
ISOLA BELLA

75 × 99 cm. Dark blue-violet tints. The bottom of a ship is being coated with tar. Compare similarly the preceding, larger work.

275 COAST VIEW
LOST. FORMERLY BRESLAU, MUSEUM, no. 257.

48 × 73 cm. Signed on the rock below the figures 'Cavaglier P. Tempesta.' Judging from the photograph, it dated from the last years of Tempesta. It disappeared during the last war, like no. 118 and a third Tempesta for-

merly at Breslau (no. 951), of which no photograph survives. For the composition, compare the larger no. 277.

276, 277 STORMY LANDSCAPE. COAST VIEW
(color plates XIV, XII)
PRIVATE COLLECTION

109 × 157 cm. A pair. The first is signed on the bundle carried by the donkey 'C.P.T. / Fecit / Ano 99 AD.' The interpretation of the last line as referring to the date 1699 is not certain, although the pair surely belongs to the last years (fancy signs on bales of goods had been a tradition since Tassi). Freshly cleaned and in excellent condition, these splendid, large pictures have the brilliant, luminous effect which so many of Tempesta's best works must originally have had.

The coast view is one of the richest and most elaborate specimens of a type recurring in a dozen other examples by Tempesta. On the right, a boat is being tarred. See no. 362 for copies of this pair.

EXH. Milan, Gall. Sacerdoti, *Capolavori*, 1965, no. 20.

278 NOCTURNAL LAKE SCENE
ISOLA BELLA

60 × 64 cm. Violet-brown tints. A ferry-boat in the center. The layout compares with no. 308.

279, 280 PASTORAL LANDSCAPE. ESTUARY VIEW
PARMA, GALLERIA NAZIONALE, nos. 281, 280.
(color plate I)

Oval, 95 × 131 cm. An important pair. The traditional designation of the coast view as a sunset is probably right, although the coloristic appearance is not far from that of a moonlight scene. Presumably from Tempesta's Parmesan sojourn, 1686/87.

COLL. The same as no. 286. LIT. Catalogs of the museum: by Ricci, 1896, nos. 280f.; by Quintavalle, 1939, p. 219. Martini, 1964, pp. 176f. ('nocturne'), 198. Donzelli, 1967, fig. 431 (landscape).

281, 282 NOCTURNAL LANDSCAPE WITH MERCURY AND BATTUS. LANDSCAPE WITH THE RAPE OF EUROPA
BRESCIA, CONGREGA APOSTOLICA

102 × 154 cm. An important, late pair. The first is rather dark; the second has bright figures, the sky is grey-blue, yellowish at the bottom. A copy of the Europa is listed here as no. 363.

COLL. Mallia, Brescia. LIT. Calabi, 1935, p. 102.

283 LANDSCAPE
PRIVATE COLLECTION, BERGAMO
126 × 165 cm. Several motives such as the bridge, the house, the waterfall, and the boat stand in the tradition of Annibale Carracci and Domenichino. The type of image continues in M. Ricci (e.g. Memphis, Tenn., *Ricci exh.*, 1966, fig. 78; Newhouse Galleries).

284, 285 PASTORAL LANDSCAPE. NOCTURNAL PASTORAL RIVER LANDSCAPE
VADUZ, PRINCE OF LIECHTENSTEIN
103 × 148 cm. and 102 × 151 cm. A pair, from the last years. The first is unusual for its symmetrical composition; compare Marco Ricci's no. 411. The pendant shows the moon in the opening on the left, a burning citadel on the hills of the opposite side; compare similarly no. 303. COLL. From the Viennese art market, 1816. LIT. Catalogs of the collection, of 1873, nos. 603, 608, and of 1927, nos. 247, 249.

286, 287 OPEN LANDSCAPE (color plate v).
WOODED VIEW
PARMA, GALLERIA NAZIONALE, nos. 243, 244.
61 × 89 cm. An important pair, presumably from Tempesta's Parmesan sojourn, 1686/87. The inner proportions of the two pictures are different. The first shows an exceptionally open landscape with a storm-laden sky, the other a closed, surface-filling interior of a wood, a type of image recurring several times in the artist's work (158, 255, 276).
COLL. Probably painted for the Boscoli family in Parma, from whom the pictures passed in 1710 to the Sanvitale. Came to the museum from the Sanvitale gallery in 1834. LIT. Catalogs of the museum: by Ricci, 1896, nos. 243 f.; by Quintavalle, 1939, p. 328 (with further lit.), and later catalogs. EXH. *Marco Ricci*, 1963, nos. 3 f.

288 PASTORAL LANDSCAPE
PRIVATE COLLECTION
120 × 175 cm. An impressive, late work.
COLL. Art market, Bergamo.

289 LANDSCAPE WITH MYTHOLOGICAL FIGURES
MILAN, AMBROSIANA
75 × 100 cm. Late. On the right, a group of five nymphs with two infants. The attire of the women and the presence of the river god indicate that the scene is mythological, but to my knowledge no story quite corresponds

(Romus and Remulus does not apply; the infant Bacchus would only demand one child).
COLL. Old Ambrosiana collection, and thus possibly from the Borromeo. LIT. Catalog of the museum, of 1907, no. 30. Galbiati, *Itinerario ... Ambrosiana*, 1951, p. 122.

290 LANDSCAPE WITH FAUNS AND NYMPHS
PRIVATE COLLECTION
98 × 143 cm. A fine, late work with figures ultimately derived from Claude (*Liber Veritatis* 55, 108, 113); nymphs and satyrs also occur in no. 334.
COLL. Haller, Wimbledon, 1914–1964. Various dealers. Sale Vienna, Dorotheum, 20 May 1965 (*Art Price Annual* 1964–1965, p. 449). LIT. Roethlisberger, in *Washington, National Gallery of Art, Report and Studies*, 1969.

291 LANDSCAPE WITH FAUNS AND NYMPHS
PRIVATE COLLECTION
75 × 100 cm. Signed on a stone at the bottom center 'Cavaliere Pietro Tempesta fecit 1700.' The composition with a framing tree trunk on the left, a central cluster of trees, and an opening into the depth on either side of it, reverts to a scheme characteristic of many landscapes of the Frankenthal school around 1600.
COLL. Sale Munich, Weinmüller, 2 May 1956, lot 1269.

292 LANDSCAPE
STUTTGART, STATE GALLERY, no. 292.
58.5 × 94.5 cm. The elongated format, exceptional for Tempesta, results in a particularly felicitous composition of wide breadth, framed on either side by groups of trees. The layout thus recalls certain elongated views by Gaspard (such as the view of Tivoli in London; exh. Bologna 1962, no. 119). But Tempesta's composition is smoother, its elegance anticipates late works by Tavella (388).
COLL. Bought in 1852 from Barbini-Breganze, Venice, as a Flemish work.
LIT. Catalogs of the museum, of 1907, no. 417, as French 17th c. school, and of 1962, no. 292, as Tempesta.

293 PASTORAL LANDSCAPE
PRIVATE COLLECTION, GENOA
150 × 198 cm. A large, important work.

294 PASTORAL LANDSCAPE
ISOLA BELLA
87 × 123 cm. Pendant to the seastorm no. 114.

295 PASTORAL LANDSCAPE
ISOLA BELLA
61.5 × 98 cm. Hangs as pendant to no. 302. The bent tree trunks on the left still evoke Flemish prototypes. The shepherdess has the facial type often encountered in Tempesta's late works.

296, 297 PASTORAL LANDSCAPES
ISOLA BELLA
98 × 122 cm. A pair. The second is signed on a rock in the center 'C. P. t. F.,' possibly followed by a date. Both pictures share the same inner proportions and the motive of tall rocks and water in the foreground.

298 LANDSCAPE
PRIVATE COLLECTION, COMERIO (VARESE)
115 × 175 cm. In the center, a burning citadel.
LIT. Nicodemi, in *L'Arte* 1958, p. 443.

299 PASTORAL LANDSCAPE
ISOLA BELLA
95 × 153 cm. Daylight; the sky dark grey.

300 LANDSCAPE (color plate XI)
ISOLA BELLA
129 × 179 cm. An important, late work. In conformity with the large size, the composition is a complex one, extending over many planes. Comparable, but simpler, is no. 294.

301 PASTORAL LANDSCAPE
BERGAMO, ACCADEMIA CARRARA, no. 924.
97 × 135 cm. The sky blue and white, the mountains blue, the animals brown.
COLL. Count Carrara, 18th c. LIT. Catalog of the museum, by Ricci, 1930.

302 LANDSCAPE WITH BRIDGE (color plate VIII)
ISOLA BELLA
61.5 × 98 cm. Hangs as pendant to no. 295. Highly refined in the execution, this is one of Tempesta's most exceptional works. The type of a landscape with prominently placed bridge goes back to Dutch Italianizing views with Ponte Molle, Ponte Rotto (including fancy views such as Asselijn's ruined bridge belonging to the Duke of Bedford) and to Rosa's so-called Ponte Rotto at Tivoli (Florence, Pitti). On the other hand, the type anticipates works of the eighteenth century (M. Ricci). The

scenery looks imaginary, but composition and coloring in gay hues give it a freshness and convincing naturalness suggestive of a work done from nature. Compare, from the same years, a fine landscape with a dominating bridge by Pandolfo Reschi (Florence, Pitti; exh. Florence 1969, fig. 74).

303 NOCTURNAL PASTORAL RIVER LANDSCAPE
ART MARKET, as Gaspard.
95 × 141 cm. A characteristic work by Tempesta. This compositional pattern was dear to the artist and occurs in several variants such as nos. 308, 285, the latter showing likewise a burning citadel at the upper right. The type of image remained influential throughout the eighteenth century.

304 PASTORAL LANDSCAPE
PRIVATE COLLECTION, GENOA
72 × 95 cm. Signed below the goat 'Cavaglier Pietro Tempesta fecit 1701.' Darkish blue-green atmosphere, but more likely sunlight than moonlight. The poses and dresses of the figures suggest that they are not merely pastoral but may illustrate a literary scene such as Granida and Daifilo.
COLL. In a French collection until 1927. LIT. Giolli, in *Rassegna d'Arte* 1914, p. 278 (wrongly as dated 1700). Haumann, 1927, p. 14. Bonzi, in *Il Raccoglitore Ligure* 1932, no. 2.

305 PASTORAL LANDSCAPE
PRIVATE COLLECTION, GENOA
60 × 75 cm. Signed at the bottom right 'Milano 1700. Cavaglier Pietro. Tempesta fecit' (no. 306). Vivid yellowish-green tints, with brown animals and blue mountains.

306 DETAIL OF NO. 305

307 NOCTURNAL LANDSCAPE
ARCUGNANO (VICENZA), COUNT GIUSEPPE CANERA DI SALASCO
38 × 63 cm. Signed on a stone at the lower left center 'Cavaglier Pietro Tempesta.' Late. Compare similarly no. 311.
COLL. Morandotti, Rome, 1965. LIT. Donzelli, 1967, fig. 432.

308, 309 NOCTURNAL PASTORAL LAKE SCENE.
PASTORAL LANDSCAPE
ISOLA BELLA
62 × 87 cm. The two pictures hang as a pair. Both have comparably dark tints, but while the first is clearly a nocturnal scene, the other shows a storm-laden daylight. The first compares, among others, with no. 278.

310 NOCTURNAL LANDSCAPE
MILAN, BRERA
52 × 81 cm. Dark blue-green tones. The motive of the fire echoes a painting by Claude (*Liber Veritatis 59*).
COLL. Oggioni, 1855. LIT. Catalog of the museum, by Malaguzzi Valeri, 1908, no. 631.

311 NOCTURNAL PASTORAL LAKE SCENE
ISOLA BELLA
43 × 63 cm. Signed below the resting cow 'Cavaglier P. Tempesta.' Hangs as pendant to no. 232. Dark green tints.

312 LANDSCAPE WITH SHEEP
ISOLA BELLA
53 × 77 cm. Yellowish tints. Possibly signed at the bottom right. Late. In the distance, peasants are seen to pursue the wolf who injured the sheep of the foreground. For a Dutch prototype, compare an engraving with sheep and a large tree on the left by F. Bloemaert after his father Abraham. The picture type continues well into the eighteenth century (Londonio).

313 PASTORAL LANDSCAPE
VIENNA, KUNSTHISTORISCHES MUSEUM, no. 1327.
56 × 70 cm. A small example of a characteristic type of pastorals with large, realistic animals in the foreground. They reflect the influence of Castiglione. The oblique tree trunk is a frequent motive in seventeenth century landscape (Tempesta, Poussin, Testa, d'Arthois, etc.).
COLL. In the museum by 1824. LIT. Catalog of the museum, of 1938, no. 1327.

314 VIEW WITH SHEPHERDESS AND FLOCKS
STUTTGART, STATE GALLERY, no. 518, as 'J. H. Roos?'
129.5 × 197.5 cm. Inscribed by a later hand on the verso 'Caval. Tempesta fecit.' A late work of a particularly realistic effect in the life-sized animals. The girl shows the familiar facial type found in many other late pictures.

Another, similar work by Tempesta was listed in 1760 in a Brescian collection (see p. 137).
COLL. Bought in 1724 from Osiander, as Tempesta. LIT. Catalog of the museum, by Lange, 1907, p. 147, no. 359, as 'J. H. Roos?'

315 PASTORAL SCENE
PRAGUE, NATIONAL GALLERY, no. O. 113.
58 × 72.5 cm. Signed on a stone block at the bottom right 'Cavaglier P. Tempesta fc. 1700.' Compare the preceding, larger picture. Similar passages of animals and figures occur furthermore in some large, late landscapes such as no. 322 (1696). The type of image anticipates the eighteenth century.
COLL. Czernin, Prague, before 1843. LIT. Catalog of the museum, of 1912, no. 427.

316 ANNUNCIATION TO THE SHEPHERDS
PRIVATE COLLECTION, MILAN
190 × 223 cm. Strong brown tints. A late work, which owes its unusual effect to the life-size animals, the warm coloring, and the strict surface structure emphasized by color and design. The type compares to nos. 321 and 323, yet the shepherds of the Annunciation may here be those of the foreground, not the minuscule distant group. The picture ultimately derives from the Bassani, Castiglione (cf. a picture in Vienna repr. by Delogu, 1928, pl. 60), Aertsen, Beuckelaer, and Vincenzo Campi.
LIT. Nicodemi, in *L'Arte* 1958, p. 443.

317, 318 ANIMALS IN LANDSCAPE, WITH IO AS A COW. ANIMALS IN LANDSCAPE, WITH MERCURY AND BATTUS
PRIVATE COLLECTION, CARATE BRIANZA (MILAN)
207 × 276 cm. The first is signed on the stone at the bottom right 'Cavaglier. Pietro Temp. FECIT. 1700.' The second is signed on the lower left border 'Cavagl.r P. Temp.ta. FECIT 1700.' Both dates are difficult to read. A pair, being Tempesta's largest extant works (after the early tempest no. 90). In conformity with the size, the handling is exceptionally broad. Both pictures have warm tones in the foreground, the first with a cool blue sky, the latter with a yellow and violet sky. The compositions complement each other. They are the culmination of a type of huge pastorals with life-size animals of a strikingly realistic effect. As in several of the following works, a rather insignificant subject is placed into the

distance–here two scenes from the story of Io, the first showing the white cow Io with nymphs and her father Inachus in a rather free rendering of the Ovidian source, the other Mercury testing Battus (pentimenti in the figures). Bassanesque inspiration is felt in the form, the handling, and the coloring.
COLL. Bought from an old Lombard collection in 1967.

319 LANDSCAPE WITH DOGS AND DYING WOLF
ROME, GALLERIA CAPITOLINA
165 × 205 cm. Dark green tones; sky pink and violet. A stately, late work.
COLL. Bequest Marquess Paolo Mereghi.

320, 321 LANDSCAPE WITH THE DESTRUCTION OF SODOM AND GOMORRAH. LANDSCAPE WITH THE ANNUNCIATION TO THE SHEPHERDS
VADUZ, PRINCE OF LIECHTENSTEIN
199 × 181 cm. The first is signed at the lower right 'Cavagliere P. Tempesta 1696 fecit.' A capital, large pair showing nocturnal scenes with supernatural light effects. The subject of the first is treated rather freely; the figures in the foreground must be interpreted as Lot and his family. The second has the same theme as nos. 316, 323, which contain similar motives.
COLL. From Baron Jos. Hugo von Hagen, Vienna, late 18th c. LIT. Catalog of the collection, of 1873, nos. 321, 323 (wrongly as 'Abraham and the angel?')

322 PASTORAL LANDSCAPE WITH THE FLIGHT INTO EGYPT (color plate IX)
GENEVA, MUSEE D'ART ET D'HISTOIRE
115 × 160 cm. Signed on the fountain 'Cavagl P Tempesta 1696.' Pendant to the seastorm no. 116. A masterpiece with a densely filled composition. Compare no. 323, which also shows the same figure types.
COLL. Gift G. Revilliod.

323, 324 LANDSCAPE WITH THE ANNUNCIATION TO THE SHEPHERDS (color plate XIII).
LANDSCAPE WITH THE CALVARY
ISOLA BELLA
136 × 165 cm. A large pair, ranking among Tempesta's masterpieces of the late period. Both show, in a supernatural illumination, large pastoral scenes in the foreground with figures watching, as mere spectators, the distant religious events which relate to the birth and death of Christ. The facial types are those often en-

countered in Tempesta's late works. Northern mannerist traits can still be felt in composition and in details (in the first work, the placing of the subject into the distance; in the second, the classicizing design of the shepherdesses). The Annunciation recalls in its layout and in numerous details the large painting of the same subject by Wtewael (Amsterdam; cf. Lindeman, *J. A. Wtewael*, 1929, p. 79).

325 LANDSCAPE WITH THE CALVARY
PRIVATE COLLECTION
136 × 210 cm. Signed on the rock in the center 'Cavaglier P.T.' An important, late painting. Compare the preceding.
LIT. Nicodemi, in *L'Arte* 1958, p. 443.

326 PASTORAL LANDSCAPE
BRESCIA, PINACOTECA, no. 646 (lent to the Loggia).
131 × 200 cm. Signed above the sleeping dog 'Cavagliere / Pietro Tempesta / Brescia 1697.' Dark brownish tints; the sun appears in the center left. Further back, a group of small fishermen pulling in their nets. The traditional title 'the rest of St. John' does not correspond to an extant iconographic scene, nor does the male figure conform to the traditional rendering of John the Evangelist or the Baptist. But the fervor expressed by this figure may account for a generic religious interpretation. Joseph besieged by doubts? The two faces are the same found in other late pastorals (322 f.).
COLL. From the church of Sta. Giulia, Brescia. Bequest Ferioli Mignani, late 19th c.

327 NATIVITY
BURGHLEY HOUSE, MARQUESS OF EXETER, no. 500.
115.5 × 165 cm. Traces of a signature on the stone at the lower left. Similar individual figures occur in several other works from the late years (322 f.), thus suggesting a date in the Lombard phase. The execution appears less fine than in other cases, but this may be owing to the unsatisfactory state of preservation.
COLL. and LIT. See no. 213. This picture only came from Signor Gabiani in Florence, presumably bought by the ninth Earl of Exeter between 1750 and 1794.

328 AGONY IN THE GARDEN
BURGHLEY HOUSE, MARQUESS OF EXETER, no. 250.
70 × 57 cm. Supernatural light on the left, moonlight

landscape on the right. This and the following four works, all at Burghley, form an unparalleled group of small religious figure pieces done in an exceptionally sweet style which brings to mind the manner of Lauri (42 ff.) and of Trevisani in Rome and certain late aspects of Luca Giordano. The whole group must date from the Lombard years and was probably the result of a specific commission. The figures show many affinities with those in late, large paintings (compare in particular the preceding, large Nativity, also at Burghley). The figures in the present picture, of pre-rococo elegance, recall the small Riposo no. 230. Two pictures among this group show outspoken Bassanesque traits (331 f.).
COLL. and LIT. See no. 213.

329   THE FINDING OF MOSES
BURGHLEY HOUSE, MARQUESS OF EXETER,
no. 278.
32.5 × 41 cm. Pendant to the next work, representing the adoration of the shepherds. The combination in a pair of these Old and New Testament subjects is unique, although both have in common the appearance of a child. See no. 328.

330   ADORATION OF THE SHEPHERDS
BURGHLEY HOUSE, MARQUESS OF EXETER,
no. 284.
35 × 42 cm. Signed on the stone at the bottom left 'Cavalier P. Tempesta.' See the preceding.

331   ANNUNCIATION TO THE SHEPHERDS
BURGHLEY HOUSE, MARQUESS OF EXETER,
no. 451.
37 × 34.5 cm. Pendant to the next work. Nocturnal light. In the distance are tiny shepherds to whom angels appear in the clouds. The picture is a small variant of Tempesta's large no. 321, of 1696, some motives being even closer to no. 323. See no. 328.

332   ADORATION OF THE SHEPHERDS
BURGHLEY HOUSE, MARQUESS OF EXETER,
no. 459.
37 × 34.5 cm. See the preceding.

333   NOCTURNAL LANDSCAPE
PRIVATE COLLECTION, GENOA
65 × 99 cm. The composition compares with nos. 295, 303. The style of this and the following work–possibly

a pendant–comes very close to the young Tavella (384).
COLL. Genoese art market.

334   PASTORAL LANDSCAPE
PRIVATE COLLECTION, GENOA
65 × 99 cm. See the preceding.

335   PASTORAL LANDSCAPE
MILAN, CASTELLO SFORZESCO
109 × 161 cm. The picture is not in optimal condition. The composition is entirely in the spirit of Tempesta; compare nos. 293 f. But some doubts arise about the execution; possibly a studio work.
COLL. Bequest Tanzi. LIT. Catalog of the museum, c. 1920, no. 241, as manner of Tempesta.

336   LANDSCAPE
PRIVATE COLLECTION, ROME
42 × 57 cm. Green and yellowish-brown tints. This delightful, small landscape is less severe and dramatic than most works by Tempesta and anticipates much of the flavor of Tavella's late paintings and of Zuccarelli. The setting compares with some other small works by Tempesta (223, 232, the former upright). In the first place, the picture is characterized by an especially fluid handling which has its closest parallel in other small works such as nos. 238 f. (Compare also no. 287.)

337   PASTORAL LANDSCAPE
PRIVATE COLLECTION, BRUSSELS
94 × 123 cm. Though hitherto considered to be by Bourdon, this richly composed work is in my opinion a masterpiece by Tempesta, comparable with nos. 300 f. for the layout, 295 for the large trees, 260 ff. for the figures, and 283 for the building.

338   LANDSCAPE
PRIVATE COLLECTION, CHICAGO
208 × 254 cm. A large, complex composition which brings to mind the even larger mountainous landscape of Lord Bute (257). Compare also the Burghley Tempestinos (364 ff.).
COLL. Bought in Florence, 1948.

339   PASTORAL LANDSCAPE
PRIVATE COLLECTION
98.5 × 132 cm. Known to me only from photograph.

The composition compares with several late works by Tempesta (258, 293, 300, 335).
COLL. Sale Milan, Finarte, 15 May 1962, lot 56.

340 STORMY LANDSCAPE
WARSAW, NATIONAL MUSEUM, no. 210279,
as Tavella.
47 × 71 cm. At the upper left, a burning citadel struck by lightning. Known to me only from the photograph. The composition and the density of the forms seem to me characteristic of Tempesta. For the figures, compare no. 251.
EXH. Warsaw, National Museum, *Italian Painting*, 1956, as Tavella. LIT. *Emporium* 1956, p. 236, as Tempesta.

341, 342 PASTORAL LANDSCAPES
LIGURIAN PRIVATE COLLECTION
Size unavailable; probably medium or small. Known to me only from the photographs. Apparently companion pieces, these works were on the Genoese art market in the 1940's, baptized Solfarolo by a dealer. Both compositions are characteristic of Tempesta. Yet, the second work, with a burning city in the distance, shows a particularly romantic mood, and though it is clearly by the same hand as the companion piece, its execution seems more unusual for Tempesta.

343 PASTORAL LANDSCAPE
LIGURIAN PRIVATE COLLECTION
Size unavailable. Known to me only from the photograph, which does not permit a definitive opinion. Setting and handling are confusingly close to Tempesta, but seem at the same time somewhat more saturated and romantic, pointing into the direction of Roncelli. The brushwork is similar to the preceding pair, which comes from the same source.
COLL. From the Genoese art market, 1940's.
The attribution of nos. 343–349 to Tempesta raises certain doubts which cannot be settled in a definitive way. The possibility of a participation by studio hands must also be considered.

344 PASTORAL LANDSCAPE
BRESCIA, PINACOTECA, no. 645, as imitator of Tempesta (lent to the Loggia).
130 × 199 cm. Orange-violet clouds. Further back on the right, a stag hunt. In accordance with the large size, the composition is complex. The picture is of good quality,

very close to Tempesta. Compare for the layout nos. 279, 335. Certain details, including the hunting scene, point to the participation of a studio hand. See no. 343.
COLL. Bequest Ferioli Mignani, late 19th century. Not listed by Calabi, 1933, among the Tempestas.

345 EXPULSION FROM PARADISE
PRIVATE COLLECTION, GENOA
77 × 100 cm. In the center, small, God on clouds, expelling Adam and Eve from Paradise. The animals are to a great extent identical with those of Tempesta's Sacrifice of Noah (240), but the arrangement of the whole, as well as the execution, are somewhat stiffer, suggesting that this may be a studio work from the Genoese years.

346, 347 SEASCAPE. COAST VIEW
PRIVATE COLLECTION
28 × 63 cm. This pair and the following work, which come from the same collection, are small pictures of good quality, extremely close to Tempesta, although possibly by studio hands. The marine with rough sea recalls the pictures of Mulier the elder (54) in the layout, but the coloring of the sky, ranging from dark grey-violet to pink, derives from Tempesta. The coast view shows the same motives as pictures of this type by Tempesta (277).

348 COAST VIEW
PRIVATE COLLECTION
48 × 71 cm. See the preceding.

349 LANDSCAPE
UNKNOWN LOCATION
95 × 135 cm. Known to me only from the photograph, which does not allow a conclusive judgment. On account of the stylistic vicinity of no. 286, this is very likely a genuine work.

349a (fig. 452) PASTORAL LANDSCAPE
PRIVATE COLLECTION, NEW YORK
33 × 42.5 cm. Yellow clouds. A small, but excellent and dense example from Tempesta's Lombard phase. The composition compares with several works, in particular nos. 279, 293 f., 335, 339.

349b (fig. 453) PASTORAL LANDSCAPE
KASSEL, Museum, no. 502.
91 × 121 cm. Much damaged. A peasant family resting

in front of the hut. I know this painting only from the photograph. On this evidence, the traditional attribution to Tempesta seems entirely justified. The composition and the small size of the figures differ from the classical style of the Lombard works and suggest a date in the Genoese or Roman phase.

COLL. It seems to be one of a pair of mountainous landscapes with animals and figures near the water, listed in the 1783 catalog of the princely Hessen-Cassel collection, p. 169, nos. 23 f. Can be traced in the museum since c. 1830. The pendant is unknown.

349c (fig. 454) ANTONIO BELLUCCI AND TEMPESTA
Bellucci: Pieve di Soligo, Treviso, 1654–1727.
DIANA AND CALLISTO
VENICE, ACCADEMIA, on loan to the Prefettura.
Lanzi (1809, vol. III, p. 264) was the first to point out the connection between Tempesta and the master of elegant mythological figure scenes: Bellucci 'worked more felicitously in small figures and added them to the landscapes of the renowned Tempesta.' The collaboration can only have taken place during Tempesta's often interrupted Venetian years, 1687–1690. In 1760, a painting in a Brescian collection was described as a landscape by Tempesta with figures by Bellucci (see here p. 137). No such picture has been identified so far, nor can the figures in any of Tempesta's landscapes be ascribed to Bellucci. Since Tempesta was an expert figure painter for his own needs, it may be that the two quoted mentions refer in reality to figure pieces by Bellucci, to which Tempesta could have added the landscape. In 1958/60, Pilo attributed to Bellucci and Tempesta a set of eight oval, upright canvases (53 × 50 cm.) with mythological subjects, coming from Palazzo Reale, Venice, and now in the private apartments of the Prefettura, Venice (Pilo, in *Arte Veneta* 1958, p. 168, and 1959/60, p. 129, one repr.; Donzelli, 1967, p. 87). Close to Liberi in the figures, these pictures were first mentioned in 1922, when two of them figured as Liberi in the *Mostra della pittura italiana del '600 e del '700*, Florence, Pitti, and were reproduced as such by Nugent in 1930 (*Alla Mostra della pitt. it.,* vol. II, p. 345 f.). The attribution to Bellucci and Tempesta is wholly convincing. Tempesta added to some of these figure pieces a discreet landscape backdrop in mellow tones, which blends in perfectly with the figures (some pictures among the group show hardly any landscape). The largest landscape portion appears in Diana and Actaeon (repr. Nugent); three works only show sky. For the foliage, cf. no. 226.

350–363 SCHOOL WORKS

A selection of landscapes by anonymous imitators illustrating the widespread wave of imitations to which Tempesta's Lombard works gave rise. Most of them go under his name.

350 COAST VIEW
PRIVATE COLLECTION
95 × 120 cm. Less thoroughly worked out than Tempesta, but similar to him in the composition (cf. 271, 278).

351 LANDSCAPE
UNKNOWN LOCATION
Size unavailable; probably medium. This work and a contrastingly arranged pendant with a shepherd in the center foreground were formerly on the art market in Bergamo. Close imitations of Tempesta's late style.

352 NOCTURNAL LANDSCAPE WITH FIRE
PRIVATE COLLECTION
40 × 54 cm. By a close follower of Tempesta. The composition compares with nos. 308–311, but the handling is less refined (compare the quality of the small no. 243).

353 LANDSCAPE
UNKNOWN LOCATION
72.5 × 102 cm. Known to me only from the photograph. Judging from the handling perhaps a school work (compare no. 339).
COLL. G. Arnot, dealer, London, by 1926.

354 LANDSCAPE
MILAN, BRERA, as Tempesta (deposited in Rome, Cassa del Mezzogiorno).
58 × 84 cm. Despite the rock formations, the composition has a serenity and classical tenor owing to the calm

green tones and the emphasis on horizontals and verticals. It imitates Tempesta (290) and the late style of Tavella (385). There is a contrastingly composed pendant, without rocks.
COLL. C.F. Longhi, 1839. LIT. Catalog of the museum, by Malaguzzi Valeri, 1908, nos. 668, 677 (pair), as Tempesta.

355 LANDSCAPE
STUTTGART, STATE GALLERY, no. 248, as Molyn.
133 × 175 cm. The traditional attribution refers no doubt to Tempesta, whose style this large painting, datable around 1700, indeed reflects. Compare similar compositions with high horizons in Tempesta (293–301). But the more detailed execution of this work and specific passages of the foreground and of the buildings point to an imitator.

356 PASTORAL LANDSCAPE
PRIVATE COLLECTION, BRESCIA
130 × 170 cm. Compare nos. 299 (setting) and 266 (figures). The handling is more fluid than in Tempesta.

357 LANDSCAPE
MILAN, CASTELLO SFORZESCO
118 × 150 cm. Compare no. 204.
COLL. Bequest Bolognini. LIT. Catalog of the museum, c. 1920, no. 240, as manner of Tempesta.

358 LANDSCAPE
PRIVATE COLLECTION, MILAN
116 × 91 cm. By an immediate follower of Tempesta. A slightly more romantic note in the loaded atmosphere already points to the direction of the early Marco Ricci and of Tavella.

359 PASTORAL LANDSCAPE
PRIVATE COLLECTION, BRESCIA
60 × 45 cm. Compare nos. 220f. There is a contrastingly arranged pendant representing a nocturnal coast view.

MUNICH, BAVARIAN STATE COLLECTIONS, nos. 922, 923, as Tempesta.
Landscape with Hagar and Ishmael. Landscape with Narcissus and Echo. 72 × 97 cm. Though traditionally ascribed to Tempesta, this broadly painted pair belongs in the orbit of Rosa.

NOTRE DAME, IND., UNIVERSITY OF NOTRE DAME, as Tempesta.
Landscape with Mercury and Argus. 168.5 × 128.5 cm. Though published several times as a work of Tempesta, this fine painting does not, in my estimate, belong in his orbit. The type of trees, the shape of the mountains, and the baroque figure style all are foreign to him. Probably a contemporary Dutch or Flemish work for which I have no conclusive attribution.
COLL. Gift Findlay, Chicago, 1956. LIT. *Handbook* of the museum, 1967, no. 25. EXH. Notre Dame, *Four Hundred Years of Landscape Painting,* 1961. Urbana, University of Illinois, Krannert Art Museum, *Paintings From … Notre Dame,* 1962, catalog by D. Miller, no. 3, repr. (Also *Art Journal* 1962, p. 259, repr.).

ART MARKET
A landscape advertised by Pars gallery, Milan, in *Burl. Mag.,* Dec. 1969, p. XXXVI, has nothing to do with Tempesta.

360–363 COPIES AFTER TEMPESTA
Only a reader unfamiliar with the abundance of copies after old masters will be surprised at the numerous copies which exist of Tempesta's paintings. As in the case of so many artists, the problem of authenticity is at times insoluble. We must, moreover, bear in mind the 'numerous young pupils who frequented his school' (Pascoli); they obviously did many of the studio repetitions and imitations. Five examples of contemporary repetitions are given here. The first pair may be a studio work done on commission, with the participation of Tempesta. The others are inferior to the originals, their brushwork is clearly not that of Tempesta. While in such comparisons the difference between original and copy is fairly evident, the problem may be difficult in cases where we cannot compare two versions.

360 COPY AFTER NO. 255.
MILAN, CASTELLO SFORZESCO
61 × 71 cm. This and the following work are contemporary copies by other hands after no. 255. They are somewhat larger and more elongated than the original; the execution is less refined. Both show slightly different figures, and the lightning is omitted in both.

361 COPY AFTER NO.255.
CREMONA, PINACOTECA, no.265, as Tavella.
100 × 122 cm. See the preceding and the marine no.123, by Tavella, which hangs as the pendant to this picture. Here, the handling does not stand up to the mastery of Tavella.

362 COPY OF NO.277.
PRIVATE COLLECTION
109 × 157 cm. This work and its pendant, which is signed like no.276, correspond in every detail to the original pair nos.276f. The contrast of appearance is emphasized by the condition: the originals are freshly cleaned, the repetitions are covered by varnish, damaged along the bottom; but they are of fair quality, only certain details such as the figures being inferior to the originals. Possibly contemporary studio works.

363 COPY OF NO.281.
PRIVATE COLLECTION, BRESCIA
98 × 109 cm. Contemporary copy of the left three quarters of no.281. The coloring is much sharper, the handling too crude for Tempesta. Possibly from his atelier. This copy is one of a series of four works by the same hand and in the same collection. The three others, at the moment still very dirty, are in the taste of Tempesta, but apparently not copies. One of them represents a coast view with a citadel and mountains on the left, an unclear mythological scene on the right (from the story of Jason?).

364–408 THE PUPILS

364–375 TEMPESTINO

The dossier of this early collaborator of Tempesta consists entirely of question marks and uncertainties. The only early mentions in the sources occur in Pascoli and Orlandi. According to Pascoli, 1730 (see here p.10), Tempestino was the prime pupil of Tempesta in Rome. The master married the pupil's sister. Later biographers merely repeat this information, except for the generally well-informed Lanzi, who specifies that Tempestino 'painted more often Poussinesque landscapes' (1795; see here p.14). Orlandi reports as early as 1704 in the *Life* of Girolamo Odam, born 1681, that Odam practiced landscape painting 'with the principles obtained from Domenico dei Marchis, called il Tempestino.' Is this the same Tempestino? In the biography of Domenico Tempesti, the Florentine portraitist (c.1655–1733), Lanzi states that the portraitist was called Tempestino and was probably identical with the Domenico dei Marchis listed by Orlandi. Lanzi was, however, mistaken, for the Florentine Tempesti was neither called Tempestino, nor did he paint landscapes. Nagler, *sub* Domenico Tempesti, gets the matter further mixed up. The question still stands whether Tempesta's pupil was identical with Domenico de'Marchis or not. Tempesta's wife was Lucia Rossi (not widowed), and her brother would hence have to be a Rossi, too, not a Marchis; it is difficult to get around this. On the other hand, Tempesta's letters from prison make several times mention of 'Domenico di Marche' and his family in Rome, who were agreeing to a reconciliation (e.g., letter of 4 August 1681); the context is never quite clear, but in view of Orlandi's statement, it would seem that Domenico de'Marchis was Tempesta's assistant Tempestino. Whatever the answer is, the sources make it evident that Tempestino was the brother-in-law of Tempesta and his pupil and collaborator in Rome at an early date. The apprenticeship must have initiated soon after 1655, when Tempesta, aged twenty, arrived in Rome. Tempestino may not have been much younger than the master. He did not live with the entire family in Tempesta's house. After the murder of Lucia, her brother, i.e., Tempestino, accused Tempesta in court in Genoa, though he did so too late. Turning to the works, we have the following mentions of paintings by Tempestino:

1690 – 'Tempestini' is being paid for landscape paintings executed in 1688 on the façades of houses at S. Quirico (which probably refers to the church of this name in Rome). See V. Golzio, *Documenti artistici sul seicento nell'archivio Chigi*, Rome 1939, p.348.

1699 – Alessandro Savorgnan at S. Agnese, Venice, owns 'two small landscapes of c.1¼ quarters, by Tempestin' (Levi, 1900, vol.II, p.97); very surprising in Venice, and perhaps a confusion with Tempesta.

1713 – The manuscript death inventory of Prince Livio Odescalchi, in the Odescalchi archives, Rome, mentions under nos.1524 and 1525 'a canvas, 2¾ palms wide, 2 palms high, represents an original landscape by Tempestino with figures. Another entirely similar.'

1786 – The death inventory of Carlo Marchionni, Rome, contains a pair of 'sea storms, 1 *testa* wide, by Tempestini' (besides a small, oblong 'maritime scene' by Tempesta; information kindly supplied by Anthony Clark).

1794 – The Doria Pamphilj catalog lists on pp. 232, 233 'a small landscape by Tempestino. And two landscapes by Tempestino' (see below).

1807 – The valuation of the Rondinini collection, Rome, lists ten landscapes by 'Tempestino scolaro di Gasparo Pusino' and 'Tempestino scola di Pusino': nos. 34 (4 pictures, 233 × 163 cm.), 56 (oblong overdoor, 93 cm. wide), 127, 234 (two oblong pictures, 93 cm. wide), 297 (*idem*). See L. Salerno, *Palazzo Rondinini*, Rome 1965, p. 283

1835 – First mention of two small sea storms (see below).

1847 – First mention of four landscapes belonging to Lord Exeter, Burghley House (see below).

1847 – Two paintings exhibited in London by Lord Bute as 'Dom. Tempesta' (here nos. 257 f.). This can only be a mistake and serves as a warning, for the paintings are known to have been done for Padua and are beyond doubt by Tempesta.

The only extant paintings given to Tempestino are two small sea storms in Valencia (119 f.), four large landscapes at Burghley, and two or three in the Doria gallery. For those at Burghley, see no. 213; they are first mentioned in 1847 as 'Tempesta or D. Tempestino,' by contrast with eight others listed as 'Molyn-Tempesta;' the four are now regarded at Burghley as by Tempestino. Difficult to appreciate because of excessive darkening, they show a close affinity with the landscapes by Tempesta – which means the landscapes of Tempesta's Lombard phase. An intimate resemblance with the works of the master is what we should expect from his closest assistant. If, then, the attribution of the Burghley pictures is correct, they reflect the art of Tempesta's Roman phase, from which no landscapes on canvas survive or can be identified. This is, however, inseparable from Gaspardism at large. In 1795 and 1807, Tempestino was in fact referred to as a follower and pupil respectively of Gaspard. The difference between the Burghley Tempestinos and Tempesta's Lombard landscapes lies in Tempestino's somewhat cruder handling, in the tiny figures, in the particularly voluminous clouds, and, mainly, in his severe, more Gaspardesque character, which in turn confirms the in-

fluence of Gaspard on Tempesta in Rome. As to the Doria Pamphilj Tempestinos, the large pair is of excellent quality but almost undistinguishable from Onofri's Roman style; whereas the third work, of lesser merit and uncertain attribution, shows a generic Gaspardesque style. Finally, there are five drawings by Tempestino. A small pair of landscapes with Old Testament stories on onyx at Orléans (nos. 1197 f.), bearing an old label 'Donato-Tempestino' are so different (reminiscent of Pynas) that they can be disregarded here.

364–367 PASTORAL LANDSCAPES
BURGHLEY HOUSE, MARQUESS OF EXETER, nos. 511, 472, 486, 487, as D. Tempestino.
All are damaged by creases and have darkened.
364: 117.5 × 160 cm. The castle is a common motive also in Tempesta (243).
365: 118.5 × 168 cm.
366: 118.5 × 171 cm.
367: 119.5 × 164.5 cm. Landscape with hurricane.
COLL. and LIT. See no. 213.

368, 369 LANDSCAPES
ROME, GALLERIA DORIA PAMPHILJ
74 × 165 cm. The two pictures do not show a complete stylistic identity, but this may be owing to differences in preservation. Of notable quality, not intimately connected with Tempesta, the pictures bring to mind a number of Roman works by Onofri in the succession of Gaspard. The compositions derive ultimately from Gaspard. Tempestino may have been a gifted imitator of several artists.
LIT. Doria catalogs of 1794, p. 232, and 1819, both times as Tempestino. Sestieri, 1942, nos. 564, 565, as 'Tempestino?.' Not in the modern Doria catalogs.

370 LANDSCAPE
ROME, GALLERIA DORIA PAMPHILJ (now in Villa Doria Pamphilj).
96 × 134 cm. Dark. On the right, a river. The composition is Gaspardesque. Compare also Claude's landscape with Narcissus and Echo of 1644 in London.
LIT. Cannot be identified with certainty in the Doria catalog of 1794 (unless it is the 'small landscape' by Tempestino, p. 233). Doria catalog of 1819, as Tempestino. Sestieri, 1942, no. 571, as 'Tempestino?.' Not in the modern Doria catalogs.

371–375 DRAWINGS BY TEMPESTINO

The following five nature drawings of trees appeared on the Genoese art market in 1966. They are of rather slight merit. They had been mounted in an album of mixed contents and were labeled Tempestino in the eighteenth century. There is no reason to doubt the accuracy of this attribution, since the style is compatible with what we might expect from a minor artist of c. 1660 in the orbit of Gaspard and Rosa. For lack of sufficient evidence, it is impossible to establish to what extent Tempestino's draftsmanship was influenced by Tempesta. But to judge from Tempesta's drawing no. 156, there is every reason to assume that he did indeed determine the style of his assistant. It is likewise difficult to draw a parallel between Tempestino's drawings and paintings.

371: 126 × 94 mm. Blue paper. Grey wash, white heightening.

372: 155 × 97 mm. (Part of the right hand side cut.) Black chalk, brown wash. Derives from certain wash drawings by Claude of about 1640.

373: 197 × 134 mm. Pen and brown ink. The refined, curly pen work and the curved hatchings still betray the influence of the circle of Bril.

374: 185 × 119 mm. Pen. The more fluid handling of this and the following sheet imitates the manner of Rosa and, to a lesser degree, of Grimaldi.

375: 177 × 120 mm. Black chalk, pen.

376–399 CARLO ANTONIO TAVELLA
Milan 1668 – Genoa 1738.

See also nos. 121–123. A special place is given here to this artist, who was not only the most gifted imitator of Tempesta, but also his principal continuator, and indeed an exquisite classicizing landscape painter. The great majority of his oeuvre being located in Ligurian and Lombard private collections, he is hardly known outside of Italy. His art is in no way less personal than that of his contemporaries Marco Ricci, Orizzonte, Locatelli, Zuccarelli. The fame which he enjoyed during his lifetime is reflected in the biography of Ratti (published in 1769), which, like everything by that author, is a fine piece of writing and our most informative source about the painter. In addition, there are some sixty letters by Tavella, in which the theme of painting holds a large place. The son of Genoese parents, he grew up in Milan, where he was the pupil of Grevenbroeck (see no. 129) from 1681 to 1688. After a Genoese sojourn, he returned to Milan in 1695 in order to study with Tempesta, many of whose paintings

he copied. Sojourns in several north Italian towns followed. In 1700–01, he again lived for some time in Tempesta's house. He soon practiced a sweeter, more delicate style than his master. In 1701, he definitively settled in Genoa and lived there a pious life until his death. His late style is increasingly classical, influenced by Claude, but lighter in character and coloring. According to Ratti (Life of Magnasco), Magnasco often added the figures to Tavella's latest landscapes. Both of Tavella's daughters were painters, too.

His oeuvre, which has not been cataloged, must be very vast. Ratti cites three hundred paintings by him belonging to De'Franchi, Genoa. Four overdoors still *in situ* are in Palazzo Balbi, ex Lomellini, Genoa (now Marquess Doria-Lamba). About 80 drawings by him are known, 50 in Palazzo Rosso, eleven minor ones in the Uffizi (nos. s. 7210–7220). Dates on them range from 1693 to 1733.

On Tavella, see Bonzi, in *La Grande Genova*, 1929, p. 181, essentially repeated in his *Il Tavella*, Genoa, ed. 1961; Delogu, 1931, p. 66, reproducing in particular a number of drawings (pl. 73–86). About 60 interesting letters by Tavella are reprinted in M. G. Bottari and S. Ticozzi, *Raccolta di lettere sulla Pittura, Scultura et Architettura*, vol. IV, Milan 1822, p. 23.

376 LANDSCAPE
GENOA, PALAZZO ROSSO

Fresco, 215 × 170 cm. Restored. In 1690–1692, the young Tavella executed in Palazzo Brignole-Sale, now Rosso, four frescoes on the walls of the *Arti Liberali* salon – three still *in situ*, one destroyed – and decorated in fresco the entire bathroom of the mezzanine. These are his earliest known works, and his only frescoes. Each of the salon frescoes forms a separate image. They were originally inserted into a painted architectural framework (partly visible above the top of the frescoes). The coloring is light, the foliage brown and green; river, mountains, and sky are blue. The style of these not yet very personal works precedes Tavella's encounter with Tempesta and is inspired by a motionless classicism derived from the late manner of Claude and from Gaspard.

LIT. *Cat. provvisorio d. Galleria di Palazzo Rosso*, Genoa 1961, p. 29. C. Marcenaro, *Gli affreschi del Palazzo Rosso di Genova*, Genoa 1966, pp. 14, 18 ff., 31, pl. 57 ff.

377 Winter Landscape
Private Collection, Genoa
74 × 62 cm. Bluish tints. An early work. The methodical composition with small motives and a rigid recession achieved by means of the diagonally displayed buildings and the horizontal planes on the left does not yet show the accomplishment of Tavella's later winter scenes such as no. 256.

378 Landscape
Genoa, Palazzo Rosso
Fresco covering the walls and ceiling of a tiny, low bathroom with continuous classicizing landscape views. Dates from 1690–92. Discussed under entry number 376. Partly owing to the unusual space, the type of these pleasant and well-preserved decorations is rather unique. It is a curious coincidence that Tavella, like Tempesta, should have started his career with a fully successful work in fresco, but never reverted to the technique later.
Lit. Marcenaro (cf. no. 376), pl. 72 f.

379 Pastoral Landscape
Genoa, Palazzo Rosso, no. 346.
90 × 127 cm. Though darkened, this is a typical example of Tavella's painting under the direct influence of Tempesta in the years between 1695 and 1700.
Lit. Catalog of the museum, of 1932, fig. 279, reproduced with later additions (oval shape) which have since been removed.

380 Stormy Landscape
Private Collection, Genoa
80 × 113 cm. Corresponds to a drawing by Tavella which was to my mind done after the finished picture (Genoa, Palazzo Rosso, no. B. 857; 267 × 431 mm.; chalk, pen; repr. Bonzi, 1961, pl. 4). A vigorous work, datable 1695–1700, done under the impact of Tempesta's stormy landscapes (252, 276).
Lit. Bonzi, 1961, p. 31.

381 Pastoral Landscape
Private Collection, Yorkshire, as Tempesta.
121 × 171 cm. Although known as by Tempesta, this large painting is in my opinion a stately work by Tavella under Tempesta's influence. The particular handling and the bold rock arch on the right (a motive not found in Tempesta) are especially characteristic for this phase of Tavella. See similarly the preceding work.

Coll. From Scandinavia. Lasson Gallery, London, cat. July 1968, no. 12.

382 Winter Landscape
Private Collection, Genoa
98 × 123 cm. Bluish-grey tints. Datable in the 1720's. The few winter scenes by Tavella derive lastly from Tempesta's no. 256 (but with purely Italianate buildings). Among other winter landscapes by Tavella, one belongs to O. Bagnasco, Genoa (repr. Bonzi, 1961, pl. 16; 50 × 75 cm.), one, dated 1732, to A. Costa, Genoa (repr. Bonzi, pl. 17; one of four seasons, 30 × 25 cm.), and the finest was exhibited in Genoa in 1969, no. 136. These works also bring to mind the few winter landscapes by Marco Ricci: an oil painting in Dresden, and a tempera (Ricci Mostra, 1964, nos. 48, 71; also *ibid.*, nos. 35, 40, are winter scenes; another, similar to the Dresden picture, is repr. in Delogu, 1930, fig. 10, another in Martini, 1964, pl. 84). Compare finally a Riccesque winter landscape by Pedon in the Correr Museum, Venice (Martini, 1964, fig. 106).

383 Pastoral Landscape
Private Collection, Milan
122 × 171 cm. A fine example of a type of large paintings by Tavella done about 1700 in a romantic manner with dominating rock formations, often also with cascades and hermits. Other examples include nos. 381, 393, and Bonzi, 1961, pl. 6, 7. Tempesta, Rosa, Gaspard, and Flemish landscape all belong to the ancestry of this type, which is paralleled at the same time by Panfi (418), the early Marco Ricci, and Magnasco. Among Tempesta's works, compare nos. 249, 287.

384 Pastoral Landscape
Genoa, Collection F. Ravano
86 × 128 cm. Green, yellow, and blue tones. Datable 1695–1700. Corresponds to the drawing no. 390. The composition still reflects the influence of Tempesta; compare, e.g., nos. 249, 301.
Lit. Bonzi, 1961, p. 29. Exh. Dayton, Ohio, Art Institute, *Genoese Masters*, 1962, no. 59.

385 Landscape
Private Collection, Genoa
49 × 75 cm. A fine, late work of the artist, characterized by an uncomplicated layout and a dense, green tonality. The style brings to mind certain late works by Claude such as *Lib. Ver.* 163, 167, 172.

386, 387   PASTORAL LANDSCAPES
GENOA, PALAZZO ROSSO, nos. 139, 140.
99 × 137 cm. An impressive pair, dating from the beginning of the eighteenth century.
LIT. Delogu, 1931, p. 69.

388   PASTORAL LANDSCAPE
GENOA, PALAZZO BIANCO, no. 350.
59 × 127 cm. Based on the heritage of Gaspard and Onofri, this style represents the north Italian equivalent of the contemporary Roman landscapes of Orizzonte and Locatelli.

389   RIVER LANDSCAPE WITH BRIDGE
PRIVATE COLLECTION, GENOA
124 × 156 cm. Reclining figures in the foreground, the *spinario*-type figure despite its Christ-like appearance probably pastoral. I reproduce this unpublished work as an example of the summits reached by the late Tavella. The type of the composition can be followed back to Tempesta (200, 232f., 265, 286). But Tavella achieves here a serenity which echoes Claude, while anticipating most of the spirit and technical brio usually credited to Boucher, Robert, Fragonard, and Vernet. The most captivating aspect of the picture, beautiful beyond words, lies in its coloring: the soft light emanating from the sun right above the bridge creates a sensation of depth prepared only by Claude.
COLL. From an old Genoese collection.

390   LANDSCAPE
GENOA, PALAZZO ROSSO, no. B. 852.
Drawing, 355 × 528 mm. Pen and brown wash on paper tinted yellow-brown. Datable 1695–1700. Corresponds to the painting no. 384, except for the absence of the figures. The lively pen work characterizes Tavella's early years.
COLL. Durazzo.

391   LANDSCAPE
GENOA, PALAZZO ROSSO, no. B. 853.
Drawing, 416 × 360 mm. Pen, brown wash, heightened, on paper tinted yellowish-brown. Nos. 390–393 are elaborate pen and wash drawings of a pictorial effect which must belong to the early years, between 1690 and 1705 by analogy with dated pen drawings (compare nos. 394f.). There are only a few examples of this style. Corresponding paintings probably existed in each case, but only one

is known at present (384). The compositions reflect the influence of Tempesta; the technique probably does also, though this is impossible to prove for lack of evidence. The nearest parallels among Tempesta's drawings are nos. 157f.
COLL. All the fifty or so Tavella drawings in Palazzo Rosso come from the Durazzo collection, Genoa (with numberings).

392   LANDSCAPE WITH ST. JOHN
GENOA, PALAZZO ROSSO, no. B. 854.
Drawing, 385 × 295 mm. Pen, brown wash, heightened, on paper tinted yellowish-brown. See the preceding.

393   ROCKS AND CASCADES
GENOA, PALAZZO ROSSO, no. B. 847.
Drawing, 470 × 362 mm. Pen, brown wash, heightened, on paper tinted yellowish-brown. See no. 391 and, for the motive of rocks, Tempesta's drawing no. 156. Rock arches occur several times in Tavella's paintings (e.g. in the landscape with the Magdalen; Bonzi, 1961, pl. 7).

394   LANDSCAPE WITH TOBIAS AND THE ANGEL
GENOA, PALAZZO ROSSO, no. A. 2124.
Drawing, 203 × 285 mm. Black chalk, pen. Inscribed by the artist on the right 'Di Pal 5. e 4. Per l'Illmo Sig. G. Batt. Torre 1693.' This and the following sheets are, in chronological order, some examples of drawings bearing autograph inscriptions which refer to a corresponding painting measuring, in this case, 5 by 4 palms, oblong. The respective pictures have not yet come to light but may well exist. Very possibly the drawings are not preliminary works, but were done as a matter of record after the finished paintings, somewhat like Claude's *Liber Veritatis* drawings. The penmanship changes very little over the years; it is vigorous in the nineties, calm later on. This drawing, preceding by a short time Tavella's apprenticeship with Tempesta, belongs to the same period as his frescoes nos. 376f.

395   LANDSCAPE WITH ST. JOHN
GENOA, PALAZZO ROSSO, no. A. 2128.
Drawing, 217 × 312 mm. (sheet). Black chalk, pen. Inscribed by the artist along the top 'Di Pal. 3 e 4. Per il Sig. Gio. Batt. Poli Bergamo 1703.' See the preceding. Saints in a wild landscape occur particularly often in Tavella's early phase.

396 LANDSCAPE
GENOA, PALAZZO ROSSO, no. B. 856.
Drawing, 294 × 426 mm. Black chalk, pen. Inscribed by
the artist along the top 'Di Pal. 5 e 7. Per il Sig. Stefano
Banfi Milano 1706.' See no. 394.

397 PASTORAL LANDSCAPE
GENOA, PALAZZO ROSSO, no. A. 2120.
Drawing, 260 × 397 mm. (frame line). Black chalk, pen.
Inscribed by the artist along the top 'Di Pal. 5 e 7. 2. mag-
gio 1729.' See no. 394. A similar composition, in the
same museum, is repr. by Delogu, 1931, fig. 86.

398 AUTUMN LANDSCAPE
GENOA, PALAZZO ROSSO, no. A. 2132.
Drawing, 215 × 310 mm. (sheet). Black chalk, pen. Inscribed by the artist along the top 'Di Pal. 2 e Pal. 1. ½.
Ottobre 1735. Auttuno. Per il Sig. Collonelo Gio. Batta.
Ulloa.' See no. 394. An example from Tavella's last
years. The painting (38 × 50 cm.) is reproduced in *Rubinacci Antichità, Genova, Pittori Genovesi, 1966,* no. 17, together with a pendant (Summer).

399 LANDSCAPE WITH VENUS AND MARS
GENOA, PALAZZO ROSSO, no. B. 855.
Drawing, 386 × 562 mm. (sheet). Pen, grey wash. This
and another sheet of the same size with Apollo and
Daphne (Palazzo Rosso, repr. *La Grande Genova,* 1929,
p. 187) are the artist's largest and most stately drawings.
They date from the middle years and were no doubt done
in connection with a set of painted overdoors.
LIT. Delogu, 1931, p. 71.

400–408 GIUSEPPE RONCELLI
Crete c. 1669–Stezzano (Bergamo) 1729.
The detailed *Vite* of Roncelli published by D. Angelo
Mazzoleni, Milan 1767, and Frc. Maria Tassi (*Vite de' pittori . . . Bergamaschi,* vol. II, Bergamo 1797, p. 41) bear witness to the considerable fame of this colorful personage,
whose life evolved between the poles of a dissipated,
mundane existence, priesthood, and religious fanaticism.
The son of a citizen of Stezzano, he was born in Crete,
returned to Stezzano at the age of six, became a doctor of
theology at the age of twenty. He taught at the seminaries
of Padua, Bergamo, and Crema, often going to Venice
in order to paint. The years from 1691 to 1701 mark his
most intense activity as a painter. About 1692, 'he stayed

for some time in Brescia, painting and also studying under the tutelage of the famous Cav. Tempesta, who was
then living in that town' (Tassi, *loc. cit.*). After 1701, he
settled in Stezzano, teaching at the seminary of Bergamo
from 1713 to his death. Overshadowed by Tempesta and
Marco Ricci, Roncelli has remained virtually ignored in
our time. He produced mainly altarpieces, not very ex-
citing examples of which survive throughout the diocese
of Bergamo (two in the bishop's palace, three in the
church of Stezzano, etc.). Of his landscapes, only a dozen
examples are known so far, but by following up the
works listed in old sources, one would no doubt discover
others in north Italian collections from Milan to Venice.
'His particular talent lay in representing with great naturalness and perfection the atmospheres – be they inflamed
at sunrise or sunset, or nocturnal views – with all kinds of
reflections of the sun and the various accidents deriving
from it, especially in the water of the sea and the rivers.
He thus had a very beautiful and pleasant manner of
painting, except that his last works, leaning towards a
single color, yellow, lack the delicacy and harmony of
his earlier works. He excelled singularly in painting nocturnal fires of cities, towns, and buildings with much
truth and with inflamed colors, rendering with unusual
mastery the fire reflected in the water and on other objects nearby . . .' (Tassi, *loc. cit.*). The documented contact
with Tempesta is confirmed by the pictures. Tempesta's
late works must have played a decisive role in the formation of Roncelli's landscape style. The art of Solfarolo,
too, must have been a source of inspiration for him.
Equally important is the impact exercised on him by
Marco Ricci, who was a few years his junior. From Ricci
come the Titianesque mountains and buildings so much
in evidence in Roncelli's pictures. But his art is less inventive, and the romantic aspects of the scenery and of the
atmosphere are over-emphasized. The Santuario group
shows Roncelli reverting to Flemish landscape formulas
from around 1600, which are rendered in a rococo handling, with incongruous results. The nocturnal fires,
which are a common effect in Tempesta, Tavella, and reputedly in Solfarolo, do not show in Roncelli's extant
works; however, some of his pictures have fiery sunset
skies. As to the dating, a firm base is lacking. After 1713,
he had little time to paint. In all probability, the works
reproduced here date between 1700 and 1713. According
to Lanzi, the figures were often added by Andrea Celesti
(1637–c. 1711, active in Brescia 1688–1700. An example

of this collaboration is in the museum of Nantes; see A. Mucchi and C. Della Croce, *Il pittore Andrea Celesti*, Milan 1954, pp. 38, 86).

LIT. The only modern citations of Roncelli are the short passages in Haumann, 1927, p. 77, and Delogu, 1931, p. 168.

400, 401 LANDSCAPE WITH TOBIAS AND THE ANGEL. LANDSCAPE WITH CHRIST CALLING JAMES AND JOHN
BERGAMO, MUSEO DIOCESANO

106 × 156 cm. A pair of discreetly contrasting compositions. The coloring in blue-green tints for the landscape and orange for the sky is striking. The first work is a rather conventional composition which does not reach the inventiveness of Ricci. The second is in spirit much closer to Ricci, from whom in particular the Titianesque buildings are borrowed. A pair of very similar landscapes is in a Genoese private collection (108 × 160 cm.)

402, 403 LANDSCAPE WITH ABRAHAM AND THE THREE ANGELS. LANDSCAPE WITH THE FINDING OF MOSES
STEZZANO (BERGAMO), COUNT MORONI

257 × 416 cm. Intense orange and green-blue tones; the atmospheres are not contrasting. Disfigured by varnishes and oxidizing. This very large pair, deeply indebted to Tempesta (283) and Marco Ricci and echoing Venetian and Ferrarese Renaissance landscapes, was already praised as one of the artist's masterpieces by Tassi, *loc. cit.* The pictures were painted for the palace in which they still are, but must at first have been in a different, large salon. The other Roncellis done according to Tassi for the same room cannot be traced at present. By analogy with no. 404 probably painted soon after 1700.
LIT. Haumann, 1927, p. 76.

404–407 LANDSCAPES WITH RELIGIOUS SUBJECTS
STEZZANO (BERGAMO), SANTUARIO MADONNA DEI CAMPI

Roncelli became chaplain of this sanctuary soon after 1701; the church had been built in 1664/67. Inserted into the present decoration are eight landscape paintings by him above the arches of the side walls and a larger one above the entrance. The whole decoration must date from soon after 1701. The large landscape (no. 404; 225 × 350 cm.) with the Flight into Egypt corresponds closely to the large pair of Count Moroni. The eight smaller pictures, badly in need of cleaning, measure c. 160 × 200 cm. They consist of two groups. The first four show densely wooded, romantic landscapes in the Flemish manner: no. 405 – the Finding of Moses (?), inspired from Flemish landscape and from Tempesta (large tree); Tobias and the Angel (?), with trees on either side, romantic buildings in the center; St. John in a wooded scenery (compare Claude's large Prado landscapes with hermits); no. 406 – Rest on the Flight, a classical landscape of Gaspardesque derivation. The other four show a type of asymmetrical landscapes with hollow rocks on one side and large figures, painted in a broad, flickering technique. Flemish compositions and Venetian eighteenth-century decoration are blended into an odd style: no. 407 – Journey to Emmaus; Christ and St. Peter; Christ and the Magdalen; the Three Marys at the Tomb.

408 LANDSCAPE
STEZZANO (BERGAMO), COUNT MORONI

65 × 87 cm. Golden sunset illumination. Differing from Roncelli's other landscapes, this personal work gives a measure of the artist's variety. The composition does not derive from Ricci. Setting and handling reveal a last echo of Gaspard, but the mountainous scenery and the bright coloring anchor the picture firmly into the eighteenth century. LIT. Haumann, 1927, p. 76.

409–451 CONTEMPORARY AND LATER ARTISTS

409–411 MARCO RICCI
Belluno 1676 – Venice 1730.
The greatest and most versatile Italian landscape artist of his time. Trained first by his uncle, Sebastiano Ricci, he came early to Venice, killed a gondoliere (a criminal record which parallels that of Tempesta and Bassi), spent

over four years with Peruzzini in Spalato or Lombardy, returned to Venice, moved around considerably, and was influenced by Magnasco. His mature years were spent in Venice, except for two sojourns in England. For lack of dates relating to his youth, there is no proof that he met Tempesta; but he may have done so during the nineties in Milan, where he was also in contact with Magnasco. Ricci certainly saw many of Tempesta's late works and absorbed their qualities to the extent that their influence on him is apparent in large portions of his oeuvre; it is most outspoken in the early phase, but recurs intermittently throughout his life. See on him p.60.

LIT. See mainly Pilo's catalog of the Marco Ricci Mostra at Bassano, publ. Venice 1964, and Zampetti's catalog *I vedutisti veneziani del settecento,* Venice 1967, pp.54ff., with complete lit.

409 LANDSCAPE
MILAN, BRERA, no.787.

106 × 142 cm. Datable around 1715. A compositional scheme of Tempesta (294–299, 333) is here transposed into a more romantic vein.

COLL. Bought 1912. LIT. Haumann, 1927, p.26. Delogu, 1930, p.93. De Logu, *Pittura Veneziana dal XIV al XVIII sec.,* Bergamo 1958, pl.99. Ricci Mostra, 1964, *sub* no.39 (as c.1720).

410, 411 LANDSCAPES
VENICE, ACCADEMIA

137 × 197 cm. One of Ricci's most impressive, mature pairs, datable about 1720. The first evokes the scenery of the Piave valley. Though no longer specifically influenced by Tempesta, the compositions and the entire character of these landscapes reveal to what a profound degree Tempesta's late manner has remained an integral part of Ricci's artistic personality. Compare the first with nos. 236, 286, the second with no.284.

COLL. Corniani-Algarotti, Treviso; bought by Count Zanetti. LIT. Catalogs of the museum, nos.457, 456. Delogu, 1930, p.95. Pallucchini, 1960, p.39. Ricci Mostra, 1964, no.39, with further lit.

412, 413 NOEL COCHIN, CALLED COCHIN DE VENISE
Troyes 1622–Venice 1695.
STORMY PASTORAL LANDSCAPE. LANDSCAPE WITH BRIGANDS
FREDERIKSBORG CASTLE, DENMARK

73 × 95 cm. A pair, bought in Venice in 1668 for the decoration of the long gallery of Frederiksborg Castle. These rather timidly done, but interesting pictures derive partly from Gaspard, partly from the tradition of Titian, to which the romantic character of the light, the skies, and the colorful distance may be credited. The buildings, of Venetian type, form the link between the sixteenth century on one hand, Marco Ricci, Roncelli (403), and Watteau on the other. The stylistic origin of the pictures points *ipso facto* to an affinity with Tempesta (298, 300), although this link may be a matter of *genius loci* and of *Zeitgeist.* The two artists may have met in Venice during the late 1680's. Another picture of a strikingly similar style is no.423. No other works are known by this artist, who is supposed to have come to Venice shortly before 1668. His name does not appear in old inventories of Venetian collections. Félibien mentions Cochin as being esteemed and active in Venice (by 1685) and as having done in Rome a copy of a landscape by Carracci's pupil Viola (*Entretiens,* ed. 1725, vol. III, p.311). According to Nagler, Cochin painted in Venice several works in Callot's manner. I submit that he is identical with the 'Monsu Cussin' praised by Boschini (1660, pp.543f., 600f.), who also reproduces a drawing of his; the latter is quite compatible with the Frederiksborg pictures. According to Boschini, 'Cussin' copied Titian and excelled in 'forests, woods, mountains, plains, lucid days, dark nights, any lovable, beautiful, and worthy site, seasons,' etc. If this identification is correct, Cochin would have settled in Venice in the 1650's, and 'Cussin' could not be identical with one Charles Cussin or Gussin known only for having competed at the Paris Academy in 1688/90.

LIT. H. Olsen, *Italian Paintings and Sculpture in Denmark,* Copenhagen 1961, p.54.

414, 415 FRANCESCO MARIA BASSI THE ELDER, CALLED IL CREMONESE DEI PAESI
Cremona 1642–Venice (?), c.1700.
LANDSCAPES
CREMONA, PINACOTECA, nos.424, 425.

215 × 310 cm. Dark greenish-brown tints. The first is close to the late Tempesta (228, 296, 301) and the earliest Tavella (383). The second is a classicizing mixture of Titianesque, Bolognese, and Gaspardesque elements; compare no.253. These large paintings are at present the only works attributed to Bassi, a landscape painter active first in Cremona, then in Venice. The paintings come from the Municipio in Cremona, where they were attributed unconvincingly to Sigismondo Benini. They are classical landscapes of a harder and somewhat cruder character than Tempesta's works, but not far from his by intention. On Bassi, see first G.B. Zaist, *Notizie istor. de pittori ... Cremonesi,* 1774, pp.113ff. A parallel with Tempesta is in the fact, reported by Zaist, that Bassi poi-

soned his wife. His cousin and pupil Francesco Bassi the younger was a landscape painter of lesser merit active in Cremona until some time after 1750 and, according to Zaist, much esteemed in the later eighteenth century; no works by him can be identified. Bassi figures rather often in old inventories of north Italian collections. Examples: Venice, Bergonzi, 1709, 'by the Cremonese two small landscapes, one with the Magdalen, the other with a shepherd; a painting with a cascade and a washerwoman; two oblong landscapes with soldiers, the other with St. John and other figures' (S. Savini-Branca, *Il collezionismo veneziano nel '600*, Padua 1964, pp. 171 f., 175). In Verona, Marquess Gherardini owned some paintings with figures and animals by him, and Count Dal Pozzo two landscapes (Dal Pozzo, 1718, pp. 286, 309). Lost pictures by Bassi in Spanish collections are described by A. Pérez Sanchez, *Pintura italiana del s. XVII en España*, Madrid 1965, pp. 554 f.

LIT. A. Puerari, *La Pinacoteca di Cremona*, 1951, nos. 424, 425. There is a further companion piece of the same size (Cremona, no. 423) with a group of card players at the lower right, too dark to be reproduced.

416 SCHOOL OF MARCO RICCI
LANDSCAPE WITH THE JOURNEY TO EMMAUS
VENICE, ACCADEMIA, as school of Tempesta.
138 × 111 cm. A work of fine painterly quality, still in search of an attribution. The composition is reminiscent of some of Tempesta's small, upright works (220, 263), but the romantic mood and the flickering handling place the picture into the orbit of the early Marco Ricci, close to Peruzzini (cf. Ricci Mostra, 1964, p. xv).
COLL. From the convent of S. Giorgio Maggiore, Venice, no. 372 (Levi, 1900, vol. I, p. CCVI, as Tempesta).
LIT. Catalog of the museum, of 1929, no. 372.

417 CRESCENZIO ONOFRI
Rome 1632?–Florence, after 1712.
LANDSCAPE
ROME, GALLERIA DORIA PAMPHILJ
136 × 71 cm. Tempera. Both this and a contrastingly composed pendant (repr. in my *Claude Lorrain, The Drawings*, Berkeley 1968, no. 1226) are ascribed in the Doria catalog of 1816 (which carries many errors) to 'Ciccio da Capua,' i.e., Francesco Graziani the elder, alias Ciccio Napoletano, pupil of Jacques Courtois, praised by Titi (*Descr. delle pitture ... in Roma*, 1763, pp. 33, 399) as a battle painter. For the few facts regarding Graziani, see

Waddingham, in *Paragone* 161, 1963, p. 54. There are two documented battle scenes by him in the Pallavicini collection, Rome. The Rondinini inventory of 1807 enumerates over a dozen paintings and 3 dozen drawings by him (landscapes, marines, battles; cf. L. Salerno, *Palazzo Rondinini*, Rome 1965, pp. 283–303).

The style of the present work and its companion is, however, indistinguishable from the Roman works of Onofri, whom I suspect to be the author of this pair, too. Only recently has his personality begun to emerge from oblivion thanks to Ilaria Toesca (*Paragone* 125, 1960, p. 51), Waddingham (*Paragone* 161, 1963, p. 49), and especially Chiarini (*Boll. d'Arte* 1967, p. 30, and exh. Florence 1969, p. 66), whose merit it is to have brought to light Onofri's activity of almost twenty-five years at the Florentine court (c. 1689 till after 1712). Like Gaspard, Onofri worked in fresco as well as on canvas. Besides a salon in Palazzo Colonna, Rome, and the Rospigliosi frescoes here ascribed to him (183 f.), his most important frescoes are continuous, wall-filling landscapes, richly adorned with trees, in four salons of the Theodoli castle at San Vito Romano; Onofri himself published engravings of them in Rome in 1696, but the actual date of the frescoes seems to lie earlier. According to Pascoli, he was Gaspard's sole pupil. His art also confirms that Gaspard was his sole teacher, whose heroic ideal was to determine his style throughout his life. (By contrast, Orizzonte, born a generation later, was to move from his Gaspardesque starting point to a more idyllic conception of landscape.) Onofri spread the heritage of Gaspard in numerous decorative paintings, often of colossal size and summary execution. See no. 418 for a possible connection with Panfi. Further insight into his art may come from the study of his many, widely scattered pen drawings, quite a few of which are signed or monogrammed (e.g. Besançon, Cleveland, Teyler Foundation in Haarlem, Holkham, British Museum, Witt coll. in London, Santa Barbara, Cal., Turin, Uffizi, Vienna, Windsor). To his Roman phase can also be ascribed the large landscape with a sacrifice at the University of California Art Gallery, Los Angeles (*Illustr. Cat. of the W.J. Hole Coll.*, Los Angeles 1942, no. 1, repr., as N. Poussin).

LIT. Doria catalog, of 1816, as Ciccio da Capua, together with a pendant (the modern no. 395). Sestieri, 1942, no. 27, as school work. Modern Doria catalogs, no. 407, as Gaspard.

418–422 ROMULO PANFI
Florence 1632–1690.

The five paintings presented here for the first time can be ascribed to Panfi, an exact contemporary of Tempesta. Notices on him are almost totally lacking. Orlandi (first in the edition of 1719, p. 384) mentions him with a few words: a pupil of Vignali, he excelled in portraits and especially in landscapes and battle pieces. He was attached to the Florentine court and lived mostly in Carmignano, near Florence. The starting point for the knowledge of this artist is a large landscape painting at the Villa della Petraia, Florence (inv. 3086; c. 2.5 × 4 m.) brought to my attention by Marco Chiarini and bearing on the verso the inscription *Romulo Panfi*. Chiarini recognized the same hand in another, large landscape deposited at the Palazzo della Provincia, Livorno, and in the two paintings at Lucca listed hereafter. Three more pictures (420–422) can be linked to this group on stylistic evidence. This nucleus reveals a gifted personality of considerable interest. While there is no personal contact with Tempesta, similar initial impulses and the same *Zeitgeist* led them to similar results. The decisive impact came from Rosa, whose Florentine sojourn (1641–1649; see exh. Florence 1969, p. 38) took place during Panfi's years of formation. Although no sojourn outside Tuscany is documented for him, the Gaspardesque side of Panfi's art also suggests a visit to Rome.

418, 419 LANDSCAPE. ESTUARY VIEW
LUCCA, PINACOTECA NAZIONALE, nos. 11, 65, as Onofri.

138 × 201 cm. and 141 × 200 cm. Much darkened and obscured by varnish. Green tones. In the first work, the sky is yellow at the upper left. Genre figures. The attribution to Onofri cannot be sustained in the light of Chiarini's rediscovery of Onofri's Tuscan activity (see no. 417). Onofri never shows an influence of Rosa (20–23) as pronounced as here. In their decorative tenor, in their complex, additive layout, and in the handling, the Lucca pictures do, nevertheless, show some degree of similarity with Onofri's Tuscan works, more than with his Roman style. Since Panfi died within a year of Onofri's arrival in Florence, this is to say that the Roman master, even at the age of almost sixty, had an open eye for the achievements of his exact contemporary from Florence. There are, from the same period, equally surface-filling landscapes by Tempesta (276, 300 f., 325); for the coast view, compare nos. 277, 299, 303.

COLL. From the Medici *Guardaroba* to Lucca, c. 1850, as Onofri. LIT. Chiarini, in *Boll. d'Arte* 1967, p. 32.

420 TREES AND ROCKS
VALENCIENNES, MUSEE DES BEAUX-ARTS, as anonymous work.

118 × 92 cm. Rich yellowish-green and brown tones. At the bottom left, illegible signs. At the upper right is a distant view with mountains. See no. 418. This is a singular type of image, rendered with a penetrating painterly handling. The weathered tree trunks, derived from Rosa and popular in the entire school of Rosa (Reschi, Coccorante) have their equivalent in Tempesta (228, 287) and the early Tavella (384).
COLL. Marquess Campana (as anonymous work), which points to an Italian origin.

421 LANDSCAPE
REIMS, MUSEE DES BEAUX-ARTS, as attributed to Gaspard.

177 × 133 cm. Greenish tones. A large, stately picture. See no. 418. The insistent handling and the frozen animation of the forms reveals the same hand as the Lucca pair. Compare Tempesta's no. 249.
COLL. Recuperated by the French state after 1945; deposited at Reims in 1953.

422 LANDSCAPE
PRIVATE COLLECTION, GENOA

148 × 133 cm. To my mind by the same hand as the preceding works, on account of the handling and of the details in the foreground. Tempesta offers many landscapes made up of similar motives. Compare also the Rospigliosi frescoes attributed to Onofri (183 f.). Two related pictures in the royal Danish collection at Fredensborg may be by the same hand (H. Olsen, *Italian Paintings and Sculpture in Denmark*, Copenhagen 1961, p. 85, pl. 62 c, d).

423 UNKNOWN ARTIST
STORMY LANDSCAPE
VENICE, PINACOTECA QUERINI STAMPALIA, no. 245, as anonymous, 17th c.

163 × 147 cm. Dark grey tones. This is a large, elegant work of classical orientation, done towards the close of the century in the northern Italian ambient. There are echoes of Gaspard (9) and parallels with Tempesta (276), Tavella (380), and Orizzonte (441 f.). The closest affinity is with the two known works by Noël Cochin de Venise

(412 f.), to whom this painting might have been ascribed, were it not for two companion pieces (Querini Stampalia nos. 244, 246) in which this link is less evident: a landscape with a ford and a castle under a pink sky, reminiscent of Dutch Italianizing art; and a more decorative, green landscape with numerous hunting figures which bring to mind Jan Miel's late works done in Turin (see L. Mallé, *Museo Civico di Torino, I Dipinti*, 1963, figs. 132 ff.). Apparently by the same hand is, in the same museum (no. 249), a somewhat smaller (130 × 95 cm.) winter landscape inscribed on the verso, in an 18th c. hand, 'Boleman.' This might refer to Pieter Bolckman, a Flemish painter listed in 1668/69 in the Roman Bent with the surname de Roeper (cf. Hoogewerff, 1952, p. 132); or is there a link with a small market scene in Turin done in the manner of Jan Miel and signed 'Bolman 1682' (Mallé, *loc. cit.*, p. 32, pl. 152)? There is no further information about these names.

424 GIOVANNI ANTON EISMAN
Salzburg 1604–Venice 1698/1700.
LANDSCAPE
MUNICH, BAVARIAN STATE COLLECTIONS, no. 1589.
93 × 137 cm. See p. 35. This work and two other paintings in the same collection form the nucleus of the very small oeuvre of Eisman, 'celebre pittore paesista,' according to Dal Pozzo (1718) and to Zannandreis. He was mainly active in Venice, where he is cited from 1644 to 1700. No forceful personality emerges from his pictures. While this landscape stands more in the line of Gaspard, the others mediate between Rosa and Peruzzini. What complicates matters is the fact that Eisman cannot be separated from his adopted son Carlo Brisighella, called Eisman (1629?–after 1718), who practiced the same genres.
LIT. Donzelli, 1967, p. 164.

425 'GIACOMO SPAGNOLO'
COAST VIEW
ROME, GALLERIA DORIA PAMPHILJ (now in Villa Doria Pamphilj).
98 × 130 cm. The ancestry of this type of a coast view with a prominent rock on one side includes Veronese's St. Anthony Preaching to the Fishes, Bril (Christ Walking on the Sea, engr. Nieulandt), Claude (*Lib. Ver.* 165), and Tassi. More directly, the picture compares with river views by Rosa (cf. Salerno, 1963, figs. 6, 78) and Gaspard (St. Anthony Preaching to the Fishes, Blunt coll., repr. *GBA* 1962, p. 280). The picture must be contemporary with Tempesta's river views such as nos. 271 f. In the Do-

ria catalog of 1816, which carries many errors, it is given to one Giacomo Spagnuolo, who is not otherwise known. LIT. Sestieri, 1942, no. 407, as unknown master.

426 PANDOLFO RESCHI
Danzig, c. 1643–Florence 1699.
COAST VIEW
ROME, GALLERIA NAZIONALE
27 × 46 cm. There is a pendant, likewise a coast view (exh. Rome 1956, fig. 42). Born in the north under the name of Resch, the artist moved early to Rome, where in 1663 he lived in Tempesta's house (see p. 16), then settled permanently in Florence, where he was attached to the court. He was a follower of Rosa and of Courtois and excelled in landscapes and battle scenes. Chiarini has published (1969) a few of his many landscapes which survive in Florence. Exquisitely soft and delicate in design and coloring, they have nothing in common with the small pair under discussion, which is, however, given to Reschi in the old Corsini inventories. A pure derivative of Rosa (compare no. 21), this coast view is thus apparently an early effort of Reschi, datable in Rome c. 1666. Perhaps not by chance, its summary handling is close to the earliest works by Tempesta (87, 108 f.). See on Reschi exh. Charlottenburg, *Deutsche Maler und Zeichner d. 17. Jhs.*, 1966, pp. 66, 160, and exh. Florence 1969, p. 62. A large battle piece of his is in Lucca, Pinacoteca Nazionale, no. 59; a fine, large landscape was sold at Christie's, 24 Nov. 1967, lot 99.
COLL. Corsini. LIT. Exh. Rome 1956, no. 57.

427 JACOB DE HEUSCH
Utrecht 1656–1701.
LANDSCAPE WITH RIVER
DESTROYED. FORMERLY VIENNA, AKADEMIE
48 × 96 cm. Was signed at the lower left 'D. Heusch f.' Nephew, pupil, and imitator of Willem de Heusch, Jacob lived for some years in Italy; he is recorded in Rome in 1674/75. The pendant of this picture, in the same museum, still exists (no. 290 of the museum; exh. Vienna, *Die römische Landschaft ...*, 1963, no. 14; Utrecht 1965, no. 157); it shows a comparable, not contrasting layout with a large rock in the center. This pair and a few other works of the artist differ from the more delicate style of the bulk of his production by a conscious imitation of Rosa's late river views (cf., e.g., Rosa's Finding of Moses, in Detroit; Salerno, 1963, fig. 84). A comparable river view by J. de Heusch in Brunswick, signed and dated 1696,

suggests that also this pair was done twenty years after the artist's return from Italy to Holland. Compared with Tempesta's coast views (271 ff.), de Heusch reveals himself more of a northerner in the small size and the detailed execution of the distant parts. This type of image was continued by Manglard (1695–1760; pictures in the Pallavicini and Spada collections, Rome, and elsewhere). COLL. Apparently Lamberg-Sprinzenstein, Vienna, 1822, as Rosa. LIT. Catalog of the museum, by Eigenberger, 1927, no.289.

428, 429 FRANCISQUE MILLET
Antwerp 1642–Paris 1679.

Born of French emigrés, Francisque was trained in Antwerp by Laurens Francken and in Paris (from 1659 onwards) by Abraham Genoels. There are no signed pictures by him, but traditional attributions of classical landscapes to him are numerous–most compositions exist in several variants–and form a distinctly personal oeuvre. He is not known to have been in Italy, and there are no pictures by him in Roman collections. Although in view of certain works of his it is hard to believe that he did not visit Italy, it must be admitted that his art may have grown out of Flemish Italianate masters, of Gaspard, of Poussin, and of the rare landscapes by Philippe de Champaigne. The starting point for attributions are 28 engravings by one Théodore after compositions of Francisque. In the only critical study of the subject, M. Davies (in *Bull. de la Soc. Poussin*, vol.II, 1948, p.13) has shown that old inventories mention, besides Poussinesque landscapes, many other, now unknown aspects of Francisque's art. Matters are further obscured by the fact that both his son and grandson, of the same name, practiced the same types of image, but next to nothing is known about them. I reproduce two unpublished examples which illustrate different facets of Francisque's art–the Poussinesque and the Flemish side. While there is no direct contact with Tempesta, the parallel between these two contemporaries is interesting and extends farther than it looks at first. In particular, the convergence of Gaspard and Rosa in Tempesta has its equivalent in Francisque's combining of classical and Flemish sources.

428 LANDSCAPE
PETWORTH, NATIONAL TRUST

81 × 107 cm. The composition is related, in reverse, to Théodore's engraving with Mercury and the daughters of Cecrops (Davies, *loc. cit.*, fig.12). It is of Poussinesque inspiration; compare Poussin's landscape with a Roman road, at Dulwich, and the landscape with a man washing his feet, in London. Another version of this composition shows in the foreground a Riposo (repr. Voss, in *Saggi e Memorie*, Venice, Istituto Cini, vol.I, 1957, p.49). The Poussinesque side of Francisque often seems like an anticipation of Orizzonte (445) and of the German heroic landscape around 1800. Compare also Tempesta's no. 305.
LIT. Catalog of Petworth House, 1920, no.79.

429 LANDSCAPE
PRIVATE COLLECTION, ZÜRICH

101 × 138 cm. The figures retouched. The composition corresponds, in the same direction, to an engraving by Théodore after Francisque (Davies, *loc. cit.*, fig.21). In the engraving, the tree on the left is omitted, and the figures differ. Although classical motives are absent, the landscape is firmly anchored along verticals and horizontals. The result makes for a very original and altogether fascinating picture. Compare Tempesta's no.300.

430 JEAN-BAPTISTE FOREST
Paris 1635–1712.
LANDSCAPE WITH BACCHUS AND THE NYMPHS OF NYSA
TOURS, MUSEE DES BEAUX-ARTS

172 × 232 cm. Only a handful of works by Forest are known at present, but the mastery of this large canvas reveals him as an accomplished artist. His style is conditioned by Foucquières and d'Arthois on one hand, by Mola, Cortona, and Gaspard on the other. Between 1654 and 1666, Forest spent seven years in Italy, where he was Mola's pupil. Tempesta might have known him in Rome. Compare no. 254.
LIT. J. Magnin, *Le paysage français*, Paris 1928, p.72. Wildenstein, in *GBA*, April 1958, p.242. EXH. London, Royal Academy, *The Age of Louis XIV*, 1958, no.234. Berne, Kunstmuseum, 1959, no.25.

431 FRANS DE NEVE
Engraving, 310 × 400 mm. Signed 'Franciscus de Neve In. e fecit.' This is the largest of fourteen engraved classical landscapes of the artist, all done in the same style, some with extant Roman buildings. There are also a few drawings which go under his name, and one of the prints corresponds to a small painting at Christ Church, Oxford, painted in the manner of F. Lauri, Cortona, and

Mola (J. Byam Shaw, *Paintings by Old Masters at Christ Church Oxford*, London 1967, no. 252, pl. 173). However, this name comprises father and son, who are impossible to separate from one another. The elder lived in Antwerp from 1601 until after 1688 and was in Rome before 1629. The younger, the presumed author of the prints and of the Oxford painting, who is sometimes cited with the dates of the elder, is recorded in Rome from 1660 to 1666, at the same time as Tempesta; later, he was active chiefly in Austria. He (or yet another artist of the same name?) is listed in Antwerp in 1690/93 (Hoogewerff, 1952, p. 140).
LIT. Hollstein, vol. XIV, p. 147, no. 13.

432 CORNELIS HUYSMANS
LANDSCAPE
FRANKFORT, STÄDELSCHES KUNSTINSTITUT
75 × 84 cm. There is a pendant in the same museum (no. 1274). Compare Tempesta's nos. 246, 253 f. Huysmans was a continuator of his teacher Jacques d'Arthois (4). Despite the occurrence of occasional Poussinesque motives, his art clearly develops within the Flemish tradition. He is not known to have been in Italy. The surface-filling character of his compositions is a northern parallel to Tempesta. See on him Thiéry, 1953, p. 152.
LIT. Catalog of the museum, of 1924, no. 1273.

433 ADRIEN FRANÇOIS BAUDEWYNS
Brussels 1644–1711.
LANDSCAPE
BRUSSELS, ROYAL MUSEUM
59.5 × 86 cm. There is a pendant in the same museum (no. 54). As is generally the case with this artist, the figures are by Pieter Bout. Baudewyns practiced at first a style similar to Huysmans, his contemporary, then developed a more refined manner, of which this painting is an example. It represents a Flemish parallel to Tempesta's landscapes (cf. no. 296).
LIT. Catalog of the museum, of 1949, no. 53.

434, 435 JOHANNES GLAUBER, CALLED POLYDOR
Utrecht 1646–Schoonhoven 1726.
ARCADIAN LANDSCAPES
FELBRIGG, ENGLAND, KETTON-CREMER COLLECTION, nos. 70, 71.
62 × 75 cm. A signed pair. Glauber was a pupil of Berchem. In 1671, he spent a year in Paris, then two years in Lyon with Adriaen van der Kabel, five years in Rome (1674–1679), two in Venice, three in Hamburg, finally settled in Amsterdam. His finely painted arcadian landscapes follow essentially the manner of van der Kabel and the refined style of French classical landscape prevailing around 1700, which Glauber contributed to render fashionable in Holland.
EXH. Norwich, 1964, no. 28 (the second work only).

436 ROSA DA TIVOLI (PHILIP PETER ROOS)
Frankfort 1657–Rome 1706.
PASTORAL SCENE
KASSEL, GEMÄLDEGALERIE
188 × 287 cm. One of a series in the same museum. Roos continued the animal genre of his father, Joh. Heinr. Roos. In 1677, he settled in Rome, where he became the leading animal painter. His northern realism, displayed in life-size pictures, goes beyond even that of Tempesta; compare, by the latter, the large nos. 316-319.
LIT. Catalog of the museum, of 1929, no. 620. On the Roos family, see in general H. Jedding, *Der Tiermaler Joh. Heinr. Roos*, Strassburg 1955 (esp. pp. 176–184).

437 GIOVANNI AGOSTINO CASSANA, CALLED L'ABATE CASSANA
Cassana c. 1658–Genoa 1720.
PASTORAL SCENE
PADUA, MUSEO CIVICO, no. 1248.
97 × 142. Detailed information about this specialist of animals and still lifes is scarce (there is a short *Vita* by Ratti, 1769), although he enjoyed a high reputation in Lombardy and the Veneto, where numerous works of his are recorded in old inventories. Active in Tuscany, Venice, and northern Italy, he practiced a style which derives essentially from Castiglione (with whom his works were often confused), but the known works show a more polished finish. Compare also Tempesta's animal scenes (315). Cassana's art parallels that of Faustino Bocchi (1659–after 1729), the Brescian specialist of small genre pieces and landscapes, whose manner was in turn continued by the Brescian animal painter Giorgio Duranti (1685–1755; for these chapters of Lombard realism, cf. Calabi, 1935, pp. 11, 33).
LIT. Delogu, 1931, pp. 61 ff. (the present picture as doubtful). Catalog of the museum, by Grossato, 1957, no. 192. Donzelli, 1967, p. 121. Cf. also exh. Naples, 1964, p. 109, and Genoa, 1969, p. 163.

438 FRANCESCO LONDONIO
Milan 1723–1783.
PASTORAL SCENE
MILAN, AMBROSIANA
35 × 50 cm. This typical example of the artist, done in
the small format in which he excelled particularly, shows
a close affinity with pastorals by Zais. The vast oeuvre of
Londonio, justly held in high esteem in Italy, represents
the finest achievement of Italian eighteenth-century animal painting and as such continues the tradition established three quarters of a century earlier by Tempesta
(compare no. 315). Londonio's work consists entirely of
animal scenes, pastorals, and genre subjects deriving essentially from Rosa da Tivoli and Ceruti. In conformity
with the trend of the time, his style is light, the handling
free and painterly. He worked mainly in Milan, with a
sojourn in Rome and Naples. His fame is furthermore
based on a hundred engravings of animal subjects (often
printed on blue paper, as in the case of Castiglione's
engravings). Prince Borromeo, the Brera, and the Ambrosiana each have about forty paintings by him.
LIT. Böhm, in *Rivista d'Arte* 1934, pp. 229 ff. (with catalog; p. 247, no. 21). Delogu, 1931, pp. 179 ff. Exh. Naples,
1964, p. 96.

439 LONDONIO
SHEEP
PRIVATE COLLECTION, GENOA
90 × 120 cm. The light brownish and blue-green tones
create an exceptional effect. The derivation of the forms
from Tempesta can still be felt (compare no. 314).

440–445 JAN FRANS VAN BLOEMEN, CALLED
ORIZZONTE
Antwerp 1662–Rome 1749.
Trained by his elder brother Pieter (Stendardo, 1657–
1720, in Rome until 1693) and by Antoine Goubeau
(1616–1698), thence active in Paris, he settled in Rome
by 1688 and became there the most important landscape
painter of his time. In his art, the gentle side of Gaspard
is transposed into a more decorative and increasingly
classical vein. Most of his pictures were done in pairs or
series. Many represent real sites from Rome and its surroundings, more are imaginary views. The figures were
often added by collaborators. Dates and/or signatures appear only on a few late works. Despite the esteem for his
works shown by collectors until the present day, his
enormous oeuvre is only now being studied by A. Busiri

Vici. The main source is Pascoli's *Vita,* written in 1732
(ed. Bombe, in *Repertorium f. Kunstwiss.,* 1925, p. 230).
Among the scarce modern literature, the most detailed
item is Busiri Vici's entry in *Dizionario biografico degli
Italiani,* vol. x, 1968, p. 793, which offers for the first
time a survey of Orizzonte's evolution. To be added to
the literature cited there are the brief passages in Calabi,
1935, p. 113; Hoogewerff, 1952; Thiéry, 1953, p. 51;
Laes, in *Revue belge d'archéol. et d'hist. de l'art,* 1958, p. 3;
and some exhibition catalogs, above all Utrecht 1965,
p. 241. I do not know the study by S. Aldana Fernandez.

440, 441 STORMY LANDSCAPES
ROME, GALLERIA DORIA PAMPHILJ
75 × 100 cm. Dark. Strongly influenced by Gaspard,
these works are datable in Orizzonte's early Roman
phase. Later, stormy scenes are rare among his oeuvre.
Compare also Tempesta's stormy landscapes nos. 203,
252, 255.
LIT. Sestieri, 1942, nos. 373, 402. Modern Doria catalogs,
nos. 299, 301.

442 STORMY LANDSCAPE
TURIN, GALLERIA SABAUDA
115 × 147 cm. Compare Tempesta's nos. 212, 258. There
is a contrastingly composed pendant, showing a serene
landscape (Sabauda no. 293).
LIT. Catalog of the museum, of 1909, no. 287.

443 LANDSCAPE
SOUTHPORT, LANCASHIRE,
ROGER F. HESKETH COLLECTION
74 × 95 cm. There is, in the same collection, a contrast-
ingly composed pendant with a mountain in the center.
Both are signed near the lower left 'V BLOEMEN ORIZONT.'
Very few other signed works by Orizzonte are known
(cf. Busiri Vici, *loc. cit.,* and exh. Utrecht 1965, under no.
161). Compare Tempesta's nos. 215, 294, 296.
EXH. Manchester, City Art Gallery, *Works of Art From
Private Collections,* 1960, no. 118 (pendant: no. 123, repr.).

444 LANDSCAPE
FORMERLY BERLIN, SCHMIDT COLLECTION, as Pieter
van Bloemen.
78 × 108 cm. The same castello as in no. 442. Among
Tempesta's works, compare no. 212. The attribution to
Pieter van Bloemen (Stendardo) must be due to a confusion.

445 LANDSCAPE
ISOLA BELLA
61 × 76 cm. Not by N. Poussin, to whom the picture is
ascribed, but by Orizzonte, strongly influenced by Gaspard (and thus also recalling certain works by Francisque).

446 ANDREA LOCATELLI
Rome 1695 (?)–1741.
PASTORAL LANDSCAPE
CARCASSONNE, MUSEE DES BEAUX-ARTS
Oval, 32 × 41 cm. There is a pendant of contrasting composition. A generation younger than Orizzonte, but deceased before him, Locatelli was, next to Orizzonte, the
principal Roman landscape painter of his time. He was a
pupil of Anesi and continued in a lighter vein the heritage
of Claude's classical landscapes. His handling is always
substantial and painterly. In the present example, the
underlying ideal of Claude is clearly felt. The extremely
voluminous oeuvre of Locatelli and the evolution of his
style are only now being studied by a Roman scholar.

447 ANTONIO DIZIANI
Belluno 1737–after 1797.
LANDSCAPE WITH MOSES AND THE BURNING BUSH
VENICE, ACCADEMIA, no. 459, formerly as Gaspare
Diziani.
55 × 98 cm. A continuator of his father Gaspare, of Zuc-
carelli, and of Zais, the younger Diziani reveals in this
work also the heritage of Marco Ricci and, indirectly, of
Tempesta (270, 286) and of Poussin (6). See on A. Diziani:
Martini, 1964, pp. 102, 257, and pl. 238 (a nocturne with a
burning citadel, close to Tempesta). There is a pendant to
the present picture with Moses receiving the tablets of
law (Accademia, no. 460).
COLL. From the Convent of S. Giorgio Maggiore, Venice.
LIT. Catalogs of the museum, no. 459, as Gaspare Diziani.
Delogu, 1930, p. 145.

In the immediate orbit of A. Diziani belongs a pair of
small landscapes in the Brukenthal Museum, Sibiu, Ru-
menia, known to me only from photograph (catalog of
the museum, of 1966, nos. 779f., as Tempesta, which
makes no sense; 34 × 50.5 cm.).

448–451 FRANCESCO ZUCCARELLI
Pitigliano (Grosseto) 1702–Florence 1788.
PASTORAL LANDSCAPES
ISOLA BELLA
85 × 104 cm. The plates of this book end with a superb,
unpublished series of four landscapes by the greatest exponent of landscape painting in northern Italy after Tempesta. In conformity with his era, the art of Zuccarelli represents an idyllic, arcadian world. At this point, we can
no longer speak of a direct influence by Tempesta; the
closest parallels are works such as nos. 212, 215. Born just
after Tempesta's death, trained in Rome and Florence,
active mostly in Venice (from 1732), Zuccarelli is not a
particularly problematic figure, has received little attention in writing, but has been all the more highly esteemed
by collectors past and present. An additional consider-
ation for the discussion of these pictures regards the Borromeo collection. It is significant that this family assem-
bled and kept not only the most comprehensive collection
of Tempesta but also an impressive group of Zuccarelli,
including a large set of pastoral *Vedute*, each of which
represents a castle or palace of the Borromeo (some are
reproduced in G. Rosa, *Zuccarelli*, Milan 1952). No mention has here been made of numerous other landscapes in
the Borromeo collection from the school of Rosa and of
Tempesta, many of which are small and of minor importance or in unsatisfactory condition (see, however, no. 445).
On Zuccarelli, see mainly Delogu, 1930, p. 116; Haumann, 1927, p. 33; Rosa, *loc. cit.*; Pallucchini, 1960, p. 196;
exh. *I vedutisti veneziani del settecento*, cat. by P. Zampetti,
Venice 1967, p. 372; and exh. *Dal Ricci al Tiepolo*, Venice
1969, pp. 274, 437.

PAINTINGS BY TEMPESTA NOT ILLUSTRATED

This list contains a selection of paintings by Tempesta
which are not reproduced here for one of the following
reasons: destroyed, unknown whereabouts, photograph
unobtainable, excessive darkening.

LOST. FORMERLY DESSAU, GEORGSGARTEN
Rape of Proserpina. Oval, 99 × 66 cm., signed and dated
1701. Collection: Hausmann.
Jacob and the Angel.
Flight into Egypt.

LOST. FORMERLY DESSAU, CASTLE
Village in the winter. 46 × 56 cm.
Two historical landscapes. 94 × 128 cm.
Landscape with sheep and goats. 30 × 41 cm.
LIT. Parthey, *Deutscher Bildersaal,* vol. II, 1864, p. 150.

ISOLA BELLA
Several Tempestas could not be reproduced because of excessive darkening and poor condition. They are listed under works of similar composition or under companion pieces. There is, in addition, a dark pastoral nocturne with two figures in the foreground, large trees on the right, trees and a hill with castle on the left; 77 × 99 cm.

MILAN, ARCIVESCOVADO
A pair of landscapes, 73 × 99 cm. And another landscape, 61 × 64 cm. Very likely by Tempesta, but too dark.

MILAN, L. LODETTI
A dark, early landscape, 40 × 60 cm.; cf. no. 109.

UNKNOWN LOCATION
Landscape. Sales Berlin, Lepke, 6 March 1928, lot 37, repr., and 5 Feb. 1929, lot 31, repr. 114 × 172 cm. Signed and dated 1697. An important, large work with a mountain landscape, trees on the right, a river on the left, a castle in the center, distant mountains.

Mountainous landscape. Sale Berlin, Lepke, 30 April 1929, lot 66, repr. 94 × 135 cm. Trees on the left.

Stormy landscape. Sale Berlin, Lepke, 23 April 1936, lot 389, repr. 72 × 118 cm. An important, late work.

Rural scene with farm house in moonlight. Sale Cologne, Lempertz, 12 Nov. 1938, lot 80, repr. 95 × 73 cm.

Pastoral landscape with an unusual diagonal composition from the lower left to the upper right. A generation ago in a Genoese collection. Photograph: Rubinacci, dealer, Genoa.

PAINTINGS BY TEMPESTA KNOWN ONLY FROM SOURCES

The following are a few early mentions of paintings which cannot be located at present.

ROME
The catalog of the Colonna palace, Rome, of 1783, lists six pictures by 'Pietro Mulier Olandese' or 'Pietro Olandese;' it could not be ascertained if they still are in the collection. These pictures were no doubt produced during Tempesta's Roman years. They are:
583. A marine. 2½ feet wide.
823. Two upright tempests. 2 feet high.
901. A marine. Wood, 2½ feet wide.
927. St. Anthony of Padua preaching to the birds. Copper, 1½ feet wide.
1157. A marine. Wood, 3 feet wide.

The death inventory of the painter Cornelis de Wael, drawn up in Rome on 2 May 1667, contains, as number 50, a landscape with sea storm, 4 palms wide. See Vaes, in *Bull. inst. hist. Belge de Rome,* 1925, p. 224.

The 1807 inventory of the Rondinini collection lists as no. 47 an oblong 'Cascade' by Tempesta, 93 cm. wide. See L. Salerno, *Palazzo Rondinini,* Rome 1965, p. 283.

The manuscript death inventory of don Livio Odescalchi, Rome, 1713/14, contains, as number 1329, an upright landscape with the moon reflected in the water, c. 50 × 40 cm. (cf. no. 222).

Cardinal Fesch sale, Rome, 1845. Seven Tempestas and a school work, all brought from France; none can be identified today.
545. Landscape. 84 × 116 cm. Large mountains, deep river with cascade, large rocks. A herdsman, a bull, a cow, two more figures. Distant mountains (cf. here no. 300).
546. Tempest. 63.5 × 94 cm. Coast view, town, lake, mountains. Tempest, tree breaking apart. Fleeing animals and figures, one on horseback, others praying under a tree.
547. Jacob returns to Canaan. 91.5 × 124.5 cm. An angel leads Jacob. Women, children, herds, mountains.
548, 549. A pair. 58.5 × 89 cm. 1) Moonlight, flanking trees, river, island. 2) Sunset, four trees, two herdsmen, dense foliage, a distant building, mountains.
550, 551. A pair. 54 × 68.5 cm. Pastoral landscapes in the manner of Castiglione. 1) Herdsman and girl seated on a rock, drinking flocks, dark sunset sky (cf. here no. 215). 2) Old herdsman leaning on a staff, a sleeping boy, flocks, pastures, mountains.

552. School of Tempesta. 96.5 × 129.5 cm. Ascending road, trees, distant river, buildings, mountains.

GENOA

A semicircular maritime tempest done on canvas for the fathers of S. Giacomo in Carignano, Genoa, shortly before 1676, mentioned there still in 1766 and 1769 by Ratti (here p. 13), does not survive. The building was secularized in 1797 and destroyed in 1905. No paintings by Tempesta figure in the old guides of Genoa.

VENICE

Fifteen paintings, probably dating from Tempesta's Venetian years (1687–190) are listed in various Venetian collections of the eighteenth century (Levi, 1900, vol. II, and S. Savini-Branca, *Il collezionismo veneziano nel '600*, Padua 1964).

Giorgio Bergonzi, inventory of 1709. The collection comprised over five hundred paintings, including numerous landscapes. By Tempesta:

198. A landscape with sheep and Diana (cf. no. 313).
216, 217. A marine and a nocturne.
224, 225. Two landscapes with animals and figures (Levi, p. 164., Savini, p. 171).

Antonio Giustinian, at S. Eustachio, 1733:
Two small landscapes. 2 quarters square, 'Anton Tempesta o Cremonese' (i.e. Bassi).
Landscape. 7 quarters high, 12 quarters wide, 'Anton Tempesta.'

Vincenzo Scroffa, at S. Lucia di Vicenza, 1741:
Maritime tempest.
Nocturne with the story of Endymion.
Calm nocturne with fishermen.
'Due altri d'architettura con figure, del Sig. Tempesta, e sono fatture del Trompei' (unclear; Levi, p. 198).

Giov. Paolo Baglioni, in S. Cassiano, 1787:
A painting with figures. (Levi, p. 252.)
No Tempestas are cited in guides of Venice such as Boschini, 1733, or Moschini, 1815.

VERONA

Marquess Gherardini, in S. Fermetto, by 1718:
'Three landscapes, in the first the voyage of Jacob with many figures and animals; in the second a sunrise; in the third a nocturne. By Antonio Tempesta, and further

small pieces by the same' (Dal Pozzo, 1718, p. 286; he no doubt confuses Antonio with Pietro Tempesta).

Count Ercole Giusti, SS. Apostoli, by 1718:
'Two landscapes with a nocturne, shepherds, and animals.' The collection included, among the landscapes, four by Rosa, four by Baldini, a Castiglione, two by Paolo Fiammingo, six by Eismann, one by Both. (Dal Pozzo, p. 298).

BRESCIA

Some twenty paintings, probably dating for the most part from Tempesta's Brescian sojourn (c. 1692, 1695), are summarily listed in 1760 in various collections of Brescia (L. Chizzola, *Le pitture e sculture di Brescia*, 1760, pp. 164–184, *passim*):

Barbisoni, Strada Lunga:
A large painting with three sheep, a goat, a woman 'al naturale' (this recalls no. 314, but cannot be the same picture).
Three landscapes; one has the figures by Bellucci.
Four landscapes of equal size.
Four small landscapes.
Two paintings, one a marine, the other a nocturne.

Counts Avogadri, near S. Bartolommeo:
Two landscapes.
Another small landscape, and another.

Benedictine monastery of S. Giulia:
In the chapter room, several paintings by Tempesta, Celesti, etc., framed in the wall.

Several now unidentified paintings by Tempesta belonged to the collection formed by Count Faustino Lechi (1730–1800). Among others: John the Baptist gathering water, with a life-size sheep, large; and a large landscape with figures and animals, both bought from Count Carlo Roncalli and lost in 1799. A sea storm, 10½″ × 1′, for sale c. 1787. A landscape with sheep. A nocturnal marine with a boat, sold to England. Two signed landscapes with figures, animals, and a hut, daylight. Two nocturnal landscapes, sold to England. A small dog asleep. Jacob's Ladder, bought by Teodoro Lechi in Milan and lost in America in the 19th century. See F. Lechi, *I quadri delle collezioni Lechi in Brescia,* Florence 1968.

None of these figures in P. Brognoli's *Nuova Guida* of

Brescia, 1826, where instead works by Tempesta are listed at the Biblioteca Quariniana and in the collection of Ottavio Ugoni ('two beautiful pictures by Tempesta, and various other small pictures of his animal studies'; p. 218).

Carboni (1776, p. 47), copied and expanded by Maggi (1794, p. 4; see here p. 14), reports that 'Bertelli's first efforts in Brescia were dedicated to copying as many pictures of Cavalier Tempesta as he could find. And these, luckily, were quite a few, that great landscape artist having spent several years in Brescia, continuously painting, so that few other cities can boast of so many pieces by that famous master.' (See also p. 63).

In 1834, A. Sala, *Pitture ed altri oggetti di belle Arti di Brescia,* cites Tempesta only in connection with landscape paintings of the Averoldi collection (p. 120).

MODENA
Campori (1855, p. 320) mentions in the ducal Este gallery of Modena two small battles by P. Tempesta; they may be the two paintings sold by the artist to Prince Foresto d'Este, Modena, in 1687. No battle scenes by Tempesta are known at present.

ROVIGO
F. Bartoli, *Le pitture, sculture ed architetture della città di Rovigo,* Venice 1793, cites in the palace of the Counts Casilini four small landscapes with elegant, spirited figures, attributed to Tempesta (p. 194).

NETHERLANDS
The sale of Petronella de La Court, Amsterdam, 19 Oct. 1707, contained ten Tempestas, including a sacrificial scene painted in Italy (lot 90), Dryope transformed into a tree (lot 99), Europa (lot 100), a small moonshine landscape, and a sea storm (lots 75, 107).

The sale of Card. Valenti, Amsterdam, 18 May 1763, contained, as lots 51 and 52, a pair by Tempesta: Annunciation of the Angels, with a woman nursing; and Moses, Aaron, with animals, 170 × 114 cm., sold to a Frenchman.

FRANCE
De Julienne sale, Paris 1767: a landscape with figures and animals. 37 × 58 cm.
Prince de Conti sale, Paris 1777: a marine, moonlight.

GERMANY
The *Catalogue Raisonné* by N. de Pigage of the Electoral Düsseldorf Gallery, Brussels 1781, lists by P. Mulier as nos. 335 f. 'Esau going to the encounter of Jacob, and Jacob going to the encounter of Esau', of contrasting compositions with mountains and valleys, 56 × 68 cm. Have since disappeared. Cf. here nos. 259–267.

ENGLAND
J. Udney sale, Christie, 25 April 1800: a sea storm, bt. Col. Murray.

ENGRAVINGS
Of the five engravings recorded after paintings by Tempesta, all issued in the eighteenth century, I have been able to find only three. One of the two missing prints records a now unknown painting (mentioned under no. 241), the other – a landscape with herdsmen and animals, engraved by G. Leonardis (1710–c. 1782) – may or may not be identical with an extant picture.

Appendix: two newly appeared works by Tempesta

STORMY LANDSCAPE (fig. 455, color plate X).
GENEVA, MUSEE D'ART ET D'HISTOIRE
115 × 160 cm. Signed on a stone near the bottom right 'Cavaglier. Pietro. Tempest. fecit 169-.' This picture constitutes a series with the sea storm no. 116 and the Flight into Egypt no. 322 (1696). The three works happen to exemplify the 18th-century concepts of the sublime, the picturesque, and the beautiful respectively, although this was surely not an intentional program of the artist. The contrast with the contemplative Flight suggests that the present picture may be understood as a Deluge. Majestic, storm-loaded clouds are spreading over the hills from the left, while lightning destroys a building at the upper right. The skillful use of chiaroscuro, with a dark ox in the foreground set against brightly lit groups further back, enhances the sense of doom, which Tempesta has never conjured as vividly as here. The nearest analogy is the destruction of Sodom and Gomorrah (320; 1696). For the dead sheep, cf. no. 312.
COLL. Gift G. Revilliod.

STORMY LANDSCAPE (fig. 456)
PRIVATE COLLECTION
70 × 84 cm. The brownish ground pierces through. Cf. no. 203. Recalls Rosa and Gaspard. Probably Roman.

BIBLIOGRAPHY

Arslan, E. *I Bassano,* Milan 1960

Bernt, W. *Die niederländischen Maler des 17. Jahrhunderts,* 4 vols., Munich 1948–62

Bock-Rosenberg: Bock, E., and Rosenberg, J. *Die Zeichnungen niederländischer Meister im Kupferstichkabinett zu Berlin,* 2 vols., Berlin 1930

Bonzi, M. *Il Tavella,* Genoa, ed. of 1961 quoted

Boschini, M. *La carta del navegar pitoresco,* Venice 1660

Burl. Mag.: Burlington Magazine

Buscaroli, R. *La pittura di paesaggio in Italia,* Bologna 1935

Calabi, E. *La pittura a Brescia nel seicento e settecento,* Brescia 1935

Campori, G. *Gli artisti italiani e stranieri negli stati estensi,* Modena 1855

Carboni, G.B. *Notizie istoriche delli pittori, scultori, ed architetti bresciani* (1776), ed. Boselli, C., in *Suppl. ai Commentarii dell'Ateneo di Brescia,* 1962

Delogu, G. *G.B. Castiglione,* Bologna 1928

Delogu, 1930: Delogu, G. *Pittori veneti minori del settecento,* Venice 1930

Delogu, 1931: Delogu, G. *Pittori minori liguri, lombardi, piemontesi del seicento e del settecento,* Venice 1931

Donzelli, C., and Pilo, G.M. *I pittori del seicento veneto,* Florence 1967

Fokker, T. In *Med. van het Nederl. Hist. Inst. te Rome,* vol.IX, 1929, p.191.

Fokker, T. Entry in Thieme-Becker, *Künstler-Lexikon,* vol.25, Leipzig 1931, p.259

GBA: Gazette des Beaux-Arts

Gerson, H. *Ausbreitung und Nachwirkung der holländischen Malerei des 17. Jahrhunderts,* Haarlem 1942

Haumann, I. *Das oberitalienische Landschaftsbild des Settecento,* Strassburg 1927

Hoogewerff, G. Entry in *Enciclopedia Italiana,* 1934, *sub* Mulier

Hoogewerff, 1942: Hoogewerff, G. *Nederlandse kunstenaars te Rome,* The Hague 1942–43

Hoogewerff, 1952: Hoogewerff, G. *De Bentvueghels,* The Hague 1952

Houbraken, A. *De Groote Schouburgh,* vol.III, Amsterdam 1721

Immerzeel, J. *De levens en werken der hollandsche en vlaamsche kunstschilders,* Amsterdam 1842

Lanzi L. *Storia Pittorica,* Bassano 1789; here quoted in the ed. of 1809, 6 vols.

Levi, C.A. *Le collezioni veneziani d'arte e d'antichità dal sec. XIV ai nostri giorni,* 2 vols., Venice 1900

Magni, E. Manuscript thesis on Tempesta, University of Bologna 1965

Martini, E. *La pittura veneziana del settecento,* Venice 1964

Moschini, G.A. *Della letteratura veneziana del secolo* XVII..., vol.V, Venice 1806

Nicodemi, G. 'Paesi del Tempesta,' in *L'Arte* 1958, p.443

Orlandi, P. *Abecedario Pittorico,* Bologna 1704

Pallucchini, P. *La pittura veneziana del settecento,* Venice 1960

Pascoli, L. *Vita de'Pittori, Scultori, ed Architetti Moderni,* vol.I, Rome 1730

Passamani, B. 'La pittura dei sec. XVII e XVIII' in *Storia di Brescia,* vol.III, Brescia 1964, p.620

Pigler, A. *Barockthemen,* 2 vols., Budapest 1963

Pilo, G. Mostra *Marco Ricci,* Bassano 1964

Pozzo, B. Dal. *Le vite de'pittori... veronesi,* Verona 1718

Ratti: see Soprani

Röthlisberger, M. 'The Colonna Frescoes of Pietro Tempesta,' in *Burl. Mag.* 1967, p.12

Röthlisberger, M. 'Le Chevalier Pietro Tempesta,' in *L'Oeil* 1970 (forthcoming)

Salerno, L. *Salvator Rosa,* Milan 1963

Sestieri, E. *Catalogo della galleria ex-fidecommissaria Doria-Pamphilj,* Rome 1942

Soprani-Ratti: Soprani, R. *Delle vite de'pittori, scultori, ed architetti genovesi,* vol.2 by C. Ratti, Genoa 1769

Storia di Milano, ed. Treccani, vol.xi, Milan 1958

Thiéry, Y. *Le paysage flamand au xviiie siècle,* Paris 1953

Ticozzi, S. *Dizionario degli architetti, scultori, pittori...,* 4 vols., Milan 1832

Voss, H. *Die Malerei des Barock in Rom,* Berlin 1924

Willis, F. *Die niederländische Marinemalerei,* Leipzig 1911

Wittkower, R. *Art and Architecture in Italy: 1600–1750,* London 1965

Wurzbach, A. von. *Neues Künstler-Lexikon,* 2 vols., Vienna 1910

Zannandreis, D. *Le vite dei pittori, scultori, e architetti veronesi* (written 1831–1834), Verona 1891

EXHIBITIONS

1956–Rome, Galleria Nazionale, Pal. Barberini, *Paesisti e vedutisti a Roma nel '600 e nel '700*

1962–Bologna, *L'ideale classico del seicento in Italia e la pittura di paesaggio*

1963–Bassano, *Marco Ricci,* cat. by G.Pilo, Venice 1964

1964–Naples, Palazzo Reale, *La natura morta italiana*

1965–Brussels, Musées Royaux des Beaux-Arts de Belgique, *Le siècle de Rubens*

1965–Utrecht, Centraal Museum, *Nederlandse 17e eeuwse italianiserende landschapschilders*

1969–Florence, Palazzo Pitti, *Artisti alla Corte Granducale,* cat. by M.Chiarini

1969–Genoa, Palazzo Bianco, *Pittori genovesi a Genova nel '600 e nel '700*

INDEX

The designations p. *and* pp. *refer to pages,* no. *and* nos. *to catalog entries*
(which are the same numbers as the illustrations).

PLATES

CONTENTS

1 Fyt. *Prado*

2 P. de Vos. *Vienna, Czernin Coll.*

3 P. de Vos. *Louvre*

4 D'Arthois. *Stockholm*

6 Poussin. *Prado*

8 Claude. *Priv. Coll.*

5 D'Arthois. *Vienna*

7 Claude. *Wildenstein*

9 Gaspard. *Rome, Galleria Doria Pamphilj*

10 Gaspard. *Rome, Galleria Doria Pamphilj*

12 Gaspard. *Louvre*

11 Gaspard. *Chantilly*

13 Gaspard. *Priv. Coll.*

14 Gaspard. *Milan, Brera*

15 Gaspard.
*Rome, Galleria
Doria Pamphilj*

16 Gaspard.
*Rome, Galleria
Doria Pamphilj*

17 School of Gaspard.
Rome, Galleria Doria Pamphilj

19 Testa. *Engraving*

21 Rosa. *Rome, Galleria Doria Pamphilj*

18 Testa. *Louvre*

20 Rosa. *Prado*

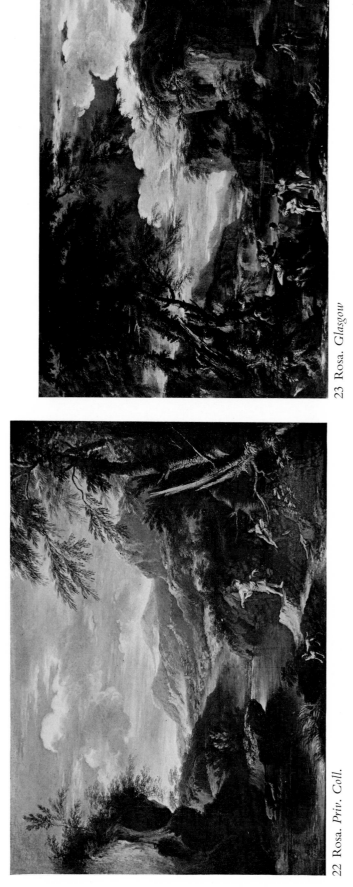

22 Rosa. *Priv. Coll.*

23 Rosa. *Glasgow*

24 School of Rosa.
London, National Gallery Reproduced by courtesy of the Trustees, The National Gallery

25 Torregiani. *Bamberg*

27 School of Mola. *English Priv. Coll.*

29 Cittadini. *Isola Bella*

26 Mola. *Sarasota*

28 Pietro da Cortona. *Rome, Pinacoteca Capitolina*

31 Francesco Bassano. *Vienna*

33 Circle of Tassi. *Bagnaia, Villa Lante*

30 Jacopo Bassano. *Lugano, Thyssen Coll.*

32 Gerolamo Bassano. *Milan, Castello Sforzesco*

34 Scorza. *Priv. Coll.*

35 Scorza. *Genoa*

36 Scorza. *Genoa*

37 School of Scorza. *Priv. Coll.*

41 School of Castiglione. *Tours*

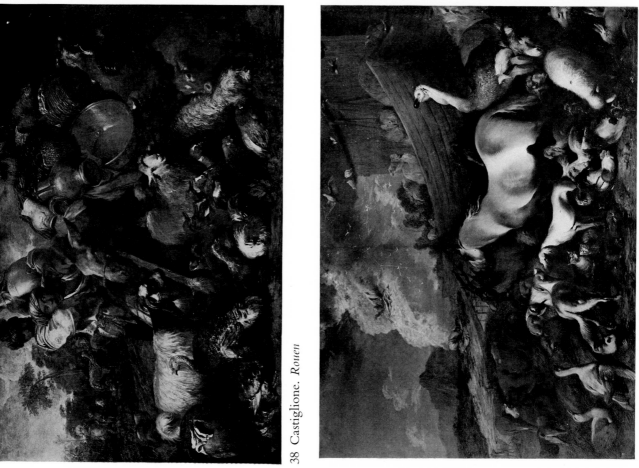

38 Castiglione. *Rouen*

39 Castiglione. *Priv. Coll.*

40 Castiglione. *Priv. Coll.*

42 Lauri. *Hampton Court (copyright reserved)*

43 Lauri. *Marquess of Exeter*

45 Lauri. *J. R. More-Molyneux Coll.*

44 Lauri. *Marquess of Exeter*

47 Mulier. *Leningrad*

49 Mulier. *Prague*

46 Mulier. *Greenwich*

48 Mulier. *Greenwich*

50 Mulier. *Priv. Coll.*

51 Mulier. *Unknown Loc.*

52 Mulier. *Priv. Coll.*

53 Mulier. *Priv. Coll.*

54 Mulier. *Unknown Loc.*

55 Mulier. *Munich*

56 Mulier. *Prague*

57 Mulier. *Karlsruhe*

58 Mulier. *Amsterdam*

59 Mulier. *Greenwich*

60 Mulier. *Prague*

61 Mulier. *Unknown Loc.*

62 Mulier. *Karlsruhe*

63 Mulier. *Priv. Coll.*

64 Mulier. *Greenwich*

65 Mulier. *Greenwich*

66 Bril. Cracow

67 De Wael. Pegli

68 Blanckerhoff. Karlsruhe

69 Blanckerhoff. Rome, Galleria Doria Pamphilj

70 Blanckerhoff. *Copenhagen*

71 Smit. *Karlsruhe*

72 Bakhuysen. *Priv. Coll.*

73 Bakhuysen. *Brussels*

74 Van Plattenberg. *Greenwich*

75 Van Plattenberg. *Greenwich*

76 Van Plattenberg. *Pommersfelden*

77 Van Plattenberg. *Greenwich*

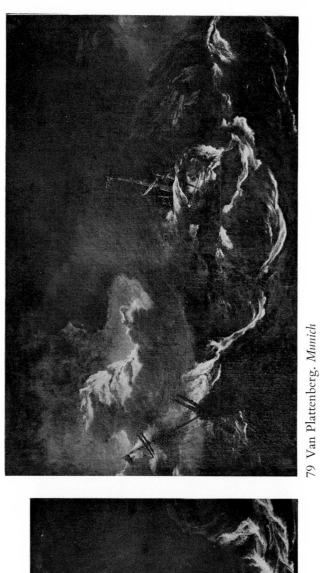

78 Van Plattenberg. *Greenwich*

79 Van Plattenberg. *Munich*

80 Van Plattenberg. *Würzburg*

81 Van Plattenberg? *Graz*

82 Van Plattenberg? *Antwerp*

83 Van Plattenberg? *Antwerp*

85 Monsù Montagna. *Angers*

84 Monsù Montagna? *Brescia*

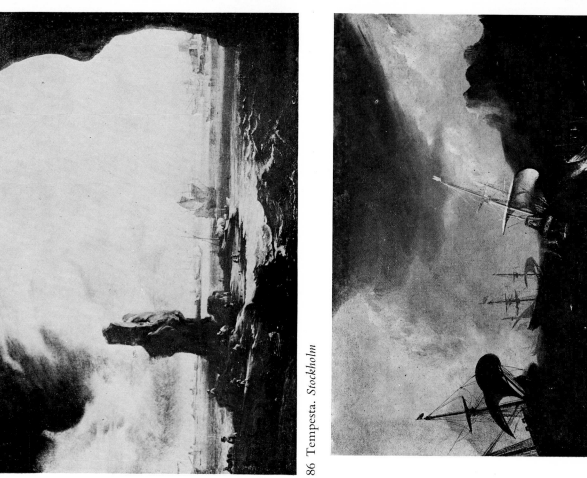

86 Tempesta. *Stockholm*

87 Tempesta. *Sens*

88 Tempesta. *Rome, Galleria Doria Pamphilj*

89 Tempesta. *Rome, Galleria Doria Pamphilj*

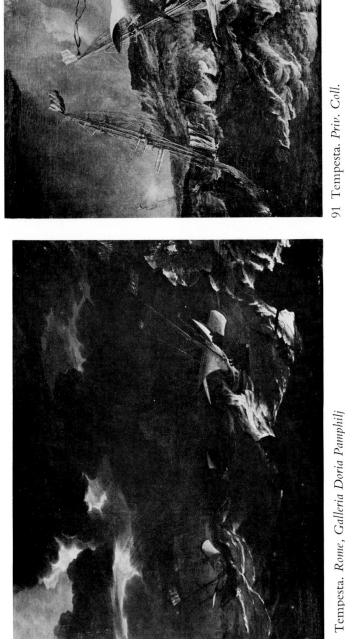

90 Tempesta. *Rome, Galleria Doria Pamphilj*

91 Tempesta. *Priv. Coll.*

93 Tempesta. *Mainz*

92 Tempesta. *Mainz*

94 Tempesta. *Genoa*

95 Tempesta. *Genoa*

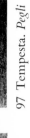

97 Tempesta. *Pegli*

96 Tempesta. *Pegli*

98 Tempesta. *Pegli*

99 Tempesta. *Pegli*

100 Tempesta. *Priv. Coll.*

101 Tempesta. *Milan, Castello Sforzesco*

102 Tempesta. *Pinacoteca Stuard*

104 Tempesta. *Modena*

103 Tempesta. *Coll. Prof. Nannini*

106 Tempesta. *Modena*

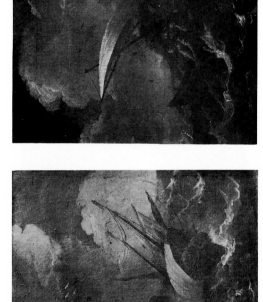

107 Tempesta. *Modena*

105 Tempesta. *Modena*

109 Tempesta. *Isola Bella*

108 Tempesta. *Isola Bella*

110 Tempesta. *Isola Bella*

111 Tempesta. *Isola Bella*

112 Tempesta. *Greenwich*

113 Tempesta. *Greenwich*

114 Tempesta. *Isola Bella*

115 Tempesta. *Priv. Coll.*

116 Tempesta. *Geneva*

117 Tempesta. *Amiens*

118 Tempesta. *Lost*

119 Tempestino. *Valencia*

120 Tempestino. *Valencia*

121 Tavella. *Genoa*

122 Tavella. *Greenwich*

123 Tavella. *Cremona*

124 Tavella? *Priv. Coll.*

125 Unknown Artist. *Priv. Coll.*

126 Unknown Artist. *Padua*

127 Unknown Artist. *Piacenza*

128 Unknown Artist. *Piacenza*

131 Grevenbroeck. *British Museum*

129 Grevenbroeck. *Alençon*

130 Grevenbroeck. *Alençon*

132 Unknown Artist. *Pegli*

133 Unknown Artist. *Priv. Coll.*

134 Manglard. *Priv. Coll.*

135 Cl.-J. Vernet. *Louvre*

137 Molijn. *Hamburg*

139 Molijn. *Hamburg*

136 Molijn. *Paris, Ecole des Beaux-Arts*

138 Molijn. *West Berlin*

140 Tempesta. *Amsterdam*

141 Tempesta. *Uffizi*

143 Tempesta. *Weimar, Schlossmuseum*

142 Tempesta. *Cape Town*

145 Tempesta. *London, Witt Library*

147 Tempesta. *Vienna, Albertina*

144 Tempesta. *Paris, Ecole des Beaux-Arts*

146 Tempesta. *Brussels*

148 Tempesta. *West Berlin*

149 Tempesta. *West Berlin*

150 Tempesta. *West Berlin*

151 Tempesta. *West Berlin*

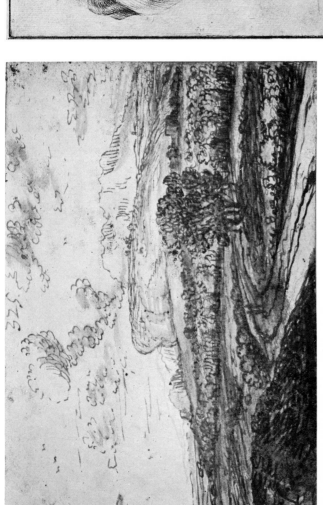

152 Tempesta. *West Berlin*

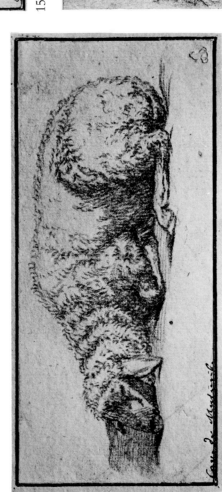

153 Tempesta. *Vienna, Albertina*

154 Tempesta. *Vienna, Albertina*

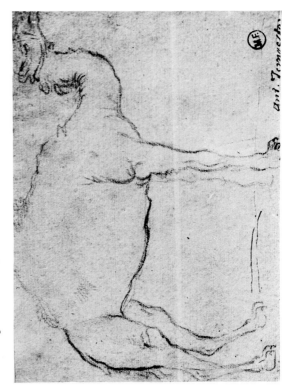

155 Tempesta. *Montpellier*

156 Tempesta. *Cologne*

157 Tempesta. *Priv. Coll.*

8 Tempesta. *British Museum*

159 Tempesta. *Amsterdam, Museum Fodor*

0 Tempesta. *Besançon*

161 Tempesta. *Haarlem, Teyler Museum*

2 Tempesta. *Hamburg*

163 Tempesta. *Hamburg*

164 Tempesta. *Leiden*

165 Tempesta. *Leiden*

166 Tempesta. *Vienna, Albertina*

167 Tempesta. *Priv. Coll.*

168 Tempesta. *Leiden*

169 Tempesta. *Leiden*

170 Gaspard. *Rome, Palazzo Colonna*

171 School of Gaspard. *Rome, Farnesina*

172 School of Gaspard. *Rome, Farnesina*

173 Tempesta. *Rome, Palazzo Colonna*

174 Tempesta. *Rome, Palazzo Colonna*

175 Tempesta. *Rome, Palazzo Colonna*

177 Tempesta. *Rome, Palazzo Colonna*

176 Tempesta. *Rome, Palazzo Colonna*

178 Tempesta. *Rome, Palazzo Colonna*

179 Tempesta. *Rome, Palazzo Colonna*

180 Tempesta. *Rome, Palazzo Colonna*

181 Tempesta. *Rome, Palazzo Colonna*

182 School of Gaspard. *Rome, Palazzo in Corso Umberto*

183 Onofri? *Rome, Palazzo Rospigliosi–Pallavicini*

184 Onofri? *Rome, Palazzo Rospigliosi–Pallavicini*

185 Manglard. *Rome, Palazzo Chigi*

187 Tempesta. *Isola Bella*

186 Tempesta. *Isola Bella*

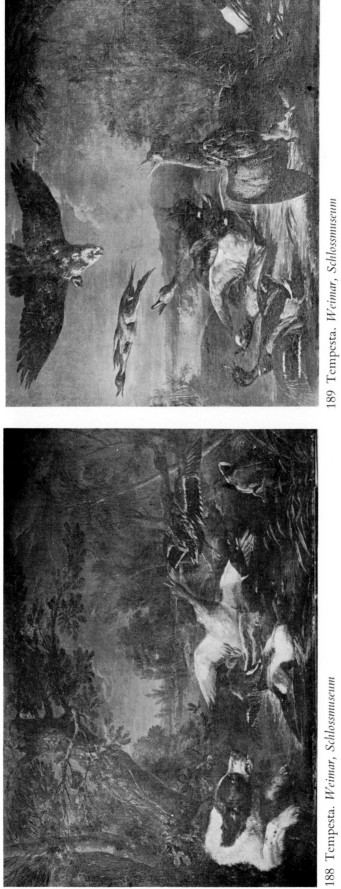

188 Tempesta. *Weimar, Schlossmuseum*

189 Tempesta. *Weimar, Schlossmuseum*

190 Tempesta. *Milan, Castello Sforzesco*

191 Tempesta. *Priv. Coll.*

192 Tempesta. *Genoa*

193 Tempesta. *Priv. Coll.*

194 Tempesta. *Priv. Coll.*

195 Tempesta. *Priv. Coll.*

196 Tempesta. *Parma, Pinacoteca Stuard*

197 Tempesta. *Parma, Pinacoteca Stuard*

198 Tempesta. *Parma, Pinacoteca Stuard*

199 Tempesta. *Parma, Pinacoteca Stuard*

200 Tempesta. *Parma, Pinacoteca Stuard*

202 Tempesta. *New York, Lynch Coll.*

201 Tempesta. *Priv. Coll.*

203 Tempesta. *Leningrad*

204 Tempesta. *Milan, Castello Sforzesco*

205 Tempesta. *Dresden*

206 Tempesta. *Dresden*

208 Tempesta. *Isola Bella*

210 Tempesta. *Isola Bella*

207 *Isola Bella*

209 Tempesta. *Isola Bella*

211 Tempesta. *Budapest*

212 Tempesta. *Budapest*

213 Tempesta. *Marquess of Exeter*

214 Tempesta. *Marquess of Exeter*

215 Tempesta. *Vienna*

216 Tempesta. *Isola Bella*

217 Tempesta. *Isola Bella*

219 Tempesta. *Isola Bella*

218 Tempesta. *Cambridge, Mass., Fogg Art Museum*

221 Tempesta. *Isola Bella*

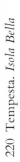

220 Tempesta. *Isola Bella*

223 Tempesta. *Isola Bella*

222 Tempesta. *Isola Bella*

225 Tempesta. *Isola Bella*

224 Tempesta. *Isola Bella*

227 Tempesta. *Isola Bella*

226 Tempesta. *Isola Bella*

229 Tempesta. *Isola Bella*

228 Tempesta. *Priv. Coll.*

230 Tempesta. *Isola Bella*

231 Tempesta. *Isola Bella*

232 Tempesta. *Isola Bella*

233 Tempesta. *Brescia*

234 Tempesta. *Brescia*

235 Tempesta. *Milan, Brera*

236 Tempesta. *Destroyed*

237 Tempesta. *Isola Bella*

238 Tempesta. *Isola Bella*

239 Tempesta. *Dresden*

240 Tempesta. *Milan, Ambrosiana*

241 Tempesta. *Kassel*

242 Tempesta. *Priv. Coll.*

243 Tempesta. *Isola Bella*

244 Tempesta. *Isola Bella*

245 Tempesta. *Isola Bella*

246 Tempesta. *Isola Bella*

247 Tempesta. *Isola Bella*

248 Tempesta. *Isola Bella*

249 Tempesta. *Isola Bella*

250 Tempesta. *Priv. Coll.*

251 Tempesta. *Isola Bella*

252 Tempesta. *Isola Bella*

253 Tempesta. *Isola Bella*

254 Tempesta. *Isola Bella*

255 Tempesta. *Stuttgart*

256 Tempesta. *Stuttgart*

257 Tempesta. *Marquess of Bute*

258 Tempesta. *Marquess of Bute*

259 Tempesta. *Priv. Coll.*

260 Tempesta. *Priv. Coll.*

261 Tempesta. *Priv. Coll.*

262 Tempesta. *Earl of Bradford*

264 Tempesta. *Priv. Coll.*

263 Tempesta. *Priv. Coll.*

265 Tempesta. *New York, Walter P. Chrysler Coll.*

266 Tempesta. *Priv. Coll.*

267 Tempesta. *Priv. Coll.*

268 Tempesta. *Priv. Coll.*

269 Tempesta. *Priv. Coll.*

270 Tempesta. *Isola Bella*

271 Tempesta. *Isola Bella*

272 Tempesta. *Genoa*

273 Tempesta. *Isola Bella*

274 Tempesta. *Isola Bella*

275 Tempesta. *Lost*

276 Tempesta. *Priv. Coll.*

277 Tempesta. *Priv. Coll.*

278 Tempesta. *Isola Bella*

279 Tempesta. *Parma*

280 Tempesta. *Parma*

281 Tempesta. *Brescia, Congrega Apostolica*

282 Tempesta. *Brescia, Congrega Apostolica*

283 Tempesta. *Priv. Coll.*

284 Tempesta. *Prince of Liechtenstein*

285 Tempesta. *Prince of Liechtenstein*

286 Tempesta. *Parma*

287 Tempesta. *Parma*

288 Tempesta. *Priv. Coll.*

289 Tempesta. *Milan, Ambrosiana*

290 Tempesta. *Priv. Coll.*

291 Tempesta. *Priv. Coll.*

292 Tempesta. *Stuttgart*

293 Tempesta. *Priv. Coll.*

294 Tempesta. *Isola Bella*

295 Tempesta. *Isola Bella*

296 Tempesta. *Isola Bella*

297 Tempesta. *Isola Bella*

298 Tempesta. *Priv. Coll.*

299 Tempesta. *Isola Bella*

300 Tempesta. *Isola Bella*

301 Tempesta. *Bergamo*

302 Tempesto. *Isola Bella*

303 Tempesta. *Art Market*

304 Tempesta. *Priv. Coll.*

305 Tempesta. *Priv. Coll.*

306 Detail of Fig. 305

307 Tempesta. *Count Canera di Salasco*

308 Tempesta. *Isola Bella*

309 Tempesta. *Isola Bella*

310 Tempesta. *Milan, Brera*

311 Tempesta. *Isola Bella*

312 Tempesta. *Isola Bella*

313 Tempesta. *Vienna*

314 Tempesta. *Stuttgart*

315 Tempesta. *Prague*

316 Tempesta. *Priv. Coll.*

317 Tempesta. *Priv. Coll.*

318 Tempesta. *Priv. Coll.*

319 Tempesta. *Rome, Galleria Capitolina*

322 Tempesta. *Geneva*

323 Tempesta. *Isola Bella*

324 Tempesta. *Isola Bella*

325 Tempesta. *Priv. Coll.*

326 Tempesta. *Brescia*

327 Tempesta. *Marquess of Exeter*

328 Tempesta. *Marquess of Exeter*

329 Tempesta. *Marquess of Exeter*

331 Tempesta. *Marquess of Exeter*

332 Tempesta. *Marquess of Exeter*

330 Tempesta. *Marquess of Exeter*

333 Tempesta. *Priv. Coll.*

334 Tempesta. *Priv. Coll.*

335 Tempesta. *Milan, Castello Sforzesco*

336 Tempesta. *Priv. Coll.*

337 Tempesta. *Priv. Coll.*

338 Tempesta. *Priv. Coll.*

339 Tempesta. *Priv. Coll.*

340 Tempesta. *Warsaw*

341 Tempesta. *Priv. Coll.*

342 Tempesta. *Priv. Coll.*

343 Tempesta? *Priv. Coll.*

344 Tempesta? *Brescia*

345 Tempesta? *Priv. Coll.*

346 Tempesta? *Priv. Coll.*

347 Tempesta? Priv. *Coll.*

348 Tempesta? *Priv. Coll.*

349 Tempesta? *Unknown Loc.*

350 Imitator of Tempesta. *Priv. Coll.*

351 Imitator of Tempesta. *Unknown Loc.*

352 Imitator of Tempesta. *Priv. Coll.*

353 Imitator of Tempesta. *Unknown Loc.*

355 Imitator of Tempesta. *Stuttgart*

354 Imitator of Tempesta. *Milan, Brera*

356 Imitator of Tempesta. *Priv. Coll.*

357 Imitator of Tempesta. *Milan, Castello Sforzesco*

359 Imitator of Tempesta. *Priv. Coll.*

358 Imitator of Tempesta. *Priv. Coll.*

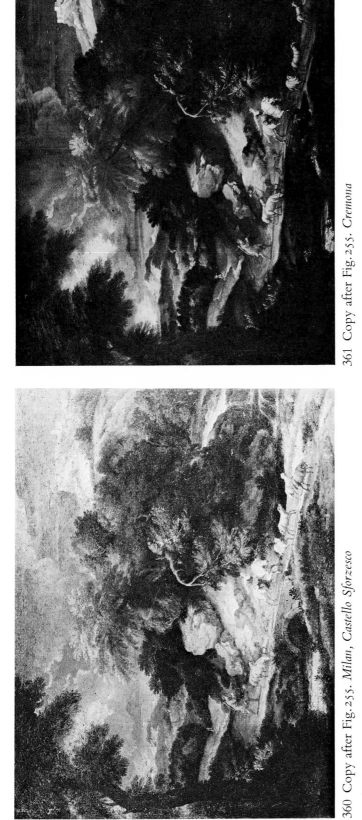

360 Copy after Fig. 255. *Milan, Castello Sforzesco*

361 Copy after Fig. 255. *Cremona*

362 Copy after Fig. 277. *Priv. Coll.*

363 Copy after Fig. 281. *Priv. Coll.*

364 Tempestino. *Marquess of Exeter*

365 Tempestino. *Marquess of Exeter*

366 Tempestino. *Marquess of Exeter*

367 Tempestino. *Marquess of Exeter*

368 Tempestino. *Rome, Galleria Doria Pamphilj*

372 Tempestino

371 Tempestino

370 Tempestino. *Rome, Galleria Doria Pamphilj*

369 Tempestino. *Rome, Galleria Doria Pamphilj*

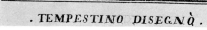

373 Tempestino   374 Tempestino   375 Tempestino

376 Tavella. *Genoa*

377 Tavella. *Priv. Coll.*

379 Tavella. *Genoa*

381 Tavella. *Priv. Coll.*

378 Tavella. *Genoa*

380 Tavella. *Priv. Coll.*

382 Tavella. *Priv. Coll.*

383 Tavella. *Priv. Coll.*

384 Tavella. *Coll. F. Ravano*

385 Tavella. *Priv. Coll.*

386 Tavella. *Genoa*

387 Tavella. *Genoa*

388 Tavella. *Genoa*

389 Tavella. *Priv. Coll.*

390 Tavella. *Genoa*

391 Tavella. *Genoa*

392 Tavella. *Genoa*

393 Tavella. *Genoa*

394 Tavella. *Genoa*

395 Tavella. *Genoa*

396 Tavella. *Genoa*

397 Tavella. *Genoa*

398 Tavella. *Genoa*

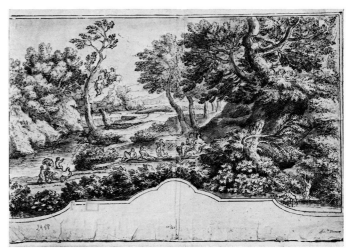

399 Tavella. *Genoa*

400 Roncelli. *Bergamo, Museo Diocesano*

401 Roncelli. *Bergamo, Museo Diocesano*

402 Roncelli. *Count Moroni*

403 Roncelli. *Count Moroni*

404 Roncelli. *Stezzano, Santuario*

405 Roncelli. *Stezzano, Santuario*

406 Roncelli. *Stezzano, Santuario*

407 Roncelli. *Stezzano, Santuario*

408 Roncelli. *Count Moroni*

409 M. Ricci. *Milan, Brera*

410 M.Ricci. *Venice, Accademia*

411 M.Ricci. *Venice, Accademia*

412 N. Cochin. *Frederiksborg Castle*

413 N. Cochin. *Frederiksborg Castle*

415 Bassi. *Cremona*

414 Bassi. *Cremona*

416 School of M. Ricci. *Venice, Accademia*

417 Onofri. *Rome, Galleria Doria Pamphilj*

418 Panfi. *Lucca*

419 Panfi. *Lucca*

420 Panfi. *Valenciennes*

421 Panfi. *Reims*

422 Panfi. *Priv. Coll.*

423 Unknown Artist. *Venice, Pinacoteca Querini Stampalia*

424 Eisman. *Munich*

425 'Giacomo Spagnolo'. *Rome, Galleria Doria Pamphilj*

426 Reschi. *Rome, Galleria Nazionale*

427 J.de Heusch. *Destroyed*

428 Francisque. *Petworth*

429 Francisque. *Priv. Coll.*

430 Forest. *Tours*

431 De Neve. *Engraving*

432 Huysmans. *Frankfort*

433 Baudewyns. *Brussels*

434 Glauber. *Felbrigg, Ketton-Cremer Coll.*

435 Glauber. *Felbrigg, Ketton-Cremer Coll.*

436 Rosa da Tivoli. *Kassel*

437 G. A. Cassana. *Padua*

438 Londonio. *Milan, Ambrosiana*

439 Londonio. *Priv. Coll.*

440 *Orizzonte. Rome, Galleria Doria Pamphilj*

441 *Orizzonte. Rome, Galleria Doria Pamphilj*

442 *Orizzonte. Turin, Galleria Sabauda*

443 *Orizzonte. Roger F. Hesketh Coll.*

445 Orizzonte. *Isola Bella*

447 A. Diziani. *Venice, Accademia*

444 Orizzonte. *Formerly Berlin*

446 Locatelli. *Carcassonne*

448 Zuccarelli. *Isola Bella*

449 Zuccarelli. *Isola Bella*

450 Zuccarelli. *Isola Bella*

451 Zuccarelli. *Isola Bella*

452 (cat.349a). Tempesta. *Priv. Coll.*

453 (cat.349b). Tempesta. *Kassel*

454 (cat.349c). Bellucci and Tempesta. *Venice*

455 Tempesta. *Geneva*. See p. 138

456 Tempesta. *Priv. Coll.* See p. 138